ENTREPRENEURSHIP AND SOCIAL CHANGE

Monographs in Economic Anthropology, No. 2

Edited by

Sidney M. Greenfield
The University of Wisconsin-Milwaukee

Arnold Strickon
The University of Wisconsin-Madison

UNIVERSITY PRESS OF AMERICA

LANHAM • NEW YORK • LONDON

Society for Economic Anthropology

Copyright © 1986 by the

Society for Economic Anthropology

University Press of America, ® Inc.

4720 Boston Way
Lanham, MD 20706

3 Henrietta Street
London WC2E 8LU England

All rights reserved

Printed in the United States of America

British Cataloging in Publication Information Available

**Co-published by arrangement with
the Society for Economic Anthropology**

Library of Congress Cataloging-in-Publication Data

Main entry under title:

Entrepreneurship and social change.

(Monographs in economic anthropology; no. 2)
Bibliography: p.
Includes index.
1. Entrepreneur—Addresses, essays, lectures.
2. Social change—Addresses, essays, lectures.
3. Economic anthropology—Addresses, essays, lectures.
 I. Greenfield, Sidney M. II. Strickon, Arnold.
 III. Society for Economic Anthropology (U.S.)
 IV. Series.
HB615.E629 1986 338'.04 85-26533 CIP
ISBN 0-8191-5165-3 (alk. paper)
ISBN 0-8191-5166-1 (pbk. : alk. paper)

All University Press of America books are produced on acid-free paper which exceeds the minimum standards set by the National Historical Publications and Records Commission.

CONTENTS

PAGE

INTRODUCTION

Sidney M. Greenfield and Arnold Strickon   4

I. Entrepreneurship in Medium and Large-Scale Japanese Firms
ROBERT MARSH and HIROSHI MANARI   19

II. Constraints on Entrepreneurship: Transaction Costs and Market Efficiency
JAMES M. ACHESON   45

III. The "Managerial" vs the "Labor" Function, Capital Accumulation and the Dynamics of Simple Commodity Production in Rural Oaxaca, Mexico
SCOTT COOK   54

IV. Entrepreneurial Agriculture and the Involution of Agricultural Dynamics in the Americas
SHELDON SMITH   96

V. Family Enterprises in Mexico
LARISSA LOMNITZ and MARISOL PEREZ-LIZAUR   124

VI. The Impressario as Entrepreneur
ERWIN H. JOHNSON   138

VII. Entrepreneurs in Public Enterprises
ALFRED H. SAULNIERS   158

VIII. Class, Political Constraints, and Entrepreneurial Strategies: Elites and Petty Market Traders in Northern Luzon
WILLIAM G. DAVIS   166

IX. Entrepreneurial Activities of Women and Children Among the Islamic Hausa of Northern Nigeria
ENID SCHILDKROUT   195

X. Political Entrepreneurs in a West African City
SANDRA T. BARNES   224

PREFACE

The chapters in this book are edited revisions of working papers presented in April of 1982 at the meetings of the Society for Economic Anthropology held at the University of Georgia in Athens, Georgia. The society had been founded the year before to establish a forum for scholars interested in economic problems who approached them from perspectives other than that of conventional economics. Anthropology had the strongest tradition of studying economic matters from either a comparative, cross-cultural, or from a multidisciplinary perspective, and so it was appropriate that anthropologists take the lead in creating the new forum while inviting colleagues in other disciplines to join with them in studying and discussing subjects of mutual interest.

At the organizing meeting at the University of Indiana in the spring of 1981, the newly formed advisory board of the society decided to devote each subsequent meeting to a specific theme. John Bennett proposed that the second of what since have become annual meetings be devoted to the theme of entrepreneurship and social change. He also proposed, with the board concurring, that the editors of the present volume, because of their previous work on the subject, be invited to organize the program for the 1982 meeting. After some brief deliberation we agreed that the meetings of the new society, given its stated desire to attract scholars from a variety of disciplines, might be an ideal place to advance the discussion of the subject. After all, the concept of entrepreneurship had first appeared in the literature of economics and business history. But following World War II it had been taken up by psychologists, sociologists, and anthropologists. Since there were few other forums where diverse positions and different disciplines could be brought together, we were tempted to accept the invitation. The willingness of John Bennett and Walter Neal to serve on the program committee with us convinced us to undertake the challenge.

We should like to thank John Bennett and Walter Neal for their assistance with the program. We also should like to express our gratitude to Arthur Murphy for his handling of local arrangements at the

University of Georgia. Our special thanks go to
Robert Aubey whose comments on the papers presented at
the Athens meeting he chose not to include in the
publication. Instead he assisted us in the
preparation of the introduction and in the production
of the manuscript. We are grateful to Professor Aubey
for the cooperation and support he has given us over
the years. Finally we should like to thank those who
presented papers at the meeting that we could not
include in this publication.

INTRODUCTION

Sidney M. Greenfield and Arnold Strickon

In the fable about the blind men and the elephant we are told about the efforts of a group of men without sight to describe the great beast. Unable to see the whole, each is limited in what he knows to the part he can touch. The one who is in front near the trunk, therefore, represents it as something long and mobile like a snake. The one near the side describes it as thick and sturdy like a wall. And so it goes, with each attempting to represent the whole in terms of the part he can comprehend. While each is right with respect to his perceptions, each also is wrong because he presents but a part of a larger whole.

Social scientists have been fond of this fable and have used it, but primarily to criticize their colleagues who have offered definitions of their subject matter that are partial and limited to a single dimension or characteristic. It has been argued, for example, that attempts to define the likes of culture, religion, society, etc. are comparable to the efforts of blind men to describe an elephant. Since the scientists are unable to comprehend the whole, it is argued, they select for their definitions characteristics from the parts with which they have experience. But in the social sciences research usually follows from the definitions of concepts proposed by leaders of a field. As a result, research tends to focus on the dimension or characteristic emphasized by whoever first defines a field and continues until someone comes along to redefine the subject by stressing another dimension or characteristic. In this way we never really get at the elephant. Instead, we develop bodies of literature each based on a characteristic used to define the whole. The results are a range of studies in many fields that, although they claim to be about the same thing, are substantatively and methodologically quite diverse. And although reference usually is made to the others, any one is comparable at best only with others that focus on the same dimension or characteristic.

Scholars then have the same problem as the blind men. And the situation is made worse when specialists come together to debate the relative merits of their respective positions. Each, as we have seen, is right while each also is wrong. But as the passion with which each puts forth his position increases, any chance at understanding decreases. Although they refer to one another, each is talking past the others. Since none has the ability to see the whole, none can appreciate the relationship between the several parts being offered as exclusive defining characteristics. The study of entrepreneurship has followed this general pattern and therefore is not unlike the effort by blind men to define an elephant. Different schools have developed each focusing on different defining characteristics. And although each makes reference to the works of the others, the outline of an elephant, assuming that one exists, is only beginning to emerge.

The concept of entrepreneurship has had a long established place in the equilibrium-oriented neoclassical thinking that until the early years of the present century dominated the study of economics. It was used theoretically to separate profits and other related elements conceptually from other returns to management in the market system.

To the theoretical economists in the neoclassical tradition, the entrepreneur was an abstract figure assumed to be unaffected by influences external to the rational operation of the firm he directed. Joseph A. Schumpeter, however, was to reconceptualize the entrepreneur and make him the focal point and key to the dynamic of economic development and and growth.

Although implicit in the writings of Adam Smith was a framework for investigating the decisions and choices of the individual as they both maintained and/or changed the socio-cultural context, neoclassical economists generally remained uninterested in the implications of this framework for change until the Great Depression. Up to that time they were "more interested in the institutional processes and arrangements that produced and sustained states of equilibrium in the 'market' than they were in the dynamics that changed the equilibrium..." (Greenfield, et al. 1979:4). Their theoretical and conceptual formulations of the behavior of the individual in the market, therefore, had stressed what they took to be the "rationally motivated" decisions the outcome of which maintained the equilibrium. With the Depression, however, change, the disturbance of an equilibrium and the creation of a new one, became for the first time a primary concern for them. This interest was reinforced a few decades later when their attention was turned to the so-called underdeveloped nations.

Schumpeter, as we (Greenfield and Strickon 1981:468) have observed elsewhere,

> postulated his theory as an alternative to what he referred to as "equilibrium theories" of economic process. His basic point was that the ultimate expansion of economic conduct was to be found in noneconomic factors...that were brought into play through actions of individuals operating in the market.

As the title of his book, The Theory of Economic Development (first published in German in 1912 and only translated into English in 1934, revised in 1949), indicates, he had turned his attention from equilibrium to questions of economic change. But he did so in terms of a set of assumptions that were shared implicitly by his fellow economists and by most other social scientists at the time as well. Following Adam Smith and most eighteenth and nineteenth century social thinkers in the Western World--as diverse as Adam Ferguson, August Comte, Herbert Spencer, Lewis Henry Morgan, Karl Marx, and Frederick Engles--he equated economic growth with progress and assumed that it was inherent in nature. He then further assumed that the task of the scholar was to formulate policies that could be presented to those in power that would enable them to facilitate and hasten the inevitable attainment of progress.

To Schumpeter (1949:66), development (to be read progress) was defined as "the carrying out of new combinations," or, more specifically, as the "spontaneous and discontinuous change in the channels of the flows, disturbances of equilibrium, which forever alters and displaces the equilibrium state previously existing" (1949:64). The key question then was: How are the new combinations brought about?

Schumpeter's answer was entrepreneurship and the entrepreneur. "The carrying out of new combinations," he wrote (1949:74), "we call 'enterprise'; the individuals whose function is to carry them out we can 'entrepreneurs'...." Entrepreneurs then were the instruments by means of which the new combinations, assumed a priori to be more progressive, were to be attained in the growth and development of economy and society.

Schumpeter's entrepreneurs then were innovators, but innovators whose actions had consequences for but a single aspect or dimension of their society. Like his fellow economists Schumpeter had separated out as the objective of his investigations the institutionalized arrangements of the Western world, to which he and his fellow economists of the period devoted themselves almost exclusively. To his credit he realized (1949:3) that all social life was a continuous flow from which academicians abstracted what came to be their separate subject matters. Since his subject matter was economics, he regularly brought the results of his analyses of the behavior of individuals back to the structured arrangements by means of which industrial technology had been harnessed to produce goods and services that were distributed by means of the market. By doing this he restricted entrepreneurship to those innovations in the flow of human activity that had consequences for the organization of the technology of production and/or the marketing of commodities. In other words, entrepreneurship in the Schumpeterian formulation focused on innovations in the production and marketing processes of the Western World. Although located in the broadest frame of social science thinking, Schumpeter in fact was looking at but a part of the elephant. Consequently, studies of entrepreneurship in the Schumpeterian tradition focused on what we shall call the technological/organizational variable or dimension.

The papers by Marsh and Manari, Acheson, Cook and Smith in Section I of this volume emphasize to greater or lesser degree this variable or dimension of the subject. All four concentrate on the organizational dimension. Working with data from contemporary Japanese factories, Robert Marsh and Hiroshi Manari take technological/organizational innovation in the Schumpeteran sense to be the hallmark of the entrepreneurial function. Therefore, they use the number of patent applications made by firms as a measure of innovation. Unlike the classical view of the entrepreneur as inventor developing and selling his own product, however, innovations in present day Japan are produced in the firm's department of research and development. Consequently, for Marsh and Manari the entrepreneurial function lies in management decisions to invest in research and development.

In the second paper, originally presented as a comment, James Acheson appeals, largely on theoretical grounds, for the recognition of still another organizational component, the constraints imposed by the size of the firm.

Scott Cook then, from a Marxist, dependency, perspective, provides us with a detailed examination of several new business undertakings in rural Oaxaca, Mexico. He defines entrepreneurship primarily in terms of its role in organizing the labor function. This enables him to examine the impact newly created firms have on the material well being of the diverse categories of workers within the communities in which they were established. In doing so he reconsiders entrepreneurship from a Marxist perspective, a perspective which traditionally has not seen it as a particularly useful concept.

Sheldon Smith in his study of Guatamalan plantations also is concerned with the organizational dimension. Unlike the others in this section, however, he examines the changes effected in agricultural "firms" in Guatamala as the result of changing relations with external forces at the national and international levels.

With the end of World War II, for political and other reasons, students of economic growth turned their attention from Western Europe and North America to the developing nations of the world. Consequently, instead of devoting themselves to formulating theories that would enable them to conceputalize and formulate policies to attain the assumed inherent movement through successive equilibrium stages towards future progress in the Western World, a new generation of students applied uncritically the evolutionary assumptions in Western social thought. Accepting implicitly the idea of inherent growth in the direction of progress, they equated the West with the more advanced stages towards which the economies and societies of the nations of the rest of the world inevitably would have to go in the universal march towards progress. The problem on which they came to focus was: How were the undeveloped nations first to become like the "more advanced" nations of the West so that after "catching up," they could participate on an equal footing in the assumed inevitable march towards more progressive stages in the future? Specifically, the task of the student of development became the creation of policies to be implemented by the authorities in the developing nations that would speed up their slow but inevitable movement in the direction of the more advanced economies and societies of the West. Needless to say, for those who chose to work within a market framework--as opposed to a socialist or communist one--entrepreneurship and the identification and encouragement of entrepreneurs came to be a matter of considerable importance.

But who, it may be asked, are entrepreneurs? Can we differentiate between their functions and their indivdual characteristics? How can they be recognized so as to be studied? What is the distribution of entrepreneurs and what are their distinctive characteristics within any given population? Which segments of society are most likely to produce entrepreneurs? Why?

These questions, and others that followed from Schumpeter's analysis, clearly extended beyond the bounds of the economics within which entrepreneurial studies first developed. They could not even be pursued without first redefining entrepreneurship in terms of some other aspect of the beast. This was done by non-economists whose research took several divergent directions. The first appeared just after World War II under the direction of Arthur H. Cole at the Center for Entrepreneurial Research at Harvard University. A. P. Usher, N.S.B. Gras, and others, abandoning the theoretical rigor of classical economics, focussed on the lives and careers of individual businessmen, firms, and even sectors of the economy. Their intent, which led to a large number of mostly simplistic studies--as can be seen, for example, listed in Henrietta Larson's <u>Guide to Business History</u> (1964)--was to provide case histories for students of management and data for friendly critics and defenders of the status quo in Europe and North America. Since none of the authors in this volume has used it, we shall not elaborate on this attempt to focus on the business sector of the Western World as the essence of entrepreneurship (for a summary see Greenfield, et. al. 1979).

Students in both the Schumpeterian and the business-history traditions followed the lead of the new generation of development economists by undertaking studies of entrepreneurship in the developing world. The first step in this process appeared to be the identification of those conditions which generated entrepreneurial talent. This, however, required analytic and research skills that were more historical, psychological, and sociological in character than economic. "Attention gradually shifted, therefore, from the functions of entrepreneurship in economic growth to the psychological traits of persons designated as entrepreneurs and to the social conditions that produced them" (Greenfield, et. al. 1979:10).

In his book, The Achieving Society (1961), David McClelland, for example, attempted to apply rigorous research procedures, using comparative analysis, to determine why some societies produce outstanding individuals (i.e., entrepreneurs) while others do not. His logic was derived from the conclusions reached by Max Weber (1930) in his classic analysis of, The Protestant Ethic and the Spirit of Capitalism. McClelland accepted Weber's formulation and extended it to examine the motives that lead individuals to behave in ways that promote development. Certain individuals, he maintains, as a result of childhood experiences, have what he calls "high n Achievement." These high achievers, he maintains, are the entrepreneurs responsible for economic growth. Governments interested in development, he advises, should seek to, "(1) break orientation toward tradition and increase other-directedness, ... (2) increase n Achievement, and (3) provide for better allocation of existing n Achievement resources..." (McClelland 1961:2).

At about the same time McClelland was examining the achievement motivation of individuals, the economist Everett Hagen (1982) turned his attention to the disadvantaged minorities living in complex, but often underdeveloped societies. He proposed that the members of marginal, usually disadvantaged minorities, such as the Dissenters in England, the Protestants in France, the Samurai in Japan, the Jews in many countries, and the Parsees in India, to mention but a few, have contributed disproprortionately to the supply of entrepreneurs. Members of these groups, he concluded, to compensate for the discriminitory way in which they are treated turned to entrepreneurial achievement.

Although these psychological studies appeared promising at the time, they have not contributed signficantly to contemporary efforts to comprehend the phenomenon of entrepreneurship. None of the papers in the present volume reflect these perspectives.

By the mid-1960s a number of scholars from diverse disciplines were experimenting with a new direction that was to result in a resurgence of interest in entrepreneurship. This was a view of the individual as neither a package of psychological characteristics nor as a projection of role requirements of social systems, but rather as a creative decision-maker. The economist William P. Glade (1967), for example, proposed that entrepreneurial, like all social behavior, be looked at at the micro-level as composed of individuals making decisions and choices within specific social and cultural settings. What he found distinctive about entrepreneurial behavior were the settings, circumstances, or situations within which the decisions and choices were made. These he termed the "opportunity structure." As these exogenous factors changed, they provided new opportunities for the individual members of a society. In their decisions and choices, some might take advantage of the new opportunities while others did not. Those who did, and were successful, came to be called entrepreneurs; they broke old equilibriums and moved economy and society to new ones.

The papers by Lomnitz and Perez-Lizaur, Johnson, and Saulniers in Section II are concerned primarily with the changing opportunity structure. Larissa Lomnitz and Marisol Perez-Lizaur trace the career of a successful Mexican family from the time of the 1910 revolution to the present. They show how the family founders and their successors mobilized personal contacts and other social resources to take advantage of new conditions brought about by changes at the national level.

In the second paper in this section Erwin Johnson shows us how the impressario in North America, with his access to both the local community and the national and international world of opera, combines the money and labor of local level elites with the national level pool of operatic talent and expertise. Johnson reminds us that "entrepreneur" and "impressario" derive from the same root and reflect the same combination of resource organization and risk taking for profit.

Alfred Saulniers' short paper, like Acheson's, also derives from comments made at the Athens, Ga. meeting of the SEA. In it he argues that the recently created publically-owned enterprises in third world societies constitute a new set of opportunities and constraints which are exploited by individuals whose behavior also can be considered entrepreneurial.

Even before the emergence of interest in opportunity structures in economics the anthropologist Raymond Firth (1964), in trying to come to grips with the subject of social change, had argued for the distinction between an abstract "social structure" and a lower level focus upon the individual which he called "social organization." This position was then elaborated by his student Frederick Barth whose "generative models" focussed on the individual as a decision-maker within his or her cultural context. Barth had written The Role of the Entrepreneur in Social Change in Northern Norway (1963). This work may have contributed to the maturation of his ideas and to formulation of his, Models of Social Organization (1966). In the earlier work the analysis, in spite of the promise in the title, was primarily institutional and structural rather than an analysis of the decisions and choices of individuals and their effect on social change.

Stimulated by Barth, but building specifically on a paper on the role of the family firm in the development process by Burton Benedict 1968), Robert Aubey, John Kyle and Arnold Strickon (1974) refocussed the study of investment behavior away from corporations, family firms, and other groups onto the activities of individuals. Integrating Barth's approach to individuals as decision makers generating social and cultural patterns and Glade's emphasis on the opportunity structure in the study of entrepreneurial behavior, they maintained that investors (i.e., entrepreneurs) mobilized and used whatever resources were at their disposal. These resources were not only financial, but also social, such as access to influential individuals, groups and social networks, and/or cultural, such as access to information and symbols. Their argument then was that entrepreneurial behavior reflects decisions and choices made by individuals within a complex yet specific social and cultural matrix.

Based upon their work, The School for American Research sponsored a seminar at which a multidisciplinary group of anthropologists, economists, and economic historians sought to consider entrepreneurial activities in a cross cultural perspective (Greenfield, Strickon and Aubey 1979). Stimulated in part by the discussions at the seminar, the editors of the present volume then attempted to carry the reformulation of the study of entrepreneurship a step further in the direction Firth, Barth and Glade had proposed when they asked for a theory of social change.

Our argument (Greenfield and Strickon 1981), rested primarily on Thomas Kuhn's (1970) use of the concept of paradigm, Colin Turbayne's 1971) admonition that we can and do fall victim inadvertently to inherited metaphors, and Robert Nisbet's (1969) explication of the root metaphor upon which the dominant paradigms in the contemporary social sciences rest. In brief, we argued that the imagery in which the paradigms that dominate contemporary social science research and thought are rooted are "essentialist." That is, they reify abstract concepts (Mayr 1976; Popper 1950). In terms of this imagery the subject matter of the social sciences are such "things" as society, culture, religion, economy, entrepreneurship, etc., which are analogues of growing organisms or of their parts. Using essentialist theories it is possible to described differences in structures from one time period to the next, but it is not possible to show the processes by means of which transformations occur. Consequently, essentialist approaches are unable to relate observed behavioral change to transformations in structural types (Barth 1967). A theory of change, as requested by Firth, Barth and Glade, we maintained, requires the establishment of a new paradigm not constrained by essentialist metaphors.

Barth and Glade had returned the study of entrepreneurship to the micro-level, but were unable to relate their analyses to the macro-level. In an effort to overcome this obstacle, we proposed a new imagery as the basis for a new paradigm. Charles Darwin faced a comparable problem when he tried to explain change in what at the time were assumed to be fixed species. His solution, as Ernst Mayr (1976) points out, was to reject the typological, essentialist view of reality then prevalent in biological thinking and concentrate upon the variability of individual organisms within the populations of which species are composed. He then was able to go further and point out that the interaction between intra-specific variability and selective forces in the environment was the mechanism that produced species change. Suggesting the advantage of this "populational" imagery for the social sciences, we proposed using Darwinian biology <u>as a metaphor</u> for the study of change.

With respect to entrepreneurship this means that we are no longer looking for a trancendent type--the analogue of the immutable species--but instead recognize existing diversity of behavior within specific populations, which at its extremes encompasses innovation and novelty. What is called entrepreneurship, from this point of view, is actually one segment of an otherwise seamless variability. This variability may be expressed in technology, organization, symbols, etc. These diverse behaviors interact with their environments--to be understood in the broadest sense--to produce outcomes which are evaluated both by the individual and others. Those "novelties" judged most advantageous in terms of the standards prevailing within the group may be copied with the result being the establishment of a statistical pattern, or a change in preexisting ones.

Freed from the constraints of the metaphors inherited from our predecessors, we suggested that new patterns emerge in response to the cumulative changes in the decisions and choices of individuals in comparable situations. That is, at any given time individuals may innovate new behaviors, adopt alternatives (at times even from outside the collective experience of their group) or copy the behavioral choices of others around them that have brought the goals or ends they also desire.

Variation, therefore, is constantly being generated. In terms of the new imagery, continuity and change are part of the same ongoing process.

Within the new paradigm no single dimension or aspect is emphasized as the essence of entrepreneurship. Instead, the approach is multidimensional in that entrepreneurship, which is seen as one aspect of continuous variation, innovation and selection, is part of the ongoing process of human life. It therefore may be analyzed directly from descriptive, ethnographic (as well as other forms of) data as demonstrated in the papers by Davis, Schildkrout and Barnes in Section III below.

Davis, in an introduction summarizing some of the arguments for and against the structuralist and individualist approaches to social phenomena, sees advantages and disadvantages to both. Using data from the Northern Philippines he tries to combine them without choosing one or the other. Instead he looks at the decisions and behaviors of market vendors responding to existing political and economic structures. We include his paper in this section because even though he incorporates essentialist concepts, he sees the necessity of relating them to an analysis of the decisions, choices and behaviors of individuals.

Schildkrout and Barnes end the volume with presentations in which they analyze data collected by traditional ethnographic means in terms compatible with the populational framework. In her paper Schildkrout examines the case of an Islamic population in Northern Nigeria. What is of particular interest is that the women are constrained by the tradition of purdah which keeps some of them housebound. In spite of this, however, or perhaps we might say because of it, both the women and their children are shown to perform a range of behaviors exploiting the "opportunities" in the situation that are entrepreneurial in character. As a result Schildkrout is able to examine for the first time to our knowledge the entrepreneurial activities of children.

In the final paper, using data from Lagos, Nigeria, Barnes shows us how some poor immigrants accumulated wealth and power by serving as brokers between the mass of their fellows and elites at the national political and economic level. In contrast with Davis, who used institutions as the context from which resources can be derived, Barnes introduces into the analysis the elites who have some measure of control over institutional resources outside the local neighborhood. In this way she shows us how the individuals she calls entrepreneurs bring together both parties in transactions that facilitate the flow of resources to the benefit of all.

At this point we should like to return to the fable of the blind men and the elephant. In terms of the inherited metaphors that dominate most contemporary social science thinking it is assumed that our definitions and research programs, as with the efforts of the blind men to describe the elephant, are based on the existence of something "out there" independent of ourselves. The problem is assumed to be that we, like the blind men, cannot comprehend its totality. Therefore, we must define it in terms of what we can grasp, its aspects or dimensions. Historically, as we have seen, students of entrepreneurship have taken these aspects or dimensions of an assumed reality "out there" one at a time, looking at them as determinants. From the perspective of the new, populational metaphor, however, we believe that they ought to be treated together as co-variables which act together in shaping the processes of innovation, variation and selection that produces both continuity and change in human behavior.

But more importantly, having freed ourselves from the essentialist assumptions of our inherited metaphors we should like to raise a question on which to end this introduction. With respect to entrepreneurship in particular, and the subject matter of the social sciences in general, we should like to ask: Is there really "something out there" beyond the behavior of individual human beings? Or are we, as Turbayne (1971) warned, being duped by our inherited metaphors into looking for "elephants" when there are none.

REFERENCES CITED

AUBEY, Robert T., John Kyle, and Arnold Strickon. 1974. "Investment behavior and elite social structure in Latin America." Journal of Interamerican Studies and World Affairs. 16:71-94.

BARTH, Frederik. 1963. The Role of The Entrepreneur in Social Change in Northern Norway. Bergen:Universitfolkaget.

_____. 1966. "Models of Social Organization. Occasional Papers of the Royal Anthropological Institute of Great Britain and Ireland." No. 23.

_____. 1967. "On the Study of Social Change." American Anthropologist. 69:661-69.

BENEDICT, Burton. 1968. "Family Firms and Economic Development." Southwestern Journal of Anthropology. 24:1-19.

FIRTH, Raymond. 1964. Elements of Social Organization. Boston: Beacon Press.

GLADE, William P. 1967. "Approaches to a Theory of Entrepreneurial Formation." Explorations in Entrepreneurial History. 2d series 4:245-59.

GREENFIELD, Sidney M., Arnold Strickon, Robert T. Aubey, and Morton Rothstein. 1979. Introduction. Entrepreneurs in Cultural Context. Sidney M. Greenfield, Arnold Strickon, and Robert T. Aubey, eds., Albuquerque: University of New Mexico Press.

GREENFIELD, Sidney M. and Arnold Strickon. 1981. "A New Paradigm for the Study of Entrepreneurship and Social Change." Economic Development and Cultural Change. 3:2.

HAGEN, Everett E. 1962. On the Theory of Social Change. Homewood, Ill.: Dorsey Press.

KUHN, Thomas S. 1970. The Structure of Scientific Revolutions. Chicago: University of Chicago Press.

LARSON, Henrietta. 1964. *Guide to Business History*.
Boston: J.J. Canner and Co.

MC CLELLAND, David S. 1961. *The Achieving Society*.
Princeton: D. Van Nostrand.

MAYR, Ernst. 1976. *Evolution and the Diversity of Life*. Cambridge, Mass.: Harvard University Press, Belknap Press.

NISBET, Robert A. 1969. *Social Change and History*.
London: Oxford University Press.

POPPER, Karl. 1950. "The Open Society and Its Enemies." *Spell of Plato*. Vol. I. London: Routledtge and Kegan Paul.

SCHUMPETER, Joseph A. 1949. *The Theory of Economic Development*. Cambridge, Mass.: Harvard University Press.

TURBAYNE, Colin M. 1971. *The Myth of Metaphor*.
Columbia: University of South Carolina Press.

WEBER, Max. 1930. *The Protestant Ethic and the Spirit of Capitalism*. trans. Talcott Parsons.
London: George Allen and Unwin.

I. ENTREPRENEURSHIP IN MEDIUM- AND LARGE-SCALE JAPANESE FIRMS

Robert M. Marsh and Hiroshi Mannari

Economists have long disagreed over the causal importance of entrepreneurship at the micro-level of production in the firm and the macrolevel of economic development. Sociologists, historians, and anthropologists have begun to study this question empirically in a variety of societies. This paper analyzes data collected in 1976 from 50 Japanese factories. We first develop an index of entrepreneurial innovation, with which the factories can be compared, and then describe instances of innovation in these factories. Finally, we test the microeconomic theory of the production function to see if entrepreneurual innovation has a significant effect on net output (value added), independent of the effect of the other factors of production in these factories, and discuss the implications of our findings.

Theory and Research on Entrepreneurship

In early French usage, as Hoselitz (1951) has shown, Cantillon held that the essence of the function of the entrepreneur was to bear uncertainty--to buy labor and materials and to sell products at uncertain prices. The entrepreneur was one who took risks and made innovations concerning the normal factors of production. J.B. Say advanced theory by showing the contribution to production made by businessmen, as distinct from the machinery and other factors of production. However, Say's theory also represents a retrogression from the insights of the physiocrats: he saw no relationship between entrepreneurial activity and capital accumulation or investment (Hoselitz, 1951).

In Britain, until the Marshaillian system rediscovered entrepreneurship, the closest equivalent terms for the French entrepreneur were adventurer, undertaker and projector. Their function was to supply and accumulate capital. The entrepreneurial--i.e., innovating, risk-bearing--function could not be fitted into British economic theory, with its assumption of

a normal state of equilibrium, established
by the multiple reactions of businessmen,
consumers, investors, and workers to the
prices of goods and services. individual
variations in behavior were seen either as
cancelled out in the aggregate or suppressed
by competition. In this highly aggregative
system, any unknown element was to be
derived from the relations of theoretically
measurable quantities. Such a system could
obviously not utilize unmeasurable social or
cultural factors such a entrepreneurship.
To say that the entrepreneur was rewarded
for risk taking, that is, for uncertainty,
was the negation of a proper theoretical
explanation (Cochran, 1968: 88-89).

Marx did not distinguish between capitalist and
entrepreneur, and was clearly more interested in
capital than in entrepreneurship. Lacking a theory of
enterprise, Marx assumed one needed to know only the
"objective" historical possibilities of capitalism's
inner logic (Belasco, 1980: 32, 184). Such a view
fails to address, much less explain, the problem of
why only some capitalists innovate, and the role of
innovation--as distinct from capital accumulation and
management--in economic development.

Contributions to the theory of entrepreneurship
were made in this century by such historical and
institutional economists as Max Weber, John R.
Commons, and of course, Joseph A. Schumpeter (1912:
1934, 1947, 1949, 1971). Schumpeter's theory held
that not all businessmen in private enterprise
economies are "entrepreneurs." He distinguished
between:

1. the capitalist, whose role is to accumulate;

2. the technologist, whose role is to invent; and

3. the entrepreneur, whose role is to innovate.

Innovation is the criterion of enterpreneurship:
"the defining characteristic is simply the doing of
new things or the doing of things that are already
being done in a new way (innovation)" (Schumpeter,
1947: 151). "...[A] study of creative response in

business becomes coterminous with a study of entrepreneurship" (1949: 150). Entrepreneurship is an analytical, not a concrete property: an owner or manager is an entrepreneur only while and to the extent s/he is making a creative or innovative response; except in the limiting case, no person is continuously an entrepreneur. When the owner or manager is maintaining the more bureaucratic, routine operations of the firm, s/he is not performing the entrepreneurial function.

Whereas classical and neoclassical economists saw economic growth as balanced, gradual and harmonious, Schumpeter realized it can occur in leaps and spurts. He distinguished three types of business cycles, named after the writers who had identified them. The duration of each type of cycle varies according to the disturbance that causes it. The shortest, or Kitchin cycle is produced by inventory accumulation and decumulation and lasts about three years. The medium, Juglar cycle of 8-11 years is brought about by individual innovations, e.g., new textile machines, dynamos, electric motors, radios, or refrigerators. The long or Kondratieff cycle is caused by the introduction of major innovations, such as railroads in the nineteenth century and automobiles in the twentieth (Stolper, 1968: 69).

Business cycles occur because equilibrium is destroyed by innovations, which appear "discontinuously in groups or swarms" (Schumpeter, 1934: 223). The fact of business cycles means that business decisions must be made in the face of risk and uncertainty. The interest rate is therefore less decisive than the indeterminancy of the future gains from investment. In this uncertainty, ordinary businessmen hesitate to invest, while a special breed--the entrepreneur--does invest. Strictly speaking, Schumpeter reminds us, it is the capitalist, not the entrepreneur, who is the risk bearer, since it is his capital that is lost through failure. The entrepreneur's "risk" derives more from the speed with which his initially high profits are eaten away by competitors who follow his successful lead.

If business cycles are influenced by innovation, the latter in turn presupposes the creation of credit. Stolper summarizes Schumpeter's (1934: ch.3) view: "Credit creation permits the entrepreneur to take resources out of the income stream [the circular flow of the economy] for productive purposes <u>before</u> he has contributed anything to the income stream" (Stolper, 1968: 69).

In summary, we define the entrepreneur as one who acts as innovator by

applying	new products
making	new techniques of production
discovering	new markets
developing	new sources of raw materials

Beveridge and Obserschall studied African businesspersons in Zambia in the early 1970s, using an explicitly Schumpeterian definition of entrepreneurship:

> "Innovation indicated not so much sound day-to-day business management techniques as the capacity to create and seize new opportunities .... Innovation was defined as a departure from established practice in a given geographic area or particular market. . . . [For example] reorganizing a medium-sized African grocery store into a small supermarket . . . .in 1959 was innovative" (Beveridge and Oberschall, 1979: 216-17).

More generally,

> "The entrepreneur is thus an innovator in economic activity: he introduces a new good or a new method of production, he opens a new market, he locates a new source of materials, he puts into operation a new organization in an industry." (1979: 276).

Although they collected data on each businessman's entire career, they found, as Schumpeter would expect, that "only about one-fifth of the Lusaka businessmen, and one-quarter of the businessmen in rural areas, ever innovated" (1979: 220). The risk element in entrepreneurship was documented in their finding that "innovations ended in failure more often than relatively conventional ventures" (1979: 227).

Beveridge and Oberschall provide an answer to the question, "What causes some Zambian businessmen to become entrepreneurs?" Unlike the situation in other countries, entrepreneurs were not drawn disproportionately from marginal groups or from certain ethnic or religious groups. Instead, after Zambian independence, new business opportunities bid local capital, and returns on investment of 50 percent or more were not uncommon. Finally, among their samples of rural traders and substantial businesspersons in Lusaka, success (measured in sales per month) was best explained by "whether a businessman ever innovated . . . . Even when other variables are controlled, innovation was by far the most important factor in accounting for success among Lusaka businessmen." (1979: 221).

Hirschmeier and Yui (1975) provide a history of business in Japan from 1600 to the present, and explain how the Japanese were able to adopt Western technology and organizational forms and adapt them to the Japanese setting. The "founder-type" executive who manifested an entrepreneurial spirit was important in Meiji era Japan (1868-1912). Market competition is a precondition for a flourishing entrepreneurship, and the growth of the Zaibatsu before 1945, with their huge complexes of corporate bureaucracies, discouraged the entrepreneurial spirit (Noda, 1966: 232, 241). After the Pacific War, the dissolution of the Zaibatsu, the increasing competition among big firms, and the rapid economic growth of the 1960s encouraged the emergence of new, colorful entrepreneurs (Noda, 1966: 243-44; Shinohara, 1968: 61).

Research Methods

The site of our research was a city of some 400,000 population in Okayama prefecture in southwestern Japan. The universe was defined as all industrial manufacturing establishments employing 100 or more persons on a site in the city. According to the city government's survey, at the time of our field work in the summer of 1976 there were 84 such establishments. When a firm had two or more factories in the city all but one were eliminated from the sample; a total of six were thus dropped. The effective universe was, then, 78.

Within our time and budget constraints, data were collected from 50 of these 78 factories, 64.1 percent of the universe. Data collection in each factory consisted of a tour of the production plant, and an interview with one or more senior officials. A structured questionnaire was left to be filled out by a key informant, requesting objective information on the organization. All interviews were conducted in Japanese, and the questionnaire consisted of standard Aston items,² as well as some items from Blau et al.'s New Jersey study (1976) and other sources, translated by others or ourselves from English into Japanese. We had time to contact only 66 of the 78 factories; 16 of these refused to allow us to tour their factory and/or to fill out the questionnaire, a refusal rate of 24.2 percent.

The city studied had manufacturing firms in 13 of the 21 two-digit industries classified in Japan's 1972 Establishment Census of Manufacturing (food, textile, clothing, rubber, transportation equipment, iron and steel, chemical, petroleum, etc.). Our sample had one or more firms in each of these 13 industries. The distribution of firms in our sample was within five percentage points of the distribution of firms in the universe (the city studied) for all but one of the 13 industries (the clothing industry firms comprised 27 percent of the 78 firms in the universe, but only 16 percent of the firms in our sample.) The sample factories ranged in size from 100 to 11,815 employees and in technology from a handicraft factory producing traditional Japanese ningyo dolls to giant, modern, automated petrochemical plants. The reader should note that our entrepreneurs innovate in the setting of medium- and large-scale firms; they are not the classic solo or small-scale businessman-innovator.

It is also important to note that our study was undertaken to investigate the relationships between size, technology, organizational structure, and performance in Japanese factories, not entrepreneurship. Fortunately, our questionnaire contained two items relevant to our concept of entrepreneur:

    1. What is your policy concerning the <u>range of products</u> to be produced in this factory? We coded as entrepreneurial the response, "expand the range of products;" and as non-entrepreneurial, the responses "maintain" or "contract the range of products."

2. How many patent applications did this factory make last year (1975)? A response of "one or more patent applications" was coded as entrepreneurial, while the non-entrepreneurial response was "no patent applications."

The distribution of the 50 factories on these two aspects of entrepreneurial innovation is shown in Table 1. The correlation between policy on range of products and number of patent applications--.27--is positive and statistically significant at the .05 level. Factories with a policy of expanding their product range tend also to generate one or more patent applications for new products, designs, processes, etc. To simplify data analysis, we combined these two variables into an Index of Entrepreneurial Innovation (hereafter, "innovation index"). This was done by assigning a factory a score of 1 for each entrepreneurial response, and 0 for each non-entrepreneurial response:

Index of Entrepreneurial Innovation

Score		N
2 High	Expand range of products and one or more patent applications	6
1	Expand range of products or one or more patent applications, but not both	12
0 Low	Neither expand range of products nor any patent applications	32
		50

Signs of Entrepreneurship

What form does innovation take in factories with a high score on this index? Let us examine three illustrative cases of factories with a policy of expanding the range of products and a record of patent applications during 1975.

Breaking into Jute. Mr. Kojima, the founder in 1962 and chief executive officer of Kojiwara Industries, has successfully broken into competition

Table 1

Relationship Between Policy on Range of Products and
Number of Patent Applications, Japanese Factories, 1975

Policy on Range of Products	Number of Patent Applications								Total
	0	2	5	7	8	10	16	29	67	
Contract range	7									7
Maintenance range	25	2	1	1				1		30
Expand range	7	1	1	_	1	1	1	_	1	13
	39	3	2	1	1	1	1	1	1	50

with jute.[4] Originally the fiber of an East Indian plant used to make rope, mats, and sacks for wheat, sugar, etc., jute had a world production of 3.8 million tons in 1975. Mr. Kojima's firm originally manufactured tatami from synthetic fibers. The provincial government assisted him to use industrial land to develop first rope, then "flat yarn." In 1964, his original plant was the first to merchandise this flat yarn, under the name of "Kojiline," although the product had been known theoretically in the Sulzer Machine Company in Germany. Kojiline flat yarn is a higly competitive innovation: like jute, it is a rough, strong fiber; but unlike jute, kojiline is seamless, and needs no sewing or welding. When material is welded, seam strength is reduced. Since Kojiline's "tarpee" sheets are seamless up to 3.6 meters' width, their strength and life are greater. Mass production reduces production costs. With the motto "Let's take the place of jute," Mr. Kojima is out to capture the market that jute producing countries like Pakistan have enjoyed.

The mass production consists of three processes: extruding yarn, weaving base cloth, and laminating or coating. The tarpee sheets produced are used in the canvas and tarpaulin fields, but cost less than one-fifth the price of canvas. Tarpee's lower price and greater strength have enabled it to open a completely new market. Weaving was traditionally done by shuttles, but Mr. Kojima introduced a waterjet loom which jets water to fill the weft yarn three times faster than can be done by shuttles. This doubles weaving speed, thereby increasing productivity; it also requires less plant space per unit of output. The company has also entered the textile machinery engineering industry, installing Kojiline Flat Yarn Manufacturing Equipment--e.g., weaving machinery--and plant in 18 countries between the late 1960s and 1976. The company's continuing innovativeness is indicated by its five applications for patents and 10 new utility designs in 1975.

Automobile Seats. The metal coil springs that used to fill car seats have been replaced by foam rubber polymer, and the Komaba Press Works, found in 1953 and still run by Mr. Komaba, is an active innovator in this area. The polyurethane mold foam made in the plant's Chemical Department has displaced not only the metal springs, but the leather and cotton that formerly went into car seats. A computer controls the color and content of the polymer that becomes the foam rubber. The company's press machines' dies bore, cut, punch, weld and mould the steel frames of car seats, home furniture, etc., which are then assembled and finished in the plant. Komaba Press Works made 10 patent applications, had two registrations of applications for patents, made 30 new utility designs, and had five registrations of utility designs during 1975. It was also engaged in a joint venture with a French firm.

Coated Steel to Prevent Rust. Demand has increased for coated steel that will resist rust. Yamazaki Steel Board Co. is entrepreneurially innovative even though it is not managed by its founder or owner: it and several other firms are wholly owned by Yamazaki Steel Company. It is a pioneer in the pre-painted galvanized steel sheet industry of Japan. High-grade synthetic resin paint is applied to the base metal of the continuously galvanized steel sheet and is baked at high temperature to secure maximum adhesion of the films to the base metal. This prevents peeling paint film and resists ultraviolet rays, acids, alkalis, salt water, etc. The company's galvanized zinc-coating and colored zinc steel plates are less expensive than prepainted aluminum sheet or stainless steel sheet, and very durable. These innovative products are sold as paneling for the exterior and interior walls of buildings and other kinds of construction material, and for television sets, washing machines, and such like. Yamazaki Steel Board Co. made two patent applications during 1975.

Causal Models

Classical and neoclassical economic theory did not recognize any systematic, direct, causal effect of entrepreneuriship on output at the level of the firm. Although historical and institutional economists like Weber, Commons, and Schumpeter argued for the impact of entrepreneurship--as distinct from the other factors of production--on output, their theoretical work was rarely subjected to rigorous empirical testing. We attempt this now.

For the individual firm, a production function can be developed between gross output, Q_G, measured in actual physical units, and various inputs: labor (L), capital (C), technology (T), raw materials (R), and organization (O):

$$Q_G = f\ (L,\ C,\ T,\ R,\ O) \qquad (Eq.\ 1)$$

The output can also be measured by value added, which is "the difference between total sales of the firm. . .and the cost of materials. . . used in producing the given level of sales" (McGuigan and Moyer, 1979: 281). Value added measures the net output (Q_N) of the firm; since it takes cost of materials (R) into account, the production function can be simplified by dropping the term R so that:

$$Q_N = f\ (L,\ C,\ T,\ O) \qquad (Eq.\ 2)$$

What is the place of entrepreneurship in the production function? Let us consider two alternative models of how entrepreneurship could affect net output Q_N. Model 1 simply adds entrepreneurship E as a term to equation 2, meaning that entrepreneurship has a direct causal impact on Q_N), independent of the influence of the other factors of production:

$$Q_N = f\ (L,\ C,\ T,\ O,\ E) \qquad (Eq.\ 3)$$

Model 2 posits that entrepreneurship has only an indirect causal effect on Q_N, through its effect on L, C, T, and O, the direct causes of Q_N. This model views entrepreneurship as antecedent to capital (and the other factors of production), a position entirely consonant with that of Schumpeter, who had that entrepreneurship "did not require antecedent ownership of capital" (Schumpeter, 1947: 151):

> Capital is nothing but the lever by which the entrepreneur subjects to his control the concrete goods which he needs, nothing but a means of diverting the factors of production to new uses, or of dictating a new direction to production, (Schumpeter, 1937: 116, where the importance of the point is indicated by its being italicized).

These models are diagrammed in Figure 1. We shall estimate the models empirically using linear multiple regression analysis. Model 1 will be accepted if, statistically holding constant the variables that measure labor, capital, technology and organization, the measured entrepreneurship of the firm has a significant independent effect on value added (Q_N). If, when these factors of production--L, C, T, and O--are held constant, entrepreneurship E has no net effect on Q_N, we can conclude that E has no direct effect on Q_N, and model 1 must be rejected. Model 2 could then be accepted if E has a significant causal effect on one or more of the L, C, T, or O variables. This would indicate that entrepreneurship's effect on Q_N is indirect, through the factors of production.

The structural form of the relationship in Model 1 can be written for ordinary least squares analysis as:

$$Q_N = a + B_1L + B_2C + B_3T + B_4O + B_5E + e$$

where net output (Q_N) equals the intercept a, plus the respective independent variables--labor, capital, technology, organization and entrepreneurship--times their regression coefficients B_1, B_2..., and e, the disturbance or error term.

These variables will be measured as follows, using data from the Japanese factory study:

Figure 1

Causes of Net Output (Value Added) of Firms

Model 1.

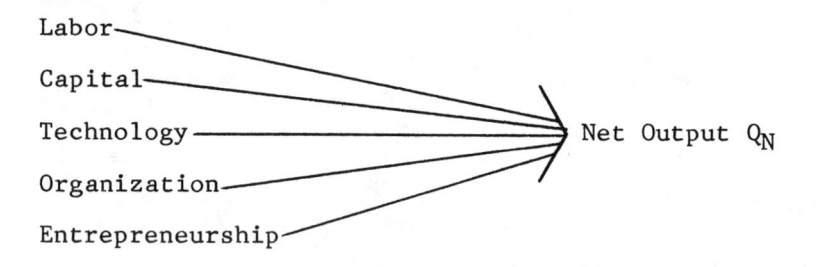

```
Labor ─────────╲
Capital ────────╲
Technology ─────── Net Output $Q_N$
Organization ───╱
Entrepreneurship╱
```

Model 2:

```
                    Labor
                 ↗ Capital       ↘
Entrepreneurship → Technology  → Net Output $Q_N$
                 ↘ Organization ↗
```

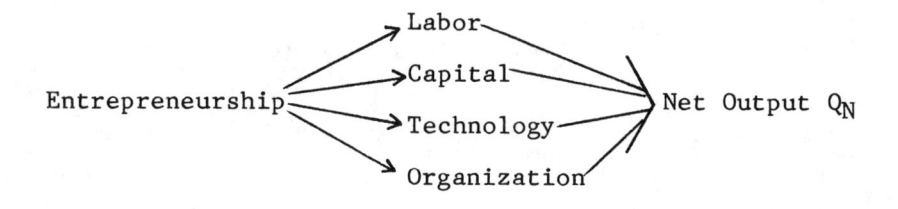

Figure 2

Empirical Test of Model 2

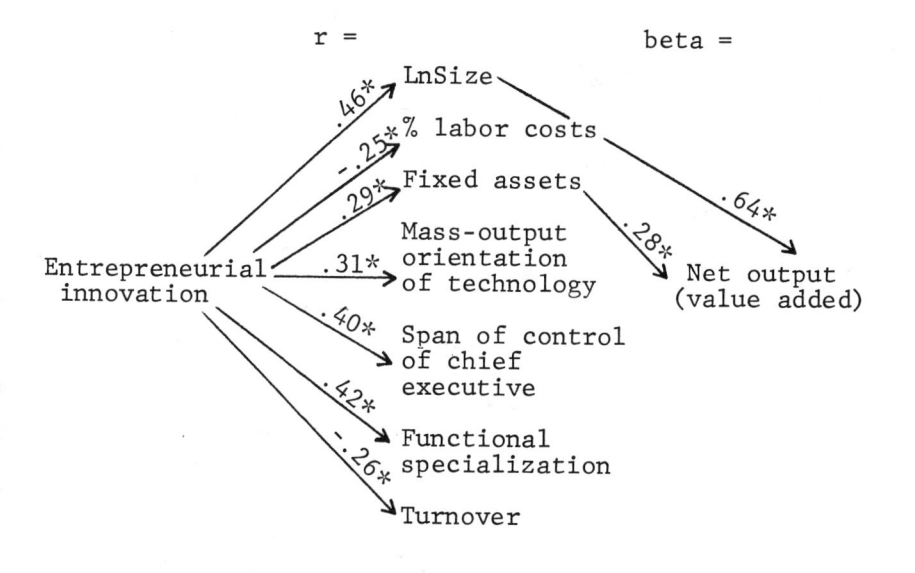

r =   beta =

                    LnSize
            .46*
              .25* % labor costs
               -.25
                .29* Fixed assets
                                                        .64*
                    Mass-output
Entrepreneurial .31* orientation   .28*
   innovation   of technology   Net output
                                                  (value added)
               .40* Span of control
                     of chief
              .42*   executive

               -.26* Functional
                      specialization

                    Turnover

Net output (Q_N) = Value added: sales minus cost of materials for the factory in 1975, to the nearest 100 million yen.

Labor (L) = LnSize: the logarithm of the number of employees in the factory, 1975.

= % labor costs: labor costs as a percent of total factory costs, 1975.

Capital (C) = Fixed assets: in machinery, tools and facilities of the factory, in million yen, end of 1975.

Technology (T) = Mass-output orientation of the factory's production technology. (This is a weighted sum of the extent to which the factory uses each of five types of production technology: custom technology, small- and large-batch technology, mass production technology, and continuous-process automated technology. In this index, factories that use primarily custom and/or small-batch technologies score substantially less than factories that use mass production and/or continuous-process technologies. Khandwalla, (1974: 81-83).

Organization (O)[6] = Span of control of chief executive: number of people who report directly to the chief executive officer of the factory.

= Functional specialization: the number of nonworkflow (administrative) task areas for which the factory has at least one full-time specialist person.

= Turnover: the total number of employees who left the factory through voluntary quits, retirement, or involuntary factors during 1975, as a percent of the average number of employees in the factory in 1975.

Entrepreneurship
(E) = <u>Entrepreneurial innovation index</u> described above (whether planning to expand the range of products, and number of patent applications in 1975.

Each of these variables has a significant effect on the factories' value added (see Table 2). Value added is increased by having more employees (r = .82), more fixed assets (r = .68), more people reporting to the chief executive (r = .57), more mass-production and automated types of technology (r = .53), more functional specialization (r = .32), and more entrepreneurial innovation (r = .29). Value added is negatively affected (decreased) by personnel turnover (r = -.33) and by higher labor costs as a percentage of total factory costs (r = - .30). These findings are what one might expect.

The further, and more central question is, "What is the net effect of each variable when the others are held constant?" and, in particular, "Does entrepreneurship continue to have a significant effect on value added, independent of the effects of the other variables in the equation?" The correlations in Table 2 indicate that entrepreneurship and the other independent variables are themselves interrelated in varying degrees. Multiple regression analysis will estimate the effect of each causal variable when the effects of the other causal variables have been statistically controlled (held constant), and thereby clarify whether some of the apparent relationships are spurious.

The results of regressing net output (value added) on all eight of these independent variables simultaneously are displayed in Table 3. The effect of number of employees (LnSize) alone on value added is so great (B_1 = .66) that when it is held constant, none of the other factors of production, or entrepreneurial innovation, has any significant additional independent effect on value added. The strongest of these other effects is that of fixed assets (B_2 = .37), but even this variable is not significant when the other variables are controlled. Most importantly, when number of employees is taken into account, entrepreneurial innovation has no net significant causal influence on value added (B_5 =

Table 2

Correlations, Means and Standard Deviations for all Variables

LOWER TRIANGLE: CORRELATION COEFFICIENTS UPPER TRIANGLE: N OF CASES FOR CORRELATION

	V15	LN71	V21	V5	V68	V106	V115	V145	V570
V15		47.	45.	43.	47.	45.	47.	47.	47.
LN71	.82		46.	45.	50.	48.	50.	49.	50.
V21	-.30	-.14		42.	46.	44.	46.	46.	46.
V5	.68	.62	-.43		45.	43.	45.	45.	45.
V68	.53	.53	-.26	.52		48.	50.	49.	50.
V106	.57	.54	-.29	.90	.65		48.	47.	48.
V115	.32	.51	.01	.20	.19	.19		49.	50.
V145	-.33	-.28	.52	-.19	-.21	-.19	-.18		49.
V570	.29	.46	-.25	.29	.30	.40	.42	-.26	
Mean	45.30	5.70	16.72	17030.73	27.12	11.31	11.10	11.69	0.56
S.D.	91.12	0.98	14.04	73139.80	8.20	19.82	4.59	9.95	0.70

Entry Identification:
  V 15 = value added
  LN 71 = lnSize
  V 21 = % labor costs
  V 5 = fixed assets
  V 68 = mass-output orientation

  V 106 = span of control of chief executive
  V 115 = functional specialization
  V 145 = turnover
  V 570 = entrepreneurial innovation

In the last column of Table 3, value added is regressed on LnSize and fixed assets only. These two variables--measures of labor and capital, respectively--each exert a significant positive, independent effect, though the effect of size (coefficient = .64) remains much greater than the effect of fixed assets (coefficient = .28). The coefficient of multiple determination adjusted for degrees of freedom lost, R^2, is .702, which indicates that 70.2 percent of the variance in value added across the factories is explained by number of employees and fixed assets. This is more of the variance than was explained by all eight variables together (69.1 percent). Thus our first conclusion is that <u>entrepreneurship has no direct effect on net output (value added) beyond that exerted by two factors of production--labor and capital inputs.</u> Model 1 in Figure 1 can be rejected. We have also seen that among these Japanese factories, once the number of employees and fixed assets have been taken into account, neither technology nor various measures of the organization of the factory have any significant causal influence on value added.

Model 2 posits an <u>indirect</u> influence of entrepreneurship on value added, through its influence on the factors of production that have a direct impact on value added. This model is estimated in Figure 2, which is based on the assumption that entrepreneurship is a cause of capital formation and affects the other factors of production, which in turn increase value added. In other words, we assume that appropriate entrepreneurial leadership can call forth these factors of production, put them together, and manage the organizations that control them. We see in Figure 2 that entrepreneurial innovation has significant correlations with all seven of the measures of the factors of production. The more innovative a factory is, the more employees it has (r = .46); the <u>lower</u> its labor costs as a percentage of total costs ($\overline{r = -.25}$); the more fixed assets it has (.29); the more it uses mass-output types of technology (.31); the larger the chief executive's span of control (.40); the greater its functional specialization (.42); and the <u>less</u> its personnel turnover (-.26).

We have seen that only two of the factors of production--number of employees and fixed assets--have a significant net causal impact on value added. Therefore, we infer that the indirect effect of

Table 3

Regression of Net Output (Value Added) on Factors of Production and Entrepreneurship, Japanese Factories

		Full Equation beta	Best Fit beta
Labor:	LnSize	.66*	.64*
	% labor costs	-.04	
Capital:	Fixed assets	.37	.28*
Technology:	Mass-output orientation	.11	
Organization:	Span of control of C.E.	-.18	
	Functional specialization	-.06	
	Turnover	-.10	
Entrenepeurship:	Entrepreneurship innovation	-.09	
R =		.867	.846
$\hat{R}^2$ =		.691	.702
Intercept =		-301.748	-301.960
Standard error of estimate =		50.617	49.774
N		42	43
F-ratio -		12.483	50.378

*Indicates the standard regression coefficient (beta) is significant at the .05 level

entrepreneurial innovation on value added operates through its effect on these two factors. Though entrepreneurship also influences technological and organizational factors, since those factors do not have a significant net effect on value added, the influence of entrepreneurship cannot be transmitted through them to value added.

The second conclusion, then, is that Model 2 in Figure 1 can be provisionally accepted. Factories that are entrepreneurially innovative--i.e., are expanding their range of products and generating patent applications--are more likely than those that are not both to increase the number of employees and to accumulate capital in the form of fixed assets (machinery, tools and other facilities). These increments of manpower and assets then increase the value added by the factory. The influence of entrepreneurship on net output is indirect, not direct.

Discussion and Conclusion

When economists ask, "What makes for increased output at the level of the firm and for aggregate economic growth?" they usually answer in terms of the crucial importance of capital accumulation, and especially "capital deepening," i.e., increased capital per worker; of technological innovation; and of market scale. When the question is, "Who makes for this output and growth in private enterprise economies?" it is capitalists (accumulators), technological inventors, and entrepreneurs (innovators) whose roles are variously stressed. (The role of government may also be stressed, but that is beyond the scope of this paper.) A central theoretical issue is, therefore, If entrepreneurial innovation has any effect on the output of the firm, is this effect direct or indirect?

Using data from 50 Japanese factories, we have empirically shown that variations in net output (value added) are explained mainly by the size of the factory work force and its machinery and other fixed assets; when these factors of production are held constant, entrepreneurial innovation has no significant net effect on value added.

The first implication of this finding is its vindication of neoclassical economic theory's neglect

37

of entrepreneurship as a direct factor of production, for it makes clear that whatever importance entrepreneurship has must derive from its impact on labor and capital inputs, the variables that economic theory sees as central causes of output and economic growth. But, to say entrepreneurship has only this indirect effect is not to say it has no effect. As J. B. Say put it: the entrepreneur's function is <u>to combine the factors of production, to bring them together</u> (Schumpeter, 1934: 76).

We must be cautious, however, in drawing even this inference. Our data are cross-sectional, whereas the inference should ideally be based on longitudinal data. Specifically, the causal model we have provisionally accepted implies the following:

(1) These are causal lags and at least three discrete time points of observation. Increases in a factory's entrepreneurial innovation between time 1 and time 2 cause more employees to be hired and more investment in fixed assets to be made. Then, between time 2 and time 3, the increased number of employees and assets cause an increase in value added. The model implies a knowledge of how long these time lags are, a knowledge which do not have.

(2) These causal processes set in motion by an <u>increase</u> in a factory's entrepreneurial <u>innovation</u> should operate to the same degree but in a reverse direction if entrepreneurial innovation <u>decreases</u>. Thus, a decline in innovation <u>between time</u> 1 and time 2 causes a reduction in the number of employees and in fixed assets, which then, between time 2 and time 3 cause value added also to decline. Insofar as it takes longer to reduce fixed assets than to reduce the number of employees, the lag time in their negative effects on value added will differ. Until we know this lag differential we cannot properly estimate the model. If the full indirect negative effect of declining entrepreneurial innovation on value added requires reductions in both labor and fixed assets, then only after both of the latter reductions have occurred can we expect to observe a decline in value added.

Another reason why the effect of declining entrepreneurial innovation on number of employees, fixed assets, and value added may not be a "mirror image" of the effect of increasing entrepreneurial innovation is what has been referred to as the "ratchet effect" (Inkson et al., 1970) or the "bumperjack effect" (Freeman and Hannan, 1975). This is the empirical observation that organizations do not exhibit identical patterns in periods of growth and periods of stability or decline. Vested interests within the organization in the larger number of employees or fixed assets act to resist the cutbacks in the work force or the physical assets that a lessening of innovation requires. These vested interests may be located among managers whose rewards are threatened by a lowering of their supervisory responsibilities occasioned by a reduction in the personnel or assets they control, or among labor unions and workers. In other words, the cross-sectional beta coefficients may obscure the fact that it is easier to add employees and fixed assets than to get rid of them.

There is, finally, the question, Is it correct to label the innovation found in some of our medium- and large-scale Japanese factories as "entrepreneurial"? Schumpeter noted that

> The entrepreneur of earlier times was not only as a rule the capitalist too, he was also often--as he still is today in the case of small concerns--his own technical expert, in so far as a professional specialist was not called in..." (Schumpeter, 1934: 77).

In other words, the innovations effected by solo or small-scale businesspersons are more unambiguously traceable to their own actions than are the innovations found in our Japanese factories. Our index of entrepreneurial innovation contains two elements, one of which--a goal or policy of expanding the range of products--is presumably still in the hands of the owner-entrepreneur. The second element, however, is patent applications, and in larger factories this function becomes progressively differentiated from ownership and institutionalized in specialized roles and departments such as Research and Development. It is likely, therefore, that the source and form of innovations--patents and the like--become transformed in larger-scale firms.

In our Japanese factories, the overwhelming cause of the number of patent applications is the size of the factory's budget for research and development (r = managers make a policy decision to allocate resources for research and development, which then "pay off" in terms of innovation. Should this be called entrepreneurial innovation? Schumpeter's answer is "yes," since it is the function--carrying out new combinations--rather than the person's status (owner, manager, or R & D staff researcher) that is the essence of entrepreneurship:

> ". . . . we call entrepreneurs not only those 'independent' businessmen in an exchange economy who are usually so designated, but all who actually fulfill the function by which we define the concept, even if they are, as is becoming the rule, 'dependent' employees of a company. . . ." (Schumpeter, 1934: 74-75).

Elsewhere, Schumpeter observed that

> ". . . . in our own time promotion [of new combinations] within the shell of existing corporations offers a much more convenient access to the entrepreneurial functions than existed in the world of owner-managed firms." (Schumpeter, 1947: 151).

There is no reason, therefore, to restrict future studies of entrepreneurship to solo and small-scale enterprises. The ways in which entrepreneurial innovation is effected in larger-scale firms is an equally important topic. It is also our hope that anthropologists will extend their range of methods from the qualitative and descriptive to the quantitative testing of causal models of the role of entrepreneurship in the economic production function. Such a shift would serve to make the findings of anthropologists more comparable to those of economists and sociologists.

NOTES

(1) This section relies on Schumpeter, 1949, Hoselitz, 1951, and Cochran, 1968: vol. 5, pp. 87-91.

(2) The Aston group of organizational researchers is so named because their initial research was done at the University of Aston, Birmingham, England. See Pugh and Hickson (1976) for a description of concepts, variables and measurement.

(3) We also asked each factory how many registrations of applications for patents, how many new utility designs, and how many registrations of utility designs they had made or received during 1975. Since all these variables are highly positively correlated, we use only the number of patent applications.

(4) Names of persons, firms, products, etc. have been altered to protect the anonymity of informants.

(5) "Organization" refers to the institutional arrangements that maximize the total effectiveness of the other factors of production. In this paper, it will refer to such aspects of the formal organization of a firm as its functional specialization, complexity, and formalization, and its personnel turnover.

(6) Organizational structure variables that were not significantly related to value added--administrative intensity, centralization of decision-making, the autonomy of the factory from its parent company, span of control of first-line foremen, and the extent to which the company recognized a labor union--were not included in the equation.

(7) The only serious collinearity--a correlation over .70 between independent variables--is the .90 between fixed assets and span of control of the chief executive. This indicates that these two variables are measuring essentially the same thing. Theoretically, it means that factories with considerable fixed assets require their chief executives to seek advice and information directly from a wider range of immediate subordinates. Collinearity clouds the issue of

precisely how much variation in value added is due to fixed assets net of span of control, and vice versa. Analyses not reported, however, show that an equation containing span of control but not fixed assets explains less of the variance in value added than one that contains fixed assets but not span of control. This suggests that the apparent effect of span of control of the chief executive on value added is somewhat spurious: i.e., partially due to the confounding of span of control with fixed assets.

REFERENCES

BELASCO, Bernard I. 1980. The Entrepreneur as Culture Hero: Preadaptations in Nigerian Economic Development, New York: Praeger.

BEVERIDGE, Andrew A. and Anthony R. Oberschall. 1979. African Businessmen and Development in Zambia, Princeton, NJ: Princeton University Press.

BLAU, Peter M. Cecilia McFalbe, William McKinley, and Phelps K. Tracy. 1976. "Technology and Organization in Manufacturing," Administrative Science Quarterly, 21 (March), 20-40.

COCHRAN, Thomas C. 1968. "Entrepreneurship," in David L. Sills, ed., The International Encyclopedia of the Social Sciences, New York: Macmillan, Vol. 5, pp. 87-91.

FREEMAN, John and Michael T. Hannan. 1975. "Growth and Decline Processes in Organizations," American Sociological Review, 40, pp. 215-222.

HIRSCHMEIER, Johannes and Tsunehiko Yui. 1975. The Development of Japanese Business 1600-1973, Harvard University Press.

HOSELITZ, Bert F. 1981. "The Early History of Entrepreneurial Theory." Explorations in Entrepreneurial History. 3, No. 4 (April 15), pp. 193-220.

INKSON, J. H. K., Hickson, D. J. and Pugh, D. S. 1970. "Organization Context and Structure: An Abbreviated Replication," Administrative Science Quarterly, 15, pp. 318-29.

KHANDAWALLA Pradip N. 1974. "Mass Output Orientation of Operations Technology and Organizational Structure," Administrative Science Quarterly, 19.1 (March), pp. 74-97.

MC GUIGAN, James R. and R. Charles Moyer. 1979. Managerial Economics, St. Paul, MN: West Publishing Company.

NODA, Kazuo. 1966. "Postwar Japanese Executives," in Komiya Ryutaro, ed., Postwar Economic Growth in Japan, Berkeley, CA: University of California Press, Ch. 11.

PUGH, D. S. and D. J. Hickson. 1976. Organizational Structure and its Context: The Aston Programme I, Farnborough, Hants: Saxon House Studies, Teakfield.

SCHUMPETER, Joseph A. 1947. "The Creative Response in Economic History," Journal of Economic History, 7, 149-59.

_____. 1949. "Economic Theory and Entrepreneurial History," in Change and the Entrepreneur, Research Center in Entrepreneurial History, Cambridge, MA: Harvard University Press, 63-84.

_____. 1971. "The Fundamental Phenomenon of Economic Growth," in Peter Kilby, ed., Entrepreneurship and Economic Development, New York: Free Press.

_____. 1934. The Theory of Economic Development: An Inquiry Into Profits, Capital, Credit, Interest, and the Business Cycle, Cambridge, MA: Harvard University Press.

SHINOHARA, Miyohei. 1968. "The Role of Small Industry in the Process of Economic Growth: Japan," in Bert F. Hoselitz, ed., The Role of Small Industry in the Process of Economic Growth, The Hague: Mouton.

STOLPER, Wolfgang F. 1968. "Joseph A. Schumpeter," in David L. Sills, ed., The International Encyclopedia of the Social Sciences, New York: Macmillan, Vol. 12, pp. 67-72.

II. CONSTRAINTS ON ENTREPRENEURSHIP: TRANSACTION COSTS AND MARKET EFFICIENCY

James M. Acheson

In virtually all of the papers presented today, emphasis has been on the strategies of entrepreneurs. Very little attention has been paid to the characteristics of the enterprises they direct, and the way the nature of those enterprises constrains the activities of entrepreneurs. In many enterprises, entrepreneurs are not free to wheel and deal indiscriminately. This is especially true in firms-- the most important enterprises from an economic point of view. The nature of the firm involved places limits on the range of incomes that can be earned and limits the kinds of strategies that must be employed if the firm is to increase in profitability.

If we are to understand the range of possible strategies open to entrepreneurs and what they need to do to increase income, we must understand something about the differences in firms and the industries in which they are embedded. The most important difference in firms concerns their degree of specialization. In modern industrialized countries, firms are highly specialized, and many are very large. Firms in peasant and tribal societies studied by most anthropoligists are small and unspecialized, as are most of the firms in all the Third World countries in general.

One way of viewing the problem of specialization and size is presented in Figure 1. Specialization here refers to component specialization. Small unspecialized firms (Type A), of the kind which predominate in the societies studied by anthropologists, make several complete products. An example of such a firm is the small peasant family farm which grows several crops, raises different types of animals, and does every step in the production process from tilling the soil to harvesting and marketing. In modern industrialized countries, there are really two different kinds of specialized firms. Some industries are dominated by small firms, each one of which makes one component part or contributes in some specialized way to the manufacture of a single product (Type C). For example, in the U.S. clothing

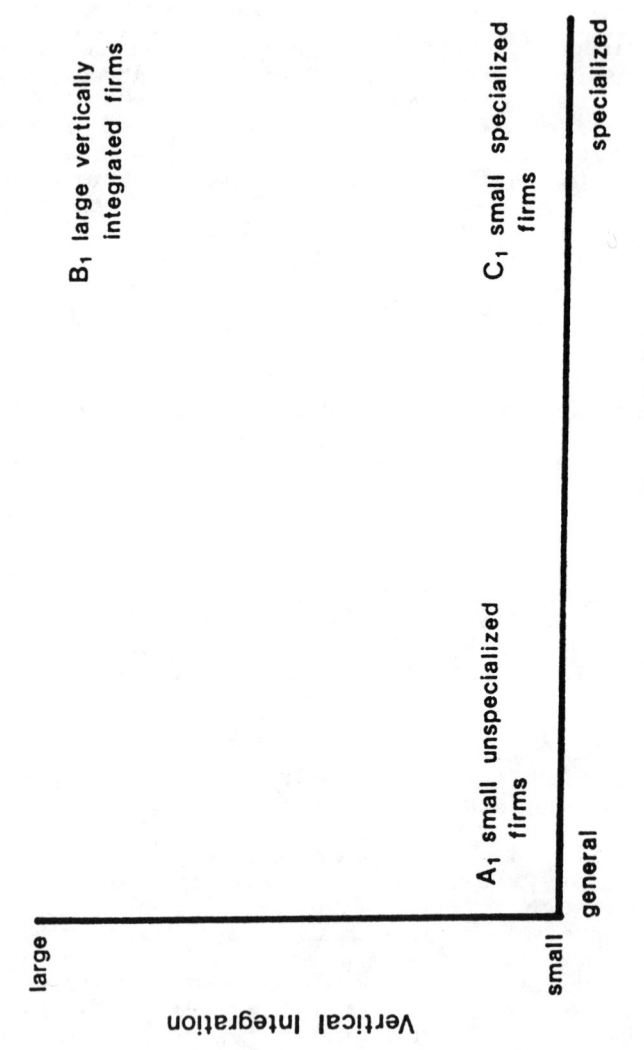

B₁ large vertically integrated firms

C₁ small specialized firms

A₁ small unspecialized firms

Vertical Integration: large, small
Component Specialization: general, specialized

Figure 1

industry one firm makes cloth, another cuts out the pieces, still a third assembles and sews the pieces into finished clothes, which are sold to consumers in thousands of individually owned stores. The second type (Type B) are large vertically integrated firms, which are simply conglomerates of small specialized units, each of which perform specialized roles (e.g., accounting, sales, production, etc.).

It is interesting to note that the papers in this symposium deal with a spectrum of firms involving different sizes and degrees of specialization. The papers by Barnes and Schildkrout deal with the tiny unspecialized firms which most anthropologists have studied. At the other extreme, Marsh and Mannari are studying firms which have achieved a high degree of specialization and some vertical integration. The enterprises discussed by Cook and Lomnitz fall someplace between these two extremes.

These different types of firms have very different capacities to generate income. The high levels of income enjoyed by citizens of industrialized countries are produced by these highly specialized firms (Types B and C), while much of the poverty in Third World countries can be traced to the limited income generating capacity of the small unspecialized firms that predominate in those societies. This has enoromous implications for development. Given this perspective, one of the key factors blocking development is the organization of firms. It also suggests that if these societies are to develop economically, some unspecialized firms must somehow become more specialized. The fact that modernization and economic development must involve a reorganization of firms has been recognized by Geertz (1963). He clearly notes that during the modernization process, entrepreneurs experiment with different types of firms, and he states that "the major innovational problems the entrepreneur faces are organizational rather than technical" (1963: 151). He does not, however, suggest any model linking organizational changes in firms to stages of development, nor has anyone else for that matter.

One of the reasons for this oversight is that no social science discipline has looked at firms along the entire continuum. Anthropologists, with very few exceptions, have studied the small unspecialized firms typical of the societies in which they work. Economists--especially those interested in industrial organization--have studied the large vertically integrated firms which which dominate such a large sphere of our own economy. Sometimes economists act as if the only kinds of firms worth studying are those in the oil, steel and auto industries. Agricultural economists have studied food production systems--primarily in industrialized states. But whatever the reason for the oversight, one of the key issues in the study of entrepreneurship (and the closely related study of development) concerns factors influencing the specialization and sizes of firms.

Economists Coase and Williamson and others interested in the elementary transaction have evolved a body of theory which is helpful in explaining the size and specialization of firms. While they have not applied their model to Third World firms or problems of development, the application of their work to these problems is obvious.

Coase agrues that the owners of firms can obtain the goods and services they require either by contracting with other firms or by hiring employees, obtaining capital, and producing the goods and services themselves. Most entrepreneurs do both. This means that entrepreneurs are involved in two kinds of transactions--those within the firm (i.e. between an employer and employee, or between departments), and those outside the firm. Both types of transactions involve costs. The size of the firm that evolves depends on the balance between internal versus external transaction costs (Coase 1952).

When internal transaction costs are smaller than external transaction costs, then entrepreneurs expand the size of their firm and produce a large number of the component parts and services they need themselves. When internal transaction costs exceed external transaction costs, then the rational entrepreneur does not expand his own firm but rather purchases the goods and services required from other firms (Coase 1952).

The key question is, What lies behind internal and external transaction costs? Williamson's work suggests that three factors influence transaction costs: the efficiency of the final product market, intermediate product market efficiency, and organization skill. Changes in each of these factors affect firm size and specialization in different ways. If intermediate product markets are efficient, than firms can buy and sell component parts and services to each other cheaply. In industries marked by such efficient intermediate product markets, small specialized firms will be the rule. Inefficient intermediate product markets will result in a tendency for firms to perform more different tasks and functions for themselves. The increase in number of component parts and services produced results in expansion of the number of sub-units in firms and an overall increase in firm size and complexity. Thus, large complex firms are the result of inefficiency in intermediate product markets.

Final product market (i.e. sales of completed products to consumers) influences the length of production runs, which has still other effects on firms. The efficiency of these final product markets depends, in large part, on the size of wholesale operations. If final product markets are efficient, then producing firms receive steady predictable orders. Under these conditions, they have long production runs, can use highly specialized machinery, and can enter into long-term contracts with employees. The result is large production operations, but not necessarily the production of a large number of different products, nor a highly complicated firm organization. The effect of efficient final product markets on firm size should not be underestimated, however. Chandler, among others, has pointed out that large firms in the United States came into being only when marketing organization was changed so that large amounts of standardized goods could be sold quickly to a mass market (Chandler 1977: 209 f.f.).

Organizational skill reduces both internal and external transaction costs. Highly educated, literate managers are more adept at dealing with bureaucracy, are able to use the legal system to effect contracts which reduce labor problems, and insure steady supplies of raw materials. They are also capable of using advanced accounting and financial management techniques to make better decisions concerning hiring labor, obtaining capital and utilizing technology. Organizational skill also makes it possible for entrepreneurs to respond appropriately to market efficiencies and inefficiencies.

The efficiency of intermediate and final product markets and the organizational skill of entrepreneurs combine in different ways to produce different types of firms. These different types of firms can be expressed in a three dimensional, eight-cell chart (Figure 2).

The firms resulting from several of these combinations are of special interest to anthropologists. The small unspecialized firms (see Figure 1, A) most anthropologists deal with are the result of inefficient final product markets, inefficient intermediate product markets and high organization costs (Figure 2, cell 4). The specific factors producing such firms in one Mexican pueblo have been analyzed in some detail in another article (Acheson 1984). In such cases, inefficient final product markets mean that orders coming into firms are small, highly specialized, and come at irregular intervals. Under these conditions, it does not pay entrepreneurs to use specialized machinery or hire labor for long periods. The inefficient intermediate product markets means they produce their own component parts. The lack of sophisticated organizational skill increases both internal and external transaction costs further.

At the opposite extreme are firms in cell 5 (Figure 2) which result from efficient intermediate product markets, efficient final product markets, and low organizational costs. Efficient intermediate product markets mean the firm can specialize in what it does best and buy other necessary components from other firms. The efficient final product markets make possible long production runs, which in turn enable the firm to use specialized machinery and labor. The high organizational skills make it possible to take advantage of both kinds of efficiencies. The result is small specialized firms operating under conditions approaching pure competition. These are the same types of firms indicated in Figure 1, (Type C).

The large vertically integrated firms (Figure 1, B) are actually two different types of firms and are the result of two combinations of factors (Cells 6 and 8, Figure 2). Such firms are, first and foremost, produced by entrepreneurs responding to inefficient intermediate product markets wherein external transaction costs are high. As a result, these

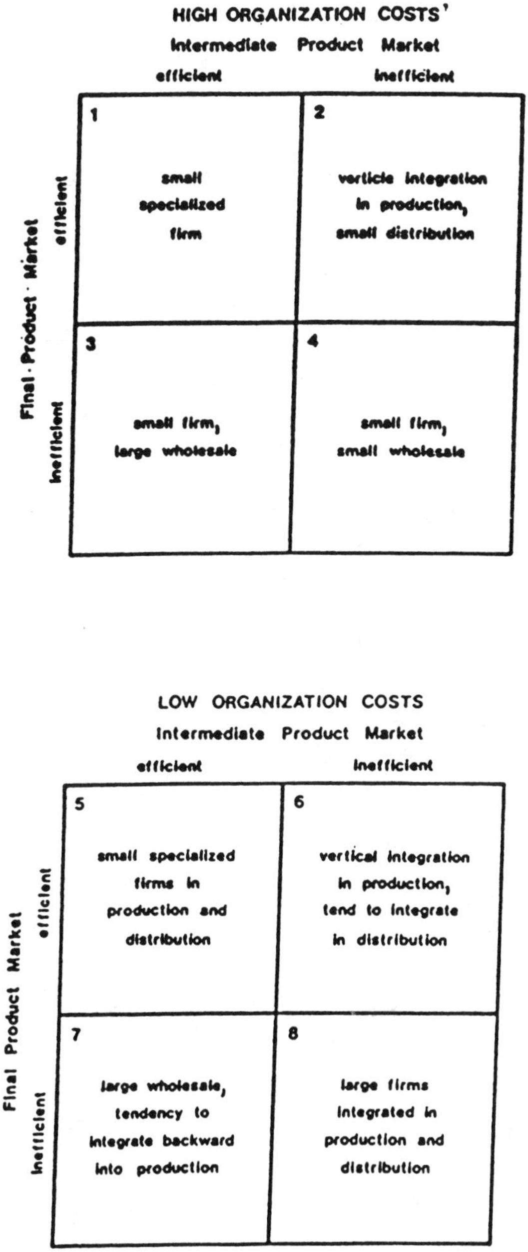

HIGH ORGANIZATION COSTS
Intermediate Product Market

	efficient	inefficient
Final Product Market efficient	1 small specialized firm	2 verticle integration in production, small distribution
Final Product Market inefficient	3 small firm, large wholesale	4 small firm, small wholesale

LOW ORGANIZATION COSTS
Intermediate Product Market

	efficient	inefficient
Final Product Market efficient	5 small specialized firms in production and distribution	6 vertical integration in production, tend to integrate in distribution
Final Product Market inefficient	7 large wholesale, tendency to integrate backward into production	8 large firms integrated in production and distribution

Figure 2

entrepreneurs integrate their firms vertically and minimize the numbers of component parts and services they purchase from other firms. Where final product markets are also inefficient, entrepreneurs find it advantageous to take over the distribution of their products as well, as has occurred with firms such as the Singer Sewing Machine Company (i.e. Cell 8, Figure 2). Where final product markets are efficient, the firm retains far looser control over marketing outlets, as is the case in the auto and oil industries.

Each of the other four cells left unanalyzed (i.e. Cells 1, 2, 3, and 7, Figure 2) represent still other types of firms resulting from still other combinations of organizational skills and market efficiency.

Two important conclusions can be drawn from this analysis and model. First, the type of firm that can be established by an entrepreneur depends primarily on organizing skill in combination with the efficiency of final and intermediate product markets. Entrepreneurs are strongly constrained by these factors and are not free to establish any kind of firm they choose. Second, economic development, with all this indicates for higher per capita income, occurs when unspecialized firms become more specialized. This occurs as firms evolve from the type represented in Figure 2, Cell 4, to those represented by Cells 5, 6, and 8, which are more profitable. From this viewpoint, economic development involves primarily increases in organizational skill which allow the entrepreneur to take advantage of market efficiencies and inefficiencies in various combinations. (Again, it needs to be stressed that increases in the earning power of firms do not always stem from market efficiencies. Vertically integrated firms are the result of entrepreneurs responding to inefficient intermediate product markets.) This, in turn, suggests that education or human capital is the critical variable in development--a point that has been made by several social scientists (Becker 1962; Schultz 1962).

REFERENCES

ACHESON, James M. 1983. "Limitations on firm size in a Tarascan Pueblo." Human Organization, 43(4): 319-329.

BECKER, Gary. 1962. "Investment in human capital: A theoretical analysis." Journal of Political Economy. Supplement 70: 9-44.

CHANDLER, Alfred D. 1977. The visible hand: The managerial revolution in American business. Cambridge, Mass. Belknap Press.

COASE, R. H. 1952. "The nature of the firm." In: Readings in Price Theory. Eds. George Stigler and Kenneth Boulding. Chicago: Richard D. Irwin Inc. pp. 337-350.

GEERTZ, Clifford. 1963. Peddlars and Princes: Social Development and Economic Change in Two Indonesian Towns. Chicago: University of Chicago Press.

SCHULTZ, Theodore. 1964. Transforming Traditional Agriculture. New Haven: Yale University Press.

WILLIAMSON, Oliver. 1975. Markets and Hierarchies: Analysis and Antitrust Implications. New York: The Free Press.

III. THE 'MANAGERIAL' VS. THE 'LABOR' FUNCTION, CAPITAL ACCUMULATION, AND THE DYNAMICS OF SIMPLE COMMODITY PRODUCTION IN RURAL OAXACA, MEXICO

Scott Cook

I. Introduction

In this paper I will discuss some preliminary results of an analysis of household survey and interview data from two villages in the Valley of Oaxaca, Mexico: Xaaga (municipio of Mitla, district of Tlacolula) which has a weaving industry and Santa Lucia del Camino (Centro district) which has a brick industry. My analysis will focus on those household-based production units within these two labor-intensive industries which regularly employ wage labor. A series of socioeconomic characteristics pertaining to the background and performance of these employer units will be examined for the purpose of contributing to our understanding of the process of capital accumulation in small-scale, labor-intensive rural craft industries.[1]

The notion of 'entrepreneur' will be employed here in a pre-Schumpeterian sense which, according to J. B. Say, assumes the entrepreneur's function to be the combination of productive factors and, according to Marshall, equates it with "management" in the broadest sense (Schumpeter 1961: 76-77). This is in distinct contrast to Schumpeter's emphasis on the "carrying out of new combinations" which singles out the entrepreneur as a unique innovator in the process of industrial capitalist accumulation (op. cit. p. 78 et passim). To avoid conflating the pre-Schumpeterian and the Schumpeterian notions I will refer to the former as the 'managerial function.'[2]

I will focus on the "managerial function" as it is realized through the labor process, that is, through the process the process by which labor-power and instruments of labor are combined to transform natural resources and raw materials into products. I further define the managerial function as operating only in labor processes geared toward commodity production, with its principal goal being the expansion of the commodity-producing capacity of the involved enterprise and, consequently, to generate more exchange-value. Ideally, when output in a given enterprise is expanded, its factor mix changes, (e.g., the ratio of investment in tools and equipment to the wages bill) and, other things remaining equal, as its labor productivity increases so does its profit potential. In short, through this focus on the managerial function and related issues, I will examine the causes, conditions, and consequences of capital accumulation in two rural craft industries which are at different phases of development from their simple commodity matrix (Cook 1982: esp. Chs. 1 & 8).

II. Employer Households in Two Village-based Industries: Weaving in Xaaga and Brickmaking in Santa Lucia

What is the rationale for selecting these two village-based industries for an analysis of the issues outlined above? Aside from the fact that I have personally spent a great deal of time on primary data collection in these two communities, I have chosen them because of the fundamentally contrasting nature of their industries: Xaaga manufactures textile products from purchased, factory-made thread which are sold almost exclusively in tourist markets, whereas Santa Lucia manufactures bricks from locally excavated clay deposits and sells them almost exclusively to contractors in Oaxaca City for urban construction projects. Although agriculture is still practiced in both villages, Xaaga is more rural and agricultural, whereas Santa Lucia which entered the 20th century as a hacienda-dependent agricultural village and was gradually transformed into a periuban agricultural-industrial community, is enmeshed in an irreversible process of urbanization under the impact of the expansion of the nearby city. At the present time it is best characterized as a semi-corporate community in the process of dissolution through urbanization (Cook 1984a: 14-22). Both villages are relative newcomers to craft production: weaving was introduced in Xaaga only 15 years ago, whereas brickmaking has been extensively practiced in Santa Lucia only since the 1930s. These are brief periods in a regional division of labor in which some communities have craft specializations with documented roots in prehispanic or early colonial times.[3]

A. The 'Employer-Weavers' of Xaaga

The settlement of Xaaga is located 5 kilometers east of Mitla in the district of Tlacolula; it is an ex-hacienda community and an ejido with all of its land controlled through the ejidal tenure regime. In 1979 it had 191 heads of household. Of the 55 households surveyed 84% participated in craft production; and, significantly, 9% (all of them weavers) did not participate in agricultural production. The craft occupation with the highest number of participants was shawl finishing (frill knotting) with 36% of the households surveyed; 32% of the latter had weavers and 20% had sewing machine operators (seamstresses). About 90% of the seamstresses were located in weaving households, a relationship which I will discuss below. The Xaaga weaving industry employs the treadle loom as its principal instrument of production; its principal product is cotton cloth which is used to make 'neo-traditional' type polo shirts, blouses, dresses, shawls and jackets. A few weavers produce and sell only cloth but most of them weave cloth and then transform it into one or more of the above-mentioned products--either in their own home workshops or in a putting-out system involving seamstresses and female finishers who are paid by piece rate. So, the female occupations of seamstress and finisher are completely integrated within a male-dominated weaving industry. This is true to such a degree in the case of the seamstresses that the typical production unit in the industry consists of the tandem couplings: loom + sewing machine and weaver + seamstress. It is skillful performance in organizing and managing production units comprised of tandem couplings between loom/loom operator + sewing machine/seamstress that the 'entrepreneur' may be separated from the non-entrepreneurs in the Xaaga weaving industry. This skillful performance usually, but not exclusively, entails the regular employment of wage labor; in other words, 'entrepreneurs' in the Xaaga weaving industry are typically, but not always, petty capitalists.

Of the 28 weaving households surveyed in Xaaga, 10 have self-employed weavers and do not employ wage-workers, 9 have self employed weavers and do regularly employ wage-workers, and 9 have between them an average (median) of three full-time hired loom operators (operarios). With regard to the distribution of income in the industry the following data are pertinent: the average weekly income of the weavers is much higher than that of the seamstresses or the shawl finishers; most shawl finishers (young girls or old women) earn less than 50 pesos (2.20 dollars) weekly, whereas the seamstresses earn between 100 and 300 pesos (3 to 12 dollars) weekly. Weaver-operarios, by contrast, earn from 300-450 pesos (12 to 20 dollars) weekly, whereas the average weekly net income for self-employed weavers (including employers and non-employers) is 650 pesos (30 dollars). There is a slightly skewed valuation of female and male labor-power operative here. The operarios are paid 3 pesos per meter for the standard type of cotton cloth and weave an average of 3 meters per hour (24 meters in an 8-hour day); seamstresses are paid 2 pesos per shirt and sew an average of 4 shirts per hour--most work only 4-hour days because of the need to do domestic tasks. So the average operario's wage is 9 pesos (40 cents) per hour or 72 pesos (3.20 dollars) per 8-hour day compared to the average wage for a seamstress of 8 pesos (30 cents) per hour of 32 pesos (1.40 dollars) per 4-hour day. By constrast, the shawl finishers earn 4-7 pesos per rebozo (2 hours work) or the equivalent to an hourly wage of 3 pesos (13 cents). However, as I discuss below, this is not the worst of it since the key to the viability of the Xaaga weaving industry is not low wages but no wages-- the inner sanctum of the family enterprise is propelled on the engine of unpaid intimate labor-power in the form of in-kind prestation or "avuda" (helping-out).

Concerning cultivated land, a comparison between weaving and non-weaving households indicates a tendency for the weavers to have less land under cultivation (70% have under 2 has.) than the non-weavers (only 53% of these households had less than 2 has. under cultivation). Nonetheless, an equal percentage of weaving households and non-weaving households have more than 3 hectares under cultivation; and two weaving households have more than 5 hectares under cultivation (compared with only one non-weaving household with this much).

Let us now examine the 'weaver-employer' households (see Table 1) and compare them with the non-employer but self-employed weaving households (see Table 2). It is worth noting that the male heads of

Table 1. Basic Socioeconomic Data on 9 Employer-Weaver Households in Xaagá, Oaxaca, Mexico

Case Number	1 No. of Years Head Worked as 'Operario'	2 Age	3 No. of Years on Own Acct.	4 Family Type*	5 No. of Looms	6 No. of Family Workers	7 No. of Sewing Machines	8 No. of Employees	9 Total Value of Owned Means of Production - Agriculture	10 Total Value of Owned Means of Production - Weaving	11 Cost of Materials of 15-Day Production Cycle	12 Cost of Labor and Other Operating Costs for 15-Day Prod. Cycle	13 Total Cost of 15-day Production Cycle	14 Sales Value of Production from 15-Day Cycle	15 Net Earnings Per Production Cycle	16 Land Ownership - Seasonal	17 Land Ownership - Watered	18 Annual Rent Value Agric. Means of Production	19 Amt. of Last Corn Harvest (Kilograms)	20 No. of Months Corn Bought Last Year	21 No. of Household Members	22 No. of Working Household Members	23 No. of Dependent Family Members	24 CW Ratio	25 Agric. Empl. Total (pesos)
1	10	32	1.5	N	2	1	1	3	3000	8710	720	480	1200	1750	550	3.1	0	2400	1500	1	6	1	5	6.0	4800
2	14	36	2	N	3	2	1	1	300	9280	1160	250	1410	2000	590	2.0	0	2100	750	3	4	2	2	2.0	0
3	19	27	4	N	2	1	0	2	0	5970	1991	1400	3391	4140	749	2.5	0	750	750	3	6	2	4	3.0	800
4	2	25	1	E	3	2	1	1	5500	15370	1600	1085	2685	5200	2515	2.0	0	0	1000	2	9	4	5	2.3	0
5	12	29	2	N	5	3	2	4	0	26650	2180	1650	3830	6505	2675	2.0	0	900	380	10	4	2	2	2.0	0
6	0		1	E	2	7	1	2	0	5210	2070	1100	3170	4875	1705	5.0	0	1700	1840	0	13	8	5	1.6	700
7	10	34	3	N	3	2	2	3	0	24740	2669	1600	4269	5760	1491	1.5	0	0	250	8	6	2	4	3.0	0
8	8	37	.5	N	1	1	1	1	0	10820	1080	720	1800	—	—	3.0	0	0	500	2	5	3	2	1.6	300
9	8	30	3	E	4	4	1	3	4000	25130	1925	1335	3260	6000	2740	4.0	1.0	0	2000	3	9	5	4	1.8	0
Totals	66		18		25	23	10	20	12800	131880	15395	9620	25015	36230	13015	22.1	1.0	7850	8470	32	62	29	33	23.3	6600
Mean	8.25		2		3.0	2.6	1.1	2.2	1422	14653	1711	1069	2779	4529	1627	2.9	.1	872	997	3.6	6.9	3.2	3.7	2.6	733

these households are young, (their average age is 30) that their careers as 'self-employed' are of recent origin but that they all had long prior experience as operarios (i.e., loom operators paid by piece rate) in the Mitla workshops. There were mixed incentives underlying their transitions from 'operario' to 'self-employed' status: two informants explained their decisions to go independent in terms of the inconvenience of the daily commute to Mitla; another cited problems with his last Mitla employer; and still another expressed his rationale as seeking to make more by selling his own products. Two of these individuals, prior to establishing their workshops, had temporarily withdrawn from the craft--both citing various physical ailments and exhaustion from long hours spent at the loom. One of them spent an entire year out of the industry working full-time as a peasant cultivator, while the other spent a somewhat longer interval as a goat trader. Yet even during this period of withdrawal, as one of them expressed it, "I had in my mind the idea of having my own loom-- I wanted a loom badly-- but couldn't figure out how to get the money."

The initial money capital required to purchase a complete loom outfit was accumulated by savings from operario earnings in three cases; in one case the source of the investment fund was goat trading; in one case a loan; and in another a wife's inheritance. Following this initial investment subsequent purchases of looms, sewing machines, and other equipment were made, in the majority of cases, with money saved from net income. In one case a sewing machine was already owned by the household prior to the purchase of the first loom and in another a sewing machine was purchased at the same time as the first loom; in all other cases sewing machines were purchased after the looms had been in operation for a year or more. The expansion of these home workshops has been steady and rapid: in one case (Table 1, no. 5) a one loom/no sewing machine/no employee operation in 1977, representing an investment of 5000 pesos (220 dollars), had evolved by 1979 into a 5 loom/2 sewing machine/4 employee operation representing an investment of 27000 pesos (1200 dollars); and in 1980 (much to my surprise on a brief visit) this unit purchased a used pick-up truck for 50,000 pesos (2200 dollars) from 'saved earnings'--thus being the first Xaaga weaving household to become a motor vehicle owner (and, incidentally, to follow in the path of several of the Mitla entrepreneurs). While material progress is usually not so dramatic as in this example, most of the other employer units in Xaaga have also experienced success in petty capital accumulation from weaving over the same period.

Why has the developmental trajectory of these nine units led to the regular employment of wage labor when it has not done so in the case of the other ten proprietor units? One might be inclined to seek an answer for this in the composition of these households and their stage in the household developmental cycle (M. Fortes 1958; Medick 1976). More specifically, income- and labor-pooling patrilineal extended households with 2 or more males between 15 and 20 obviously are less apt to employ weavers than households with one or no males in that age bracket or than those which may have the available labor-power but which do not pool income and labor. Among the nine employer households only three (nos. 4, 6 & 9) are patri-extended--but in two of the cases where labor and income pooling is practiced, the patriarch is a full-time peasant cultivator with one married resident son who is the proprietor of the weaving enterprise. Obviously in these two cases, as in those of the nuclear households--all of which either have no or underage male offspring--the acquisition of an additional loom, or a decision by the proprietor to reduce or eliminate his own loom work-time, necessitates the recruitment of hired labor. Of the four patri-extended households among the non-employers, two practice income- and labor-pooling and have sufficient able-bodied males to fill their weaving labor requirements. Two, however, do not practice income- and labor-pooling; and there, like the six nuclear household units, the expansion of weaving activity to include an additional loom necessitates the recruitment of a hired laborer.

The next question that arises about these units is, 'Why haven't they expanded?' Various factors may come into play here. In some cases the units are recently established and have not had time to expand (five were one year or younger at the time of the study); in others weaving is looked upon strictly as a part-time occupation by a peasant-cultivator; in still others the weaver-proprietor is especially skilled and seeks to increase earnings by making high quality products himself rather than by expanding production of lower quality products through employing others; and, finally, one weaver-proprietor explained his failure to buy an additional loom and hire an operario in terms of his dislike for spending time looking for new customers, buying materials, and, in effect, managing a business rather than working at a craft.

An examination of the data presented in Table 1 suggests that expansion of the scale of the weaving enterprise increases net income but at a rate below that of the rate of increase in investment in tools and equipment; thus the mean value of means of production owned by the employer units is more than twice that owned by the non-employers, whereas their net income per production cycle is roughly 1/3 larger. Also, eight of the non-employer units (see Table 2) had net earnings per production cycle substantially above those reported for three of the employer units (1, 2, & 3). Moreover, half of the non-employer units had net earnings of 1000 pesos (40 dollars) or more, the aggregate mean net profit being 1506 pesos (67 dollars) which is close to the average reported for all of the employer units. It might be argued that this higher rate of profit for the non-employer units is artificial since it fails to valorize family labor power. The rate would clearly decline, and profits might disappear entirely in some cases, if this were done.

But un-valorized family labor-power, especially that of seamstresses, is also important in the employer units. Indeed, there are an average of 2.6 family workers in weaving per employer household as opposed to 2.0 per non-employer household. In other words, the rate of returns for both types of units would be affected similarly by non-valorization of labor. Of course, the other side of the coin is that the three most successful employer units (4, 5 & 9) have an average net income per production cycle of over 2500 pesos (111 dollars) which is substantially above that of any of the non-employer units. This is a level of income which has been regularized in their operations and which permits a significant degree of capital accumulation. Another factor which might be at work here is suggested by the relatively low consumer-worker ratio of the employer units vis-a-vis the non-employer units (2.6 vs. 3.4); other things remaining equal, it stands to reason that those

Table 2. Basic Socioeconomic Data for Non-Employer Self-Employed Weavers in Xaagá, Tlacolula, Mexico

Case Number	1 Age	2 No. Yrs. Operario	3 No. Yrs. Own Acct.	4 No. of Looms	5 Family Type	6 No. of Sewing Machines	7 No. of Family Workers	8 Total Value of Owned Means of Production — Agric.	9 Total Value of Owned Means of Production — Weaving	10 Materials Cost-15 Day Cycle	11 Labor/Other Costs-15 Day Cycle	12 Total Cost - 15 Day Cycle	13 Sales Value	14 Net Earnings	15 Land Worked Seasonal	16 Land Worked Watered	17 Rent Ag. Means	18 Corn Harvest	19 Corn Bought	20 No. of H.H. Members	21 Family Workers	22 Family Deps.	23 C.W. Ratio	24 Agric. Emp. Tot.
1	22		3	1	E	1	2	0	15720	740	1050	1790	3450	1660	2.1	0	0	300	0	3	2	1	1.5	0
2	42	1	1	1	N	0	3	3000	5750	720	60	780	1680	900	2.0	0	450	750	5	6	2	2	3.0	0
3	23	0	1	2	E	2	5	23500	13100	1320	50	1370	1840	470	4.0	0	0	2500	2	11	7	4	1.6	120
4	30	5	1	1	N	0	1	0	1100	890	200	1090	1980	890	1.0	0	450	300	8	5	1	4	5.0	0
5	43	0	1.5	1	N	0	1	0	3350	720	30	750	1600	850	2.0	0	700	250	9	5	2	3	2.5	0
6	45	15	1 mo.	1	E	0	2	0	3730	1000	0	1000	2000	1000	6.0	0	2000	1000	3	9	2	7	4.5	2000
7	33	8	3 mo.	1	N	0	0	0	4060	180	25	205	250	45	1.3	0	950	500	5	6	1	5	6.0	0
8	52	3	2	1	N	0	2	300	10080	1130	130	1260	2400	1140	3.0	0	300	750	10	5	2	9	2.5	320
9	26	3	2.5	1	E	0	1	0	3600	1030	200	1230	3000	1770	0	.1	0	100	8	5	1	4	5.0	140
10	37	16	2	1	N	1	3	0	9340	890	10	900	2860	1960	0	1.1	1250	500	10	6	3	4	2.0	0
Total	353	51	14.3	11		5	20	26800	69830	9500	1225	10725	21060	10335	21.4	1.2	6100	6950	60	61	23	37	33.6	2580
Mean	35	5.7	1.4	1.1		.5	2	2680	6983	950	122.5	1072.5	2106	1033.5	2.1	.1	610	695	6	6.1	2.3	3.7	3.4	258

households with a relatively favorable ratio of workers to consumers will presumably be able to allocate more of their income to investment in the expansion of the commodity-producing capacity of their enterprise than will units with less favorable ratios.

A comparison of the employer and non-employer households with respect to agriculture also yields mixed results. On the one hand, it is clear that in terms of amount of land worked, amount of harvest of shelled corn, and the number of months corn was purchased, the employer units seem to be better off (either as a cause or consequence of their success in weaving?). On the other hand, a glance at the annual rental of agricultural means of production and the amount spent on hired agricultural workers shows that they pay more for this 'advantaged' status.

Just as a bifurcation between an agrarian and a craft ideology characterizes the general population of weavers in Xaaga, so it is present (though with a decided bias against participation in agriculture) within that segment of the population with the highest stake in the weaving industry--the employers. Two of five successful employers, each with more than 11 years of experience as weavers, adhere to the dominant peasant-artisan ideology of the Oaxaca Valley which views a dual occupational involvement as complementary and necessary for survival--though one of them noted, "We lose our work in the fields but not in weaving" [implying, of course, the risk element in rainfall agriculture]. A third employer-informant argued this same point about the greater risk of agriculture but summed up his attitude by observing that "We were born in the countryside and don't dare to abandon it." Nevertheless, he also told me that when he inherits his father's land, he plans to sell his ox team and to cultivate the land with hired hands. Other weaver-employers were less ambivalent in expressing negative views about agriculture, as well as about peasants who double as weavers. I will quote more extensively from these two statements among the younger male weavers and are, perhaps, illustrative of an embryonic trend toward the separation of agriculture and industry in the regional division of labor as a consequence of capitalist development:

1. In agriculture one works too much and often doesn't harvest anything; but in weaving that

never happens. When one sells his products one gets back the pennies that he invested. Those who work in the fields have only the hope that their work will yield something. The gentlemen who work in the fields often find themselves with the need to sell their crops . . . . within 2, 3 months following harvest they're already buying corn; I definitely don't work in agriculture because I dedicated myself to this trade; this way I'm sure that I'll be able to feed my family from my work. When peasants find themselves in need they to sell the food they've grown for their family. Then they suffer doubly because they have to look for another job to feed their family.

2. If I work in agriculture I can't work in weaving. Peasants must work the land every day, they don't have time for other work. There are many of them who do some weaving without understanding it. There are a few who are real weavers. Others are peasants by trade but, because their sons more or less can halfway move the loom, well they went and bought a loom. I don't think they understand the time that it takes to become a weaver. And, they need to sell quickly if they are going to keep on weaving, so they sell at low prices.

As this latter statement implies there is an undercurrent of resentment among the full-time weavers--and, especially, among the most successful ones--against the peasant interlopers in the industry whose cardinal sin, from the viewpoint of the professionals, apparently is their failure to properly valorize the labor-power embodied in the products they so recklessly "undersell" (malbaratar).

Yet here we find our professional weavers impaled on a contradiction. Their own long experience as exploited piece-workers in Mitla sweatshops has taught them well the value of labor-power; but the viability of their own operations, in a market controlled by the Mitla wholesale buyers, revolves around their ability to produce with unwaged family labor--especially with that of their seamstress wives and daughters [as well as upon a non-capitalist accounting calculus which focuses only on current labor and material costs and writes off investment in tools and equipment as simply a non-reimbursable fee for the privilege of entering the trade]. The following statement by one of the two most successful employer-weavers expresses various facets of this crucial role of 'family labor':

> In weaving one can benefit and help oneself substantially when one's wife and children cooperate. I am convinced that if my wife didn't help me I couldn't do anything--this help is an important factor in the trade and in the home. There is work that one cannot do alone so it's necessary that the family cooperate. I have observed that there are families where the husband works hard but where the wife doesn't collaborate . . . and that's where there is little progress. Let's assume that my wife earned 2 pesos for each shirt she sewed; if we sold only our cloth [without sewing it into shirts] those 2 pesos would pass into the hands of the merchant who buys the cloth [to make shirts]. I have thought about this; I have analyzed that those 2 shirts benefit one's own household. The man or the weaver weaves and the woman is the seamstress and finisher--that's the foundation of it.

This is an incisive statement of what I call the petty bourgeois strategy of "endofamilial" accumulation (Cook 1984a, 1984b, and 1984c).[4]

The ideology of these petty bourgeois rural industrialists is contradictory in other areas as well. For example, they are uniformly ambivalent in their views about intermediaries in general and especially so about those from Mitla. One must sympathize with the Xaaga weavers here, if only because the Mitla merchants represent the epitome of the aggressive, cunning, egocentric and suspicious Zapotec trading class. In the days of the hacienda the peones of Xaaga were at the very bottom of the Mitla-centered sub-regional class structure. First as charcoal sellers to the wealthier Mitla families, then as operarios in Mitla textile workshops--and always as indebted customers in Mitla stores--the men of Xaaga learned the tricks of the weaving trade and nursed desires to emulate their Mitla patrons someday. That day may be dawning but still even the most ambitious, successful and intelligent Xaaga weaver-employer is dependent upon the Mitla merchants (most of whom are their ex-employers but are now their principal buyers and creditors) whose prior accumulation of capital and marketing prowess, reinforced by their monopolization of the tourist trade, give them a dominant position in the regional, national, and international markets for locally produced textiles.

Xaaga weaver-employers express resentment against, as one of them put it, the "middlemen who are dedicated to living off of the artisans" and who take a disproportionate share of the profits from the sale of Xaaga products. In the words of another Xaaga weaver: "The real earnings go to the resellers. They travel to the ports, to the beaches where they sell a shirt for two to three times the price they pay us for it. That's real profit but we have to accommodate ourselves to the prices that they offer us." So, in the last analysis, the Xaaga weavers view the profits of the Mitla traders as just rewards for their marketing skills and the risks of travel--and while they realize that a local producer's organization might give them the ability to bargain for higher prices from the Mitla traders they still harbor dreams of emulating them through individual enterprise and initiative.

This posture is also evident in their wives on the sources of inequality in Xaaga and Mitla. There is a consensus among them that poverty among their fellow villagers is attributable to large family size (i.e., too many dependents) and to the absence of hard work either by the household head, his wife or both. The following response is representative of those made to a question about why poverty exists in the village: "There are households that have too many members; the head is a day laborer because he never learned to work in a trade (oficio)." They were also unanimous in expressing a belief that a poor family can progress materially through hard work. As one of them put it: "One won't make progress with his hands at his sides but by working and achieving every day. Everything depends on work and on the form of managing it." It's true that in Xaaga one gets the impression that the consistency with which these views are expressed may reflect the influence of the Adventist religion which has many proselytes in this village but I encountered similar views in many other villages without organized Protestant cults. I am inclined to believe, therefore, that this is, in essence, a classic petty bourgeois ideology spawned by the hegemonic regime of private property and private accumulation.[5]

B. The Brickmaker-Employers of Santa Lucia del Camino[6]

Those of you who have driven by day east from Oaxaca City on the Pan American highway will probably have observed clouds of thick black smoke hanging in the air on both sides of the highway just at that point where you sense that you are leaving the city and are headed for the attractions of the Zapotec countryside. Sometimes the sources of this smoke are hidden from view but often they are clearly identifiable as kilns located in the midst of what looks like an ecological disaster zone--a gouged and cluttered landscape which, upon closer examination, proves to be a labyrinth of clay pits interconnected by a network of paths and dirt roads, the latter plied by a constant traffic of flatbed trucks. You are, in short, passing through the heartland of the Oaxaca Valley brick industry--a zone encompassing several square kilometers both north and south of the highway within the territorial jurisdictions of Santa Lucia del Camino, San Agustin Yatareni, Santa Cruz Amilpas, San Sebastian Tutla and San Francisco Tutla. My field work was conducted mostly in Santa Lucia which is the original center of brick production in the area, although its position as the largest production center has been eclipsed in recent years by Yatareni.

The kiln-fired bricks produced in this industry have replaced sun-baked adobe bricks in urban construction throughout the region; and while cement blocks and poured concrete are used in the regional construction industry their use has not seemed to dampen the demand for hand-made, kiln-fired bricks. In recent years at least one major highly capitalized joint government and private venture into mechanized brick production in the area has collapsed. So it appears that labor-intensive brick production is not in any immediate jeopardy from capital-intensive production; indeed, its demise may ultimately have more to do with the supply of cheap labor than it does with the availability or the investment of capital.

Before I review some selected data for a sample of employer units in the Santa Lucia del Camino branch of the Oaxaca Valley brick industry, a few additional general points should be made. There is a marked contrast between a labor-intensive extractive and transformative industry like brick-making, which supplies a basic utilitarian product for the booming construction industry in Oaxaca City, and a labor-intensive transformative industry like weaving which supplies a luxury product for the tourist-oriented 'handicrafts' market. This contrast is conveyed concretely by juxtaposing some of the things the two industries call to mind: picks, shovels, crowbars, pits, clay, mud, kilns, smoke, fire, heat, bricks, storage sheds, and flatbed trucks vs. skeins of thread, spinning wheels, spindles, looms, shuttles, cloth, and clothing. In essence, brickmaking evokes images of 'heavy industry' (drudge work) whereas weaving evokes images of 'light industry' (craft work).

If we follow the circulation of bricks from clay pit to kiln to consumer we are drawn into the guts of the regional political economy, a location we bypass by following the circulatory routes of cloth and clothing products. First, in the brick industry we must deal with a more crystallized and polarized class structure [the status of destajista or milero (brickmaking pieceworker), unlike that of operario, more closely approximates that of a true proletariat--and the relationship patron/milero is more formalized in 'class' terms than that between patron/operario. Second, in the brick industry we are confronted head-on with powerful urban interests and a political-economic subterfuge involving millions of pesos in construction contracts which are up for grabs by politicians, bureaucrats, police, truck drivers, architects, construction bosses, and last but not least, the brick merchants themselves. What this means is that the most successful entrepreneurs in the brick industry are those whose political contacts and 'generosity' in the manipulation of kickback funds assure them of substantial shares in the brick traffic for urban construction projects. In other words, this is one of those cases where the appearance of small-scale industry often yields to the reality of big-time money and interests. Needless to say, my study makes only an exploratory probe into these complexities.[7]

Although Santa Lucia del Camino is on the outskirts of Oaxaca City and undergoing a process of urbanization, the brickmaker-employers there are, with few exceptions, also engaged in agricultural persuits. Only one of the nine households listed in Table 3 did not cultivate any land--and this is a case of recent 'depeasantization'; most of them also raise animals-- especially pigs, cows and poultry. This is not surprising considering, among other things, that the primary natural resource in the brick industry is land and more specifically, a particular type of clay which lies beneath the topsoil and which is the basic raw material for the manufacture of bricks. The typical brickyard (ladrillera) lies on flat arable land; its vertical and lateral expansion occur at the expense of the arable. The brickyard + kiln combination, the industry's fundamental production unit, is, in essence, a 'factory in the fields'. Incidentally, the conversion of arable land into brickyards is not irreversible. The lower limit of excavation is set by the water table; at some point a few feet above the latter, clay excavation ceases and the remaining soil (which is now more humid and easily irrigable) is recycled back into agricultural production (usually planted with alfalfa) and is probably more productive agriculturally than it was as unwatered seasonally cultivated land before excavation.

The employer units shown in Table 3 represent only the top half of the socioeconomic hierarchy in the industry which begins with the brickmaker-employee, who is paid in accordance with a piece rate for each 1000 unfired bricks produced. These pieceworkers (mileros), the true brickyard proletariat, are either permanent employees who have migrated to Santa Lucia from other districts or regions and who live with their families in the brickyards (in housing provided rent-free by their employer), or are casual day-laborers who live in Santa Lucia or nearby settlements and who circulate between different brickyards on a temporary basis. The next stratum consists of self-employed brickmakers called "ladrilleros" who work in a brickyard owned by someone else and who pay the owner a set fee per 1000 bricks for the clay excavated. The third stratum is made up of those self-employed ladrilleros who lease brickyards from their owners for a year or longer; and the fourth stratum consists of those who manage to acquire ownership of brickyards but who do not own kilns. An examination of the work histories of many ladrilleros discloses a similar career trajectory

Table 3. Basic Socioeconomic Data on Nine Employer Households in the Brick Industry in Santa Lucia del Camino, Oaxaca, Mexico

		Case Number	1	2	3	4	5	6	7	8	9	Total	Mean
1		No. of Years as Brick Maker Before Being 'Own Account'	39	0	0	3	15	5	25+	2	11		
2		No. Yrs. on 'Own Acct'	20	2	7	10	10	2	11	1	5		
3		Present Age of Employer	58	60	35	40	58	50	57	22	56	436	48
4		No. of Brick Yards Owned	2	1	1	2	1	1	1	1	1		
5		No. of Kilns Owned	1	1	1	1	1	0	1	1	1		
6		No. of Employees	3	2	3	2	2	1	1	1	3	18	2.0
7		Type**	E	N	N	N	N	N	E	N	E		
8	Family	No. of Brick Yard Workers	3	3	0	1	6	7	0	3	1	24	2.7
9	Total Value of Owned Means of Production (pesos)	Agriculture	0	0	24100	0	0	0	415	0	0		
10		Brickmaking	40000	60790	25600	29300	90000	48930	31620	92860	95940	515040	57227
11	One-Month Production Cycle	Cost of Materials (pesos)	1000	1500	1200	1550	1500	0	1200	1500	1900	11350	1261
12		Labor and Other Costs (pesos)	7000	5500	7550	6600	6850	4000	8350	4600	9980	60430	6714
13		Total Cost (pesos)	8000	7000	8750	8150	8350	4000	9550	6100	11880	71780	7976
14		Value of Output (pesos)	21000	15000	15000	17000	12300	10200	20000	12000	20000	142500	15833
15		Net Returns (pesos)	13000	8000	6250	8850	3950	3400	10450	5900	8120	67920	7547
16	Land Worked (Hectares)	Seasonal	0	.8	1.0	.8	1.0	4.0	1.0	.5	1.0	9.1	1.0
17		Watered	2.0	.3	0	0	0	0	1.5	0	0	3.8	.4
18		Annual Cost of Rental Agricultural Means of Production (pesos)	4600	3000	0	2250	800	0	6000	0	2000	18650	2072
19		Annual Cost of Hired Agricultural Labor (pesos)	800	0	0	0	0	0	0	1000	1800		200
20		Amt. of 1979 Shelled Corn Harvest (kilos)	400	600	500	1500	2000	0	2500	300	300	8400	933
21		No. of Months Corn Bought in 1979	0	2	0	7	12	12	3	0	4	40	4.4
22		Size of Family	5	4	4	11	6	14	6	5	13	68	7.6
23		No. of Family Workers (all categories)	1	3	0	0	6	9	6	3	3	31	3.4
24		No. of Dependent Family Members	1	1	3	10	0	5	0	2	10	32	3.6
25		C.W. Ratio	1.3	1.3	4.0	11.0	1.0	1.5	1.0	1.6	4.3	27	3.0

**N = nuclear, E = extended

which, in effect, transforms these strata into stages in the developmental cycle of the family brick-making enterprise. That is, many direct producers who entered the industry as mileros became self-employed clay-buyers, then renters or leasees (arrendatarios) and, eventually, achieved the status of private proprietors of brickyards. This developmental cycle is still operative but my impression is that the proportion of mileros who actually experience it is small and diminishing. What the self-employed usufructuaries have in common with the first-stage private proprietors is the lack of ownership of kilns which means that they all tend to sell crude bricks since if they want to sell fired bricks they have to rent a kiln, which of course, adds to their production costs.

The fifth stratum in the brick industry hierarchy is occupied by those employer units which own at least one brickyard and one kiln, and which employ both family and hired-labor to produce bricks which are sold to trucker-merchants (transportistas or revendedores) or to buyers for own-use. Some of these units may also own old trucks which are primarily used for hauling bricks within the brickyard area and only occasionally for hauling bricks to construction sites outside the village (case nos. 2, 5 & 9). Finally, the sixth and top stratum encompasses the most highly capitalized employer units which combine the ownership of multiple brickyards, kilns, and trucks, and whose business includes selling bricks produced in their own brickyards as well as reselling bricks produced by other units. In addition there are a series of trucker-merchants who haul bricks for a fee and may or may not regularly operate as resellers.

Returning for a moment to the issue of the agricultural involvement of the employer units, it is apparent that most of them do not have capital invested in agricultural means of production and, consequently, must rent these. However, most units perform lighter agricultural work (e.g., weeding, cutting alfalfa, harvesting, planting) themselves rather than with hired labor. Also, the amount of land under cultivation is small, even by Valley of Oaxaca standards, with only three units working more than one hectare or reporting shelled corn yields of 1 metric ton or greater, a fact that is not surprising given the high ratio of population to arable land in

Santa Lucia and its semi-urban life style. On the other hand, in five of the nine cases the sale of animals, crops, or arable land was the source of money capital used to buy a brickyard and to initiate production. Some of these ladrilleros expressed an anti-agrarian ideology similar to that of the Xaaga weavers, but most of them simply considered brickmaking to be a much less risky enterprise than agriculture. Also, most of them agreed that agriculture was a helpful supplement to brickmaking for domestic provisioning. Their agricultural involvement is mostly in animal-raising and the growing of alfalfa (and some corn) on irrigated land, and not in planting corn, beans, and squash by the traditional dry-farming method.

It is clear from a comparison of Tables 1 and 3 concerning the total investment of means of production and net earnings per production cycle (two weeks in weaving vs. four weeks in brickmaking), that the employer units in brickmaking are more highly capitalized (mean of 14,653 pesos for weaving vs. 57,227 pesos for brickmaking) and more profitable (mean net income per month of 3254 pesos or 145 dollars in weaving vs. 7547 pesos or 335 dollars in brickmaking). Interestingly enough, the mix of family to hired labor in the weaving and brickmaking units is nearly identical (2.6 to 2.2 in weaving vs. 2.7 to 2.0 in brickmaking); but it should be noted that the brickmaking units employ additional hired labor during every production cycle to load and unload the kilns, to stoke the kilns, and to load trucks (which is reflected in the much higher monthly labor costs for the brickmaking units: 6714 pesos (298 dollars) vs. 2138 pesos (95 dollars).

With regard to the background of the individual ladrillero-employers only two of them did not work as brickmakers prior to establishing their production unit. But individually (with few exceptions) and collectively, they have had longer careers as proprietors, as well as a wider range of work experiences (especially in jobs in modern industries), than have their counterparts in Xaaga weaving. This reflects partially the fact that the ladrillero-employers are an older population than are the weavers (mean age of 48 years vs. 33 years) but also the proximity of Santa Lucia to the City. The following summary of some highlights from a portion of the life history of one ladrillero (case no. 5, Table 3) illustrates not only this diverse work background but also the dynamics of success and failure in the brick industry:

>Alberto's work career in the brickyards began at the tender age of 5 when his father gave him various light but necessary tasks like scraping and stacking bricks. He describes how he began to make 50 bricks a day and then progressed by stages to reach a daily output of 300. By that time he was in his early teens and had reversed roles with his father who was, at that point, helping Alberto rather than vice-versa. He describes the division of tasks between his father, himself and his three brothers as follows: "Some of my brothers went with my father to the fields while others of us remained in the ladrillera. When there was a lot of work in the campo, like stripping leaves from the corn stalks, all of us would go to help. The rest of the time some would go with my father to the fields and others would work in the ladrillera."

As the second oldest brother of the family, Alberto was expected to work to help his two younger brothers study fulltime and qualify for careers. One succeeded in becoming a maritime technician, and the other a petroleum engineer. Alberto got fed up with the brickyard routine by the time he was 18 and took an opportunity to learn to drive and get a job as a truck driver in Oaxaca City. This job lasted for ten years. In 1958 he left for Mexico City to find a better paying job (by this time he was married and had one son). His first job in Mexico City was as a newspaper vendor. This lasted 1 1/2 years. Next he got a job in a pencil factory which lasted for 8 years. He began as a mechanic's assistant and ended up as the factory's chief boiler operator. He also established and ran a 'snack' business at the factory for his co-workers. The factory was sold and his seniority was lost under the new management so he decided to return to Santa Lucia in 1968. His first job after returning was as a truck driver and route salesman for a bottled water company in Oaxaca City. He quit this job after two years when he decided to lease out a parcel of land inherited from his father and with the proceeds made a down payment on a truck. Thus he embarked on a career as a brick hauler and reseller which was to last for four years.

In 1969 Alberto was elected to be <u>Presidente Municipal</u> against his wishes. This both helped and hindered his business. He explains what happened as follows: "When I was <u>presidente</u> some good opportunities came my way; I not only hauled bricks but I also resold them. Since I was born and raised here many people had confidence in me. I didn't have any capital but I would stop at the kilns in my truck and tell the <u>ladrilleros</u> that I had arranged a contract in Oaxaca City for 25,000 bricks. Then I would make a proposal: 'I'll take your bricks and when the contractors pay me I'll repay you.' As I said, I personally didn't have any capital but I did have possibilities of supplying orders; so with the bricks I hauled I earned my hauling fee plus an additional profit. In that way I began climbing rapidly; I was lucky."

Alberto emphasizes that his business success derived from his use of the prestige of the municipal presidency and of his knowledge of the brick industry. He selected only prime quality bricks to sell to his special clients in Oaxaca City; he sought to build a clientele through the quality of his merchandise. He explains how his success led to his acquisition of a second flatbed truck: "Some gypsies offered me a Chevrolet for 6000 pesos. I took money I earned from the bricks which the <u>ladrilleros</u> had 'loaned' me to sell for them. Then I would tell the <u>ladrilleros</u>: 'Look, the contractors haven't paid me the full amount they owe me so all that I can give you now is a partial payment.' But, in reality, I had all of their money in my hands, so I was able to pay cash for the second truck which I knew would help me make more money to repay my debts to the ladrilleros. I started to work both trucks; we'd load up one and then the other. We hauled lots of bricks."

Within a year of the purchase of his second truck he purchased a third truck in the same manner or as he says "by taking money from others because I didn't have any of my own. One guy would consign to me his entire firing of bricks; I would owe 1500 pesos to one, 1000 to another, 2000 to a third and I would explain to them: 'Within 15 days I'll get your money to you.' I had already calculated that I'd pay one back first, then another, and then the third."

But the burdens of elected office began to damage his business. He had to hire drivers and helpers and they didn't look out for his interests with his clients. His clientele began to dry up. Near the end of his period of tenure as presidente he sold one of his trucks, called in the lease on his land, and for the first time since he was 18 he took up brickmaking once again. Then came a problem regarding his handling of a local school construction project. He was accused of illegally expropriating land from a private owner for the school, was sued, sent to the state penitentiary for two days, and had to sell another of his trucks to meet his legal expenses.

Alberto came out of this situation essentially broke and humiliated; he was faced with the necessity of starting from scratch in the brickyard to earn his livelihood. In his words: "To raise myself up again in the brick business, since I was broke, I started making bricks myself; my wife and children came to haul the clay, to scrape and stack the bricks though sometimes I worked alone. We completed the first kiln-load, loaded the kiln and then I asked the guy who sells sawdust to advance me a load so that I could fire up the kiln. I told him that I'd repay him when the bricks were sold. He agreed. Afterwards, I paid him in bricks since I didn't have any money. It took us three years working that way to raise ourselves up again."

As the data in Table 3 show Alberto (no 5) is in reasonably good shape once again. Indeed, he recovered sufficiently to put his eldest son through law school and to support his second son in medical school (though both of them put in long hours in the brickyards when they weren't studying). The last time I visited this family they were together in the brickyard; Alberto, his wife, his son and his two teenage daughters were working diligently as a coordinated team to load their kiln.

Approximately half of the employers listed in Table 3 do not perform any physical labor in brickmaking. Aside from Alberto, only three others are true 'worker-owners'; the rest spend much of their time away from the brickyards attending to agricultural or other tasks. For example, employer no. 7 has a small store in his house and spends a few hours daily waiting on customers there. These individuals check up on their mileros on Saturday. As noted above, several of these employers have resident workers who they provide with housing in the brickyard; these resident mileros are, in most cases, paid according to the prevailing piece rate. They pay no rent but do provide the patron with round-the-clock surveillance of the brickyard. Another real advantage of his arrangement to both parties is that the milero's productivity is enhanced by the assistance of his wife and children who, given the location of their living quarters in the brickyard, are a sort of 'captive' labor force who can (and invariably do) perform various tasks which reduce the milero's work load. In these cases, then, the Saturday wage is a payment to the milero household head for labor performed by himself and his family.

The patrones, given their recognition of the difficulty of recruiting and maintaining competent, reliable workers adopt a very paternalistic posture which includes making loans and interacting with workers in the egalitarian way. As one of them expressed it: One has to 'live together' (_convivir_) with the _milero_; one shouldn't bother them or coerce them. One should treat them as members of one's family and help them with their problems. That way they'll be content, they'll work quietly and do a good job." There appears to be competition among the _patrones_ for good workers; some _patrones_ use piece rates and cash advances to lure away _mileros_ from competitors. As this implies, there is no formal association of brick industry employers nor of the _mileros_--but there is a great deal of informal discussion among members of both groups about wages and prices. Information about piece rates and prices travels quickly from brickyard to brickyard, with the truckers or their helpers often being the messengers. Wage hikes demanded or granted quickly become common knowledge and provide new ammunition for _mileros_ in the bargaining process. In inflationary times the wage-price spiral impacts directly on life in the brickyards. For example, following the Mexican government's decision to increase the price of sugar in 1980 there were almost immediate demands by the _mileros_ for a compensatory hike in the piece rate. As one employer explained with some resentment: "My _mileros_ are telling me that they can't live on what I'm paying them. They're bothering me with demands that they want a 50 pesos (per 1000 bricks) increase because sugar is now more expensive!" Such demands for wage increases are usually taken seriously and are often conceded if only because, as another _patron_ put it, "If we don't grant them a raise they'll leave and find another _patron_ who'll pay them more."

I do not want to give the impression here that the _mileros_ are in the saddle in the brick industry but I do want to emphasize that the relations between capital and labor in the brickyards are fluid and open.

III. Tentative Conclusions and Some Theoretical Considerations

A. Conclusions

One conclusion which should be emphasized because of the prevailing tendency to explain 'entrepreneurship' (or the 'managerial' function) in terms of individual behavior or psychology, and to reify it as separate from labor (e.g., as a discrete 'factor' of production), is that with few exceptions the 'employer' status in the weaving and brickmaking industries is inextricably bound up with labor in two ways. First, employers are, both individually and collectively, creatures of the labor process in their industries; they began their careers in the industry as direct producers and learned the trade from from their personal involvement in the labor process. Second, and without exception, the existence and viability of the employer units in both industries is predicated upon the availability of a pool of labor-power which can be hired at either a low wage, an "inferior wage" (i.e., below the socially average cost of reproduction--Cook 1982), or for no wage at all. The brickyard proletariat in Santa Lucia is paid a wage which approximates the cost of its reproduction (i.e., necessary labor)--but which does so only because of the regular contribution of family labor power to the production process. In other words, the surplus labor/necessary labor ratio in this industry hovers around the survival minimum and would fall below this minimum without the unpaid labor of the <u>mileros'</u> dependents. Given the external social origins of the majority of this brickyard proletariat [who are <u>avecindados</u> or outsiders who have taken up residence in Santa Lucia] and their completely landless status, there appears to be little opportunity for them to progress materially through endo-familial accumulation as did some of their counterparts in earlier generations. In this industry, then, we find a tendency toward crystallization or polarization of its class structure which is manifested in a perpetual struggle over the piece rate as the prices of wage goods rise. We also find that some of the brickyard enterprises have crossed the from the space threshold where 'family labor' is the principal source of capital accumulation and have entered the space where 'wage labor' has assumed that role.

In the Xaaga weaving industry, on the other hand, the prevailing piecework wages are 'inferior': they are below the level of 'necessary labor' because they are paid either to young men (i.e., the <u>operarios</u>) or to the women (i.e., the seamstresses) who are, in every case, natives of Xaaga and who either directly or indirectly reproduce part of their own labor-power from non-wage sources (e.g., their own agricultural production or that of some other member or members of their extended families). It will be recalled that many of today's employers in Xaaga were yesterday's operarios; and that the past and present trajectories of their weaving enterprises reflects some degree of "endo familial accumulation. So the achievement of their current employer status and its continued viability hinge upon their use of non-waged family labor-power. One implication of this is that class relations in the Xaaga waving industry are incipient and, therefore, less polarized than those obtaining in the brick industry. Consequently, there is more possibility for upward mobility among today's operarios than there is among the mileros.

There is a larger reality here which relativizes or contextualizes this apparently idyllic petty bourgeois scenario in weaving, namely, the hegemony of Mitla merchant capital over the Xaaga industry. What we have here is a sort of accumulation by proxy which has been established by the partial de-industrialization of Mitla. Unlike their counterparts in 17th or 18th century England (e.g., Dobb, 1963; Goody 1982), the Mitla worker-owners turned sweatshop operators appear to have rejected the path of 'rationalization' which would have presumably led them from workshop to manufactory to factory and, rather, have tended to gradually disband their workshops--which were substantially dependent on imported labor-power from Xaaga anyway--to sell their well-used looms and equipment to their ex-operarios (not aspiring patrones), and concentrate on redeploying their capital toward the consolidation of their local monopoly over the sale of thread and other raw materials and over the marketing of locally-produced textiles. According to this view, then, the ex-operario from Xaaga becomes, in effect, an engager of labor-power in his own village labor-pool for Mitla merchant capitalists who were willing to retreat in the field of production so as to exploit the cheap labor-power of Xaaga by proxy. So the Xaaga industry can, to some extent, be considered to be comprised of 'castaway shops' which are held hostage by oligoponistic merchant capital centered in Mitla. The burdens of proprietorship and managership of the means and process of production are increasingly being carried by the Xaaga patrones but the lion's share of profits flow in the Mitla direction. Only time will tell whether or not the Xaaga industry will be able to break these bonds of dependency, simply accommodate itself to them or, perhaps, through persistent "endofamilial accumulation" [or outside help] drive Mitla capital into greener pastures outside of weaving.

It is interesting to note that what is happening sub-regionally in the weaving industry between Mitla and Xaaga is also happening regionally between Oaxaca City and its hinterland. Recently, in fact, one of Oaxaca City's largest textile-product enterprises built a facility in Xaaga to house a manufactory to employ the weavers there as operarios. This undertaking was short-lived since the Xaaga weavers found it more profitable to work on their own or in conjunction with the Mitlenos rather than in the manufactory. The future of the Oaxaca City firm will apparently depend upon its success in exploiting prison labor in outlying district towns, a practice which it had initiated prior to its abortive Xaaga effort. Many smaller enterprises, including nearly all of the family workshops, have disappeared from the City and many of their looms have been sold to rural buyers like those from Xaaga. The driving force here seems to be the cost of labor-power; the urban proletariat must receive higher wages than the rural semi-proletariat--thus a competitive advantage for rural small enterprise. Also, it should be noted that there is significantly less susceptibility to government harassment about work regulations, social security, and taxes, in the village sanctuary than in the City or large towns (Cook 1984 : Ch6).

With regard to the relationship between agriculture and industry, I will posit three roles for agriculture: (1) as a partial reproducer of labor-power--especially among the operarios and some of the patrones in Xaaga, and to a lesser extent among the self-employed ladrilleros of Santa Lucia; (2) as an arena for possible capital accumulation--especially during the early phases of development of the independent brickmaking enterprise but also in some of the self-employed weaving units; and (3) as an industrial 'cloaking' device to the extent that small industrial and/or merchant capital use the 'peasant' agricultural status as camouflage or a decoy to evade taxes, work regulations, and so on [which, in any case, are poorly adapted to the realities of small-scale, labor-intensive enterprises] or, on the other hand, to benefit from certain agrarian reform or other agricultural promotion programs. Given the evolution of official Mexican agrarianism since the Revolution, both ideologically and organizationally, it is to the advantage of those who live in the countryside to emphasize their 'peasantness' even though they, in fact, are no longer peasants either objectively or subjectively. On the other hand, there is probably a material disincentive for rural Mexicans to identify themselves as petty industrialists or for that matter, as merchants, and few incentives, material or otherwise, to identify themselves as artisans. This reflects an agricultural bias in the rural policies of the government, as well as the latter's unquenchable thirst for new sources of tax revenue or to regulate productive and commercial activities in the countryside.

B. Theoretical Implications and Considerations

The small-scale, labor-intensive production of non-agricultural commodities in the countryside--which we identify by a variety of labels like cottage or domestic industry, simple or petty commodity production, home production, etc.--is usually shown or considered to be an adjunct to agriculture; during the annual production cycle it waxes as agricultural production waves and vice-versa. The direct producers themselves are defined as 'peasants' or 'peasant-artisans' whose principal economic involvement and ideological make-up are dominated by agriculture; and whose performance is geared to simple reproduction of the means of production and subsistence, not to accumulation or investment. Many of us have participated in the study and, perhaps, the 'celebration' of this social type (see Cook 1984b).

But another prominent feature of life in the countryside of the contemporary capitalist 'Third World' is, of course, social differentiation and class formation which imply capital accumulation (see Cook 1984c). Rural life in the so-called 'capitalist periphery' is by no means stagnant or passively replicative of past forms but, on the contrary, is dynamic and generative of new forms and of contradictory processes. This life is not a creature and any one set of exogenous or endogenous conditions, nor of any one level of structural integration but of many conditions and levels operating serially or simultaneously and directly or indirectly. Presumably the job of social scientists is to avoid being intimidated by this complexity to the point of nihilism or even of empirical relativism [i.e., the doctrine that my data about situation X indicates this and your data about X, Y, or Z indicate that; neither is right or wrong, both are equally valid, and that's that]. But we should also approach this complexity with humility born of a recognition that there are finite limits to our ability to produce valid knowledge and that there is nothing new under the intellectual sun (though there is quite a bit that has been ignored or forgotten).

An issue pertinent to the theme of this paper is the significance of the managerial function in contemporary Third World economies and, to a lesser extent, what its selection as a problem for study implies for economic anthropology. Its "problematization" inevitably evokes a lot of intellectual baggage from the heyday of developmentalism in the 1950s and 1960s which many of us would rather forget. This ranges from the naive Rostowian unilineal gradualist approach, which had such sophisticated anthropologists like Clifford Geertz (1963) searching for the socioeconomic sources of the "take-off into sustained growth" (Rostow 1960) in Indonesia, to the well-intentioned psychologism and behaviorism of McClelland (1961) and Hagen (1962), which led anthropologists like George Foster (1967) to seek the sources of "underdevelopment" in rural Mexico within the cognitive structure of the peasantry--and hosts of others to search for the roots of development in individual decision making. For all of the weaknesses in the Marxist-influenced "dependency" and "world system" approaches of the last fifteen years, we at least recognize more clearly through them the fundamental flaws in the developmentalist approach (e.g., Roxborough 1979; Taylor 1979; Wolf 1982: Ch. 1).

Yet, this Marxist critique notwithstanding, I doubt whether the entrepreneurship problem deserves the oblivion and ridicule it has suffered as a consequence of the rise to 'fashionability' of Marxist-oriented thought in economic anthropology and development studies. This has probably been a classic case of throwing out the proverbial baby with the bathwater. Indeed, if we take the time to re-read sources like Schumpeter (1950) [who was himself influenced by Marx if, also, a confirmed anti-Marxist and quasi-monarchist], W. A. Lewis (1955), and Staley and Morse (1965) in economics or, for example, C. Geertz (1962; 1963) and Milton Singer (1960) in anthropology, we find some potentially fruitful ideas about capitalist development from the simple commodity matrix. Actually, one is almost driven to these earlier sources to find analyses of economic development which emphasize the role of endogenous factors and which single out the importance of rural industry in that process.

Together with the tendency over the last 15 years to celebrate the role of exogenous factors in economic development, there has been a parallel tendency among 'peasantists' to agrarianize the countryside, that is, to study and write about rural peoples and their problems as if these involve exclusively agricultural pursuits. Of course, there has been a persistent interest in craft production among anthropologists but mostly from a 'culturalist' perspective which has had little or no impact on the mainstream of theory and analysis in rural or peasant studies. The dominant concerns of the period were the "peasant dilemma" (Wolf 1966)--not the 'peasant-artisan dilemma'--and in the Marxist literature we have the "agrarian question" or the "agrarian problem" and never the problems of 'industry' in the countryside, even though the latter was a prominent topic of concern in the pioneering works by Lenin (1964) and Kautsky (1974) and in seminal works by economic historians like Dobb (1963) and Thompson (1966). One result of this major oversight has been, in my opinion, a tendency to ignore the mutually reinforcing and compatible elements in simple commodity and capitalist forms, the extent to which capital accumulation may occur in the simple commodity form, and the extent of rural labor-power's involvement in simple industrial capitalist circuits. All of this has resulted in a mis-characterization of the peasantry and of its role in national economic development in Asia, Africa, and Latin America (Cook).

According to this 'peasantist' view peasants are typically conceived as being inserted in a non-capitalist mode of production which revolves around the intensive use of family labor, the non-accumulation or investment of capital, and simple reproduction (i.e., the quest for subsistence and replacement, with commodity production geared exclusively toward the recircuiting of value from other-use to own-use circuits). We need only to mention the peasant studies tradition in Mesoamerican anthropology--from Redfield (1956), Foster, and Wolf (1955, 1966) to Stavenhagen (1978), Barta (1974), and Warman (1980)--to see this model at work; and, interestingly enough, in a way which cross-cuts Marxist and non-Marxist labels as a 'peasant mode of production' (Harrison 1977; Cook 1977).

This lack of attention to rural non-agricultural small industry in the peasant and rural development literature of the past fifteen years or so is paradoxical given its well-known importance in the development of capitalism in Western Europe between 1750 and 1850 (and earlier in many cases) and in Russia after the 1860's agrarian reforms. The hallmark Western European case is England; one need only recall Maurice Dobb's (1963: Ch. 1) thesis of the 'petty commodity bridge' between feudalism and industrial capitalism to confirm this. E. J. Hobsbawn (1969: 29) in discussing the so-called textile phase in the industrial revolution in Great Britain starting around 1750 reminds us that on the eve of this revolution, ". . . a good deal - perhaps most - of the industries and manufacturers of Britain were rural, the typical worker being some kind of village artisan or small holder in his cottage, increasingly specializing in the manufacture of some product . . . and thus by degrees turning from small peasant or craftsman into wage laborer." Finally, we need look no further than Marx's Capital to find earlier support for such an emphasis; with reference to the rural direct producers in the transition from feudalism to capitalism in England, he reminds us that, ". . . the new wants he acquires . . . and the increasing assurance with which he disposes of . . . his labor-power will spur him on to a greater exertion of his labor-power, whereby it should not be forgotten that the employment of his labor-power is by no means confined to agriculture, but includes rural home industry" (1967: 794). And he adds with reference to "rural home industry" that, "The possibility is here presented for definite economic development taking place . . ." (ibid.).

Schumpeter (1950) is critical of Marx for his ridiculing of the importance of saving by small proprietors as a mechanism of primitive capitalist accumulation and, while I disagree with Schumpeter's failure to link entrepreneurship to labor during subsequent phases of capitalist development, I think his criticism of Marx on this point is valid. Moreover, I believe that the following statement by Schumpeter (1950: 16), which emphasizes the labor origins of the proto-capitalists, has a great deal of relevance for our understanding of incipient, local-level capitalist development in areas of the contemporary Third World like Oaxaca:

> Many a factory in the 17th and 18th centuries was just a shed that a man was able to put up by the work of his hands, and required only the simplest equipment to work it. In such cases the manual work of the prospective capitalist plus a quite small fund of savings was all that was needed--and brains, of course.

On the basis of my examination of the data from the Santa Lucia del Camino brick industry and the Xaaga weaving industry, I would add two additional elements to Schumpeter's list: family labor-power plus a sub-wage labor pool in other local households.

A cautionary note is in order here: it is one thing to study European economic history with a view toward deriving possible insights or hypotheses about capitalist development in places like contemporary Oaxaca, but it is quite another to assume that the former established a trajectory which the latter can, should or must replicate. The heuristic approach is fruitful; however, as the career of developmentalism shows, the replication approach is analytically sterile. The role of the entrepreneur in the British textile industry between 1750 and 1850 was not only important for the textile branch of British industry and for the British economy but was of world historic importance because it directly contributed to the transformation of the British social formation and humanity at large to a new level of socioeconomic organization in which industrial capital was dominant (Wolf 1982: Ch. 9). The rise of industrial capital to hegemony in the British economy had profound effects outside of Britian; it irreversibly transformed the structure and dynamics of the world capitalist system. There is no way that this transformative role in textiles, or, for that matter, in any other branch of industry can be repeated in the contemporary Third World. Nor can the mangerial function in particular branches of production in contemporary Third World economies, dominated as they are by advanced forms of industrial capital in the metropolitan centers, impact upon those branches as it did during the formative period of European (and, later, of U.S.) industrial capital. For example, textile production in the contemporary Oaxaca countryside is geared to satisfying a social demand for handmade textiles which, of course, cannot be met by capital-intensive industry. What the latter does is supply labor-intensive industry with its basic raw material, thread--the rising price of which is a major problem confronting the would-be or budding entrepreneur; and it's a problem which they can do very little about. Any managerially mediated technological revolutions in the future of Mexican textile production will originate in the industrial capitalist sector, located in central and northern Mexico (or outside Mexico in countries like the U.S. and Japan), and not in Oaxaca's petty industrial sector. The latter serves only as a laboratory for observing a contemporary version of a process that has been going on in Oaxaca since the colonial period when the Spanish introduced the treadle loom, namely, the rise, climax, and decline of weaving enterprises in the city and the countryside--a process in which entrepreneurship has played some role (Chance 1978; cf. Villanueva 1985).

In the last analysis the future of small-scale labor-intensive industries like those in Santa Lucia del Camino and Xaaga lies in a combination of external and internal factors, just as did their past. Nationally, advanced forms of industrial capital control the construction materials and textiles industries: labor-intensive forms persist at the regional and local levels either because the market is not conducive to capital-intensive forms (as, for example, is the case with handicraft products which can only be produced by labor-intensive methods, e.g., handicraft products must be produced in labor-intensive industries) or because it is not attractive to capital-intensive enterprise, given the availability of low-cost labor to sustain the labor-intensive form (e.g., as in brick production). Nevertheless, an economic future with higher degrees of capitalization is not totally preempted by or dependent upon external capital. Santa Lucia's brickyard entrepreneurs could conceivably develop more vertically integrated, capital-intensive brick-producing enterprises by investing internally generated capital and by loans [indeed, several of them mentioned the possibility of purchasing diesel-fueled burners to eliminate manual stoking from the brick firing process]; and Xaaga weaver-entrepreneurs could possibly develop more capital-intensive, vertically-integrated clothing enterprises, though probably not without external assistance in both production and marketing. In other words, these small industries are not quite so retrograde in nature as Baran (1973: 316) and Kautsky (1974: 217 et passim) before him have argued. They may, in fact, play a moderately progressive role in improving over time the material conditions of life of their rural populations but with an inevitable cost in terms of increasing socioeconomic inequality and class antagonism (see Kitching 1982 for an extended discussion of controversies over possible outcomes of labor-intensive industrialization).

NOTES

(1) The field work upon which this analysis is based was conducted through a project entitled "Petty commodity production, capitalist development and underdevelopment in the 'Central Valleys' region of Oaxaca, Mexico," of which I was Principal Investigator, from 9/78 - 8/81 funded by National Science Foundation grant BNS78-18948. The project's primary data corpus includes a principal component consisting of a survey of 947 households in 20 villages in the districts of Ocotlan, Tlacolula, and Centro. In addition, the primary data corpus includes the following six (6) components: (1) transcribed texts of tape-recorded, structured interviews with 160 craft producers (74 men, 82 women) from 8 villages and towns and representing the following occupations: backstrap loom weaving, treadle loom weaving, embroidery, wood carving (utensils), palm-weaving (mats and baskets), broom-making, fireworks-making, sandal-making, blacksmithing, and carpentry; (2) a special questionnaire for merchants/intermediaries was administered to 31 respondents involved in the embroidery industry in five separate localities, and to 72 proprietors of craft businesses (many of which were also engaged in production in Oaxaca City (the businesses included pottery, weaving, and other types of workshops, stalls in various city marketplaces, and stores); (3) the main survey questionnaire was also administered to a small non-random sample of weavers in the town of Mitla, to a few assorted artisans in the town of Ocotlan, and to 23 artisans in the town of Tlacolula; (4) Fifteen detailed household budget studies were carried out in 4 villages ranging from 4 to 10 weeks each; and (5) a series of observational studies - most important in a treadle loom weaving village, a palm-harvesting and weaving village, an ixtle fiber producing village, and a brickmaking village.

Publications to date dealing with data from this project are: Cook 1984a, 1984b, and 1984c.

(2) Schumpeter refers to the "entrepreneurial function" (1961: p. 78 et passim) which he defines as follows: ". . . to reform or

revolutionize the pattern of production by exploiting an invention or . . . an untried technological possibility for producing a new commodity or producing an old one in a new way, by opening up a new source of supply of materials or a new outlet for products, by reorganizing an industry and so on . . .. This function does not essentially consist in either inventing anything or otherwise creating the conditions which the enterprise exploits. It consists in getting things done" (1950: 132). Schumpeter emphasized that entrepreneurs were not necessarily capitalists even though they clearly function vis-a-vis capitalist enterprises. I am inclined to agree with his thesis that the entrepreneurial function performed its major historical role during the 19th century rise of industrial capital and has essentially ossified during the 20th century trajectory of capitalist development (until, perhaps, the advent of the computer/micro-chip age with its 'high technology' industry). But I disagree with his apotheosis of the private entrepreneur as a species of economic magician at the expense of the worker in the ascendancy of industrial capital. See Robert Marsh's paper in this volume for an excellent rendition of Schumpeter's approach to entrepreneurship in terms of the 'production function.'

(3) Oral tradition in Xaaga indicates that the weaving occupation was temporarily practiced there for the first time around 1950 when several looms were set-up in the adjacent ex-hacienda property by the brother of the owner, a weaver whose Oaxaca City workshop was closed due to a labor dispute. This imigrant weaver, who I was able to interview, managed to recruit five apprentices from Xaaga to work with him and had the support of the authorities there. But the experiment failed partly out of disputes over compensation, and one of the Xaaga apprentices continued to work as weavers after this failure. In 1953 this same master weaver was invited to relocate his looms from the hacienda to the famous <u>Hotel Sorpresa</u> in Mitla by E. R. Frissell, an American expatriate and devotee of traditional Oaxaca culture, for the purpose of establishing a weaving school on the premises. This enterprise

was more successful; all of the principal treadle-loom entrepreneurs of Mitla today were trained as apprentices in this school--and the hallmark product of the Mitla treadle-loom weaving industry, the fine white-wool shawl (which tourists are led to believe is an authentic artifact of traditional Mitla culture) was developed--by our peripatetic Oaxaca master (who, by the way, was born in a remote mountain village in the district of Yautepec and came to Oaxaca City via Tlacolula where he learned to weave as a boy). Ironically, the Mitla apprentices trained in the Sorpresa school became in the 1960s and early 70s the principal loom owners and entrepreneurs in a 100-loom industry (Beals 1975: 258) and, as such, the employers and teachers of young men from Xaaga (some of whose elders were participants in the failed hacienda experiment)--many of whom in turn became the pioneer loom-owners and weaver-employers in their home village. Meanwhile, the original maestro - now 70 years old - is back in Oaxaca City employed as a pieceworker in what will surely be one of the last old time weaving sweatshops or mantelerias in the City.

(4) Some readers may wonder why I have coined a new term for a notion which Chayanov (1966) labelled "self-exploitation." There are three reasons why I have done so: (1) it is not so much "self-exploitation" as it is reliance on the labor-power of others in the worker-proprietor's household which is occurring in the Xaaga situation; (2) exploitation is a term best restricted to the relationship between capital and labor that is mediated by a wage payment and in which the purpose is the appropriation of surplus-value; and (3) to emphasize that the family labor-power expended may result in capital accumulation and not just simple reproduction as Chayanov's approach implies.

(5) The Seventh Day Adventist religion has entrenched itself in Xaaga over the past decade. There is a tiny, recently constructed Catholic chapel but - unlike almost every other community its size in the region - Xaaga has no patron saint and no operative cult of the saints (i.e., mayordomia system). According to oral tradition Catholic

worship was centered in the nearby hacienda (which had a large chapel) and, when it was eventually abandoned during the post-revolutionary agrarian reform period, the hacendado sold the patron saint to the Mitla church. The people of Xaaga were obliged to pay a tithe to the latter for many years but they eventually abondoned this practice. It is noteworthy that the religious division within the village population is mirrored within the division of labor: all of the households which have weaving as their principal occupation are Adventistas whereas the Catholic households that weave consider themselves, without exception, to be campesinos and their principal occupation to be agriculture.

(6) Since this section was first written, I have published a book (Cook 1984a) on the Santa Lucia brick industry.

(7) There is another element present in the brick industry which is lacking in weaving: danger. No job in the entire village-based division of labor is more physically punishing and dangerous than that of stoker (atizador) in the brick industry; these individuals work under prolonged exposure to intense heat with no protective clothing and are always in danger of being consumed by a firestorm which results when sudden downdrafts force flame out of the fire box into the highly volatile sawdust staging area from which the stoker fuels the kiln. Over the years several stokers have been incinerated or seriously burned in this fashion. Few can make a career out of stoking because of the punishing effects on the organism from the combination of intense heat, smoke, and dust.

REFERENCES

BARAN, P. 1973. The Political Economy of Growth. Pelican.

BARTA, R. 1974. Estructura Agraria y Clases Sociales en Mexico. Mexico, D.F.: Serie Popular Era.

BEALS, Ralph L. 1975. The Peasant Marketing System of Oaxaca, Mexico. Berkeley and Los Angeles: University of California Press.

CHANCE, J. 1978. Race and Class in Colonial Oaxaca. Standford University Press.

CHAYANOV, A. V. 1966. The Theory of Peasant Economy. Homewood, Ill.: Irwin.

COOK, S. 1977. "Beyond the Formen: towards a revised Marxist theory of precapitalist formations and the transition to capitalism," Journal of Peasant Studies, 4, 4:360-89.

_____. 1982. Zapotec Stoneworkers. Washington, D.C.: University Press of America.

_____. 1984a. Peasant Capitalist Industry, Lanham, MD and London: University Press of America.

_____. 1984b. "Peasant economy, rural industry and capitalist development in the Oaxaca valley, Mexico," Journal of Peasant Studies, 12, 1:3-40.

_____. 1984c. "Rural industry, social differentiation, and the contradictions of provincial Mexican capitalism," Latin American Perspectives, Issue 43, Vol. 11, 4:60-85.

DOBB, M. 1963. Studies in the Development of Capitalism. New York: International Publishers.

FORTES, Meyer. 1958. "Introduction" to J. Goody (ed.), The Develpomental Cycle in Domestic Groups, Cambridge, pp. 1-14.

FOSTER, George. 1967. Tzintzuntzan. Boston: Little, Brown and Co.

GEERTZ, C. 1962. "Social change and economic modernization in two Indonesian towns: a case in point." Ch. 16 of E. E. Hagen, On the Theory of Social Change, Dorsey Press, pp. 385-407.

_____. 1963. Peddlers and Princes. Chicago: Univ. of Chicago Press.

GOODY, E. 1982. "Introduction in From Craft to Industry, ed. E.N. Goody, Cambridge University Press.

HAGEN, E. E. 1962. On the Theory of Social Change. Homewood, Illinois: Dorsey.

HARRISON, M. 1975. "Chayanov and the economics of the Russian peasantry." Journal of Peasant Studies 2,4: 389-417.

_____. 1977. "The peasant mode of production in the work of A. V. Chayanov." Journal of Peasant Studies 4,4: 323-336.

HOBSHAWN, E. J. 1969. Industry and Empire. Pelican.

KAUTSKY, Karl. 1974. La Cuestion Agraria. Mexico, D. F. Siglo Veiniuno.

KITCHING, G. 1982. Development and Underdevelopment in Historical Perspective. London and New York: Methuen.

LENIN, V. I. 1964. The Development of Capitalism in Russia. Moscow: Progress Publishers.

LEWIS, W. A. 1955. The Theory of Economic Growth. London: George Allen & Unwin.

MARX, Karl. 1967. Capital. Vol. 3. New York: International Publishers.

MEDICK, Hans. 1976. "The proto-industrial family economy: the structural function of household and family during the transition from peasant society to industrial capitalism." Social History 1,3: 291-315.

MC CLELLAND, D. 1961. The Achieving Society. New York: VanNostrand.

REDFIELD, R. 1956. Peasant Society and Culture. Chicago: University of Chicago Press.

ROSTOW, W. W. 1960. The Stages of Economic Growth. London: Cambridge University Press.

ROXBOROUGH, I. 1979. Theories of Underdevelopment. Atlantic Highlands, N.J.: Humanities Press.

SCHUMPETER, J. A. 1950. Capitalism, Socialism and Democracy. New York: Harper.

SINGER, M. 1960 "Changing craft traditions in India." In Moore, W. E. and A. S. Feldman (eds.), Labor Commitment and Social Change in Developing Areas, Social Science Research Council, pp. 258-276.

STALEY, E. and R. Morse. 1965. Modern Small Industry for Developing Countries. New York: McGraw-Hill.

STAVENHAGEN, R. 1978. "Capitalism and peasantry in Mexico," Latin American Perspectives. Issue 18, Vol. 3:27-37.

TAYLOR, J. 1979. From Modernization to Modes of Production. London: MacMillan.

THOMPSON, E. P. 1966. "Chayanov's concept of peasant economy." In Thorner, D., B. Berblay, and R. E. F. Smith (eds.), Theory of Peasant Economy By A. V. Chayanov, pp. xi-xxiii, Homewood, Ill.: Irwin.

VILLANUEVA, M. 1985. "From calpixqui to corregidor: appropriateion of women's cotton textile production in early colonial Mexico," Latin American Perspectives, 12, 1:17-40.

WARMAN, A. 1980. We Come to Object: The Peasants of Morelos and the National State. Baltimore: Johns Hopkins.

WOLF, Eric. 1955. "Types of Latin American peasantry: a preliminary discussion," American Anthropologist, 57, 3:452-78.

_____. 1966. *Peasants*. Englewood Cliffs, N.J.: Prentice-Hall.

_____. 1982. *Europe and the People Without History*. Berkeley and Los Angeles: University of California Press.

IV. ENTREPRENEURIAL AGRICULTURE AND THE INVOLUTION OF AGRICULTURAL DYNAMICS IN THE AMERICAS

Sheldon Smith

Traditional developmental theory clearly supports the idea that capitalist entrepreneurial activities will lead to economic growth and development (Schumpeter 1961). The net result of national policy based on developmental theory in many third world countries, however, has not been growth and development but growth and revolutionary violence. This paper presents the perspective that economic growth in many (but by no means all) third world countries can have no result other than political destabilization because instead of bringing about the transformation of traditional social structures, as occurred in the "core countries" (Chirot 1978, Wallerstein 1972, Levy 1972), it brings about the involution of national social structures and political instability.

The concept of involution was introduced into human ecology and anthropological economics by Clifford Geertz in 1963, to describe agricultural and social processes in Indonesia. He, in turn, borrowed the concept from Alexander Goldenweiser "who devised it to describe those cultural patterns which, after having reached what would seem definitive form, nonetheless fail either to stabilize or transform themselves into a new pattern but rather continue to develop by becoming internally more complicated" (Geertz 1963: 81). In this paper, entrepreneurial economic growth in Guatemala (and elsewhere in Central America) is shown to lead, not to modernization (transformation), but to involutionary processes which, in turn, are tied to revolutionary violence.

Growth and Revolution

The link between economic growth and revolution has been made many times by Marxist as well as non-Marxist writers. Studies of revolutions in the 20th century have shown that in many instances, it was not economic devolution (a dropping of the G.N.P.) which brought about revolution, but, surprisingly, economic growth (Wolf 1968). Mexico supplies a classic case. Mexico, in the late 19th century and early 20th century, had a rapidly growing economy, thanks to the national policies of the director Porfirio Diaz. Of particular importance to that growth was the introduction of railroads and the expansion of hacienda agriculture (Coatsworth 1974, 1978). This period was followed by a deadly revolution which lasted, off and on, from 1910 into the mid-1930's. Other countries which have suffered national revolutions on the heels of periods of economic growth are Vietnam, China, Russia, and Cuba (Wolf 1968). The following case study will show that similar growth patterns have been occurring in Guatemala and are having similar consequences for similar reasons. However, before presenting the case for involution in coastal Guatemala, it is important to look at the two contrasting theories dealing with development and underdevelopment: diffusion theory and dependency theory.

Diffusion Theory and Dependency Theory

The basic theoretical perspective behind policy making in third world countries can be referred to as "diffusion" or "development" theory and is clearly expressed in the writings of formal economic theorists such as W. Arthur Lewis (1955), W. W. Rostow (1962), and B. F. Hoselitz (1952), to name but a few. A current application of the positive entrepreneurial assumptions from these theories to Guatemala is found in Fletcher, Graber, Merrill, and Thorbeck´es *Guatemala's Economic Development: the Role of Agriculture* (1970). While on the one hand denouncing the intolerable working conditions found on rural estates as well as the poverty of *minifundistas* in Guatemala, they go on to assert that increased production of export oriented agricultural goods will lead, sooner or later, to positive economic development.

The theoretical model which underlies the assumptions about the positive benefits of entrepreneurialism has been called the "diffusion model" by dependency theorists (Chilcote and Edelstein 1974: 19-26). A diffusion model assumes that the growth of first world core countries, through increased demand for the export goods of third world countries, will pull third world economies to ever higher levels of development (a form of "trickle down" theory). Thirty years ago, frustrations over the evident lack of economic development led Celso Furtado and the Economic Commission on Latin America (E.C.L.A) to declare formal diffusion theory bankrupt (Furtado 1965). More recently, writers like Lappe' and Collins (1977) have tried to show that entrepreneurial agriculture, rather than leading to economic development, often leads to economic underdevelopment. As the dependent economy of a third world country becomes more dependent, it also becomes more underdeveloped. Dependency theory was developed and popularized in the writings of Andre Gunder Frank (1968), Bodenheimer (1970), Petras (1973), and Dos Santos (1970). Dos Santos' definition of dependency theory has been widely cited:

> By dependence we mean a situation in which the economy of certain countries is conditioned by the development and expansion of another economy to which the former is subjected. The relation of interdependence between two or more economies, and between these and world trade, assume the form of dependence when some countries (the dominant ones) can expand and can be self-sustaining, while other countries (the dependent ones) can do this only as a reflection of that expansion, which can have either a positive or negative effect on their immediate development (Dos Santos 1970: 231).

However, dependency theory itself is loaded with a priori assumptions about the relationships between growth sectors and non-growth sectors in the world economy. The attack against dependency theory is most vigorous in the writings of Latin American economic historians who have used rigorous quantitative economic analyses to study various periods and regions of Latin America. Their studies tend to show that neither diffusion theory nor dependency explain economic growth or non-growth. Growth, or a lack thereof, is the result of the interaction of local and international conditions and not just the one or the other.

Among recent studies which can be cited contesting both dependency theory and diffusion theory are John Coatsworth's studies of Mexican railroads during the Porfiorato. He shows that a large number of obstacles to Mexican economic development were Mexican in nature and that a considerable amount of development occurred despite them (Coatsworth 1974, 1979). Duncan and Rutledge's collection of papers on rural workers in Latin America shows that the exploitation of rural workers in Latin America is largely an indigenous phenomenon not explained away by such outside influences as a United Fruit Company (Duncan and Rutledge 1977). Holloway's (1977) study of coffee agriculture near Sao Paulo, Brazil, not only demonstrates the success of former landless workers in developing coffee plantations but also suggests linkages of that development to the industrialization of Sao Paulo. William McGreevy has made similar arguments about the development of coffee agriculture in highland Colombia and the industrialization of Medellin, following Parson's earlier suggestions (McGreevy 1971, Parsons 1968). Spaulding has shown, on the other hand, that class stratification and the ownership of large hacienda estates in the southern highlands of Peru are responsible for holding back economic development (Spaulding 1980). Irving Stone has shown that while there was considerable outside British investment in Argentina prior to 1914, investments and errors leading to underdevelopment were made locally, often to the detriment of British investors who learned not to invest in Argentina (Stone 1977: 690-722). Shane Hunt, in a fascinating study, showed how the guano industry of 19th century Peru, which had been thought to be an enclave of an outside country, in fact was mismanaged by local elites who dissipated the short term wealth instead of investing it (1973). Flavio Rabelo Versiani has demonstrated the initial success of industrial development in Brazil (1979), while Nathaniel Leff has shown its long term success (1969), countering the underdevelopment argument of Andre G. Frank (1966). Warren Dean (1969) and Albert Fishlow (n.d.) have added more background on the success of Brazilian industrialization.

It is clear that neither develomental theory nor diffusion theory explain either economic development or underdevelopment, and by the same token, they cannot explain political instability in Latin America. In the case of both theoretical positions we may have, as Peter Berger has pointed out in __Pyramids of Sacrifice__ (1974), not two theories, but two myths with attendant mythologically based national policies. The main myth is that of modernization (diffusion theory) which historically brought up the counter myth of dependency. For Berger (who is borrowing his idea of myth from Sorel) ". . .a myth is any set of ideas that infuses transcendent meaning into the lives of men. . ." (Berger 1974: 17). Developmental theory and dependency theory, which is a reaction to developmental theory more than it is a theory, are projections of the histories of core countries which may have little application to the countries of the periphery (Berger 1974: 17-113).

If developmental theory and dependency theory are myths, then our entrepreneur may very well be a mythological hero who is deemed to have the power to transform national economic and political structures. The diffusionist would argue that entrepreneurs are intermediaries between core countries and satellites who act to produce economic growth and development in both (I am separating "growth" from "development" in this essay; development refers to an improvement in human living conditions, growth refers to an expansion of the G.N.P.). The "dependistas" would argue that if outside economies did not penetrate the economies of third world countries, indigenous entrepreneurs (both economic and political) would bring about the coming of the millenium.

In a recent article, Sidney Greenfield and Arnold Strickon also question the myth of modernization and the entrepreneur (1981):

> The Schumpeterian formulation of economic development singles out entrepreneurship (and the entrepreneur) as the critical factor in the process. Put bluntly, the implicit assumption is that is entrepreneurs do what they are supposed to, new combinations are assumed to be better than the previous ones-that is, to bring about progress-it is important that entrepreneurs be encouraged and facilitated. Should they not, for whatever reason, the better, more developed economic states that follow growth would not be brought into being. The future good of humanity, according to the model, is in the hands of entrepreneurs (Greenfield and Strickon 1981: 470).

The critique of entrepreneurship and of the assumptions of development theory underlying much of the modernization literature should not be restricted to the diffusionist model. A balanced perspective requires an equal critique of revolutionary socialist models as well since the state bureaucrats who attempt to transform underdeveloped economies may actually interfere with the development process (Berger 1974: 76-110).

Goal of the Paper

In this paper, I seek to show how entrepreneurial activity can lead to involution, underdevelopment, and revolution. To accomplish my ends, I will lift the concept of "entrepreneur" out of a strictly economic context (as did Barth, 1972) to place it into a broader cultural context within which the economy is embedded (Polanyi 1944: 43-55). An entrepreneur, in this paper, is one who seeks to re-organize the sources of production in a novel way by using economic or political means. In the end, the entrepreneur seeks personal advantage. However, in the process of seeking that advantage, there may accrue benefits to society or there may not. There is no way to predict the impact of entrepreneurial decision making on society until after the transformation has taken place. As Greenfield and Strickon perceive entrepreneurial decision making, the large benefits to society may be positive (developmental) or negative (anti-developmental). Evolutionary assumptions may be entirely misplaced (Greenfield and Strickon 1981: 481).

There is, however, a larger issue here. Entrepreneurs rarely operate in the singular. In both capitalist and socialist economies, there are those who intervene in countries' economies to create, or to help create, the economic and political environments which attract the activities of entrepreneurs. For example, John Bennett has shown in his Northern Plainsmen how the movement of farmers and ranchers west into Saskachewan was determined not by economic or ecological or social factors but by the decisions of politicians and bureaucrats who opened the West (Bennett 1968: 103). However, just as economic theoretician cannot predict the impact of entrepreneurial activities on society, neither can the higher level decision makers, the people who make national policy. In Guatemala, as we shall see, decisions by national and international politicians

and bureaucrats brought about the transformation of
the economic environment of the south coast making it
attractive to agricultural entrepreneurs who moved in
to create a new plantation economy. But, if the new
system of organization was supposed to bring benefits
to the people of the region, so far the opposite has
been true.

The Historical and Ecological Context of Siquinala, Guatemala

   This case study is an analysis of the history of
land tenure in the municipio of Siquinala, Guatemala,
located on the south coast. The south coast,
particularly the department of Escuintla, where
Siquinala is located, presents a pattern of middle
class (medium sized) and cosmopolite (elite)
controlled "fincas" with patches of minifundios
scattered here and there, mostly developed by
government redistribution programs. Map 1, which is
based on a cadastral survey carried out by the
Guatemalan government, shows in detail what the land
tenure pattern looks like. It has been described in
detail by following the vertical lines from the lower
coast to the piedmont elsewhere (Smith 1982). It is
fairly clear, from a study of the map, where the old
land grants of the fifteenth and sixteenth centuries
were. Recently, the region has suffered considerable
political turmoil and violence. The towns of the
coast and the small aldeas (hamlets) have been subject
to continuous right wing and left wing attacks for
well over a decade.

   Plantation agriculture is the predominant
socionatural system (see Bennett 1980: 22-23 for an
explanation of "socionatural") found on the coast of
Guatemala. The particular system of plantation
agriculture found on the south coast of Guatemala has
been given the name of "central-satellite plantation
system" and has been described elsewhere (Smith 1982).
Le Beau has written that plantation agriculture
constitutes the economic backbone of Guatemala (La
Beau 1956). More than 90 percent of all exports are
derived from plantations. However, while there have
been a few large plantations on the coast such as the
United Fruit Company's La Bananeria and the Herrera
owned Pantaleon, the majority of plantations in
Guatemala were primarily located along the western
piedmont and were exclusively devoted to coffee up

until the 1950's, when a new pattern of plantation agriculture spread to the coast.

Historically, on the coast, the earliest export agriculture plantations were specialized in the growing of indigo or cattle, neither of which were raised intensively. Indigo was ideally suited to the coast because transportation was extremely difficult and the dye was a compact good which could easily be carried by horse. Cattle were also a logical product for the region because they could transport themselves to market. In the late 19th century, however, indigo growers had to turn to cattle and foodstuffs because of the German invention of analine dyes. However, much of the land was not used at all. There are several reasons for land being kept out of production, some of which are still true today. First, the infrastructure of the region was very poorly developed making it uneconomical to grow goods that were difficult to transport. Second, by keeping land out of production but under the ownership of the few, the cost of labor was kept down since rural workers had no alternative except to work for the wealthy. Third, the region was not considered healthy.

Labor policies on the plantations were those of debt peonage, common throughout Latin America. Landless workers were loaned foodstuffs and clothing in return for the work they did on the plantations. Plantation workers who lived on the estates were usually given up to an acre of land (milpa) and raised much of their own food. Surpluses could be sold during emergencies. The relationships between owners and workers were paternalistic and there is evidence that owners took relatively good care of their workers. This is particularly true of those plantations owned by members of the local elite. The local elite consisted primarily of landowners who moved into the region during the period between 1860 and 1890 when the collectively owned ejido lands of the Indian population were given to individual Indian families. These families, for a variety of legal and non-legal reasons, lost their properties to the local elites during the period from 1860 to 1890. The properties of the local elite ranged in size between 160 to 1,000 acres and were worked by owners and landless laborers. At the turn of the century, the local elite controlled approximately one third of the land in Siquinala and also had considerable control

CADASTRAL MAP OF SIQUINALA, GUATEMALA: 1900

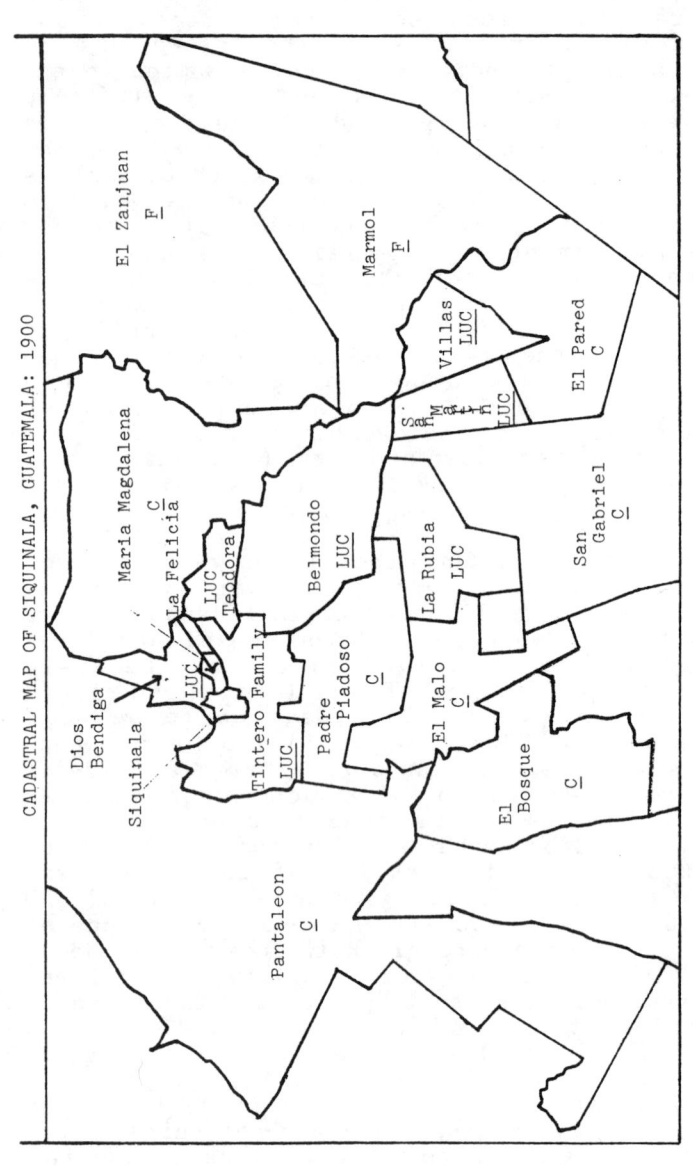

Map No. 1

C = Cosmopolite
EMC = Emerging Middle Class
LUC = Local Upper Class
F = Foreigner or Foreign Owned

over local political events. For the most part, however, the south coast was lightly populated with little access to Guatemala City or to the ports. The coastal city of Puerto San Jose has deep water facilities, but these were only constructed since World Was II.

During the 1900's and on through the first part of the century, the pace of the coastal economy quickened because of the establishment of the United Fruit Company's banana plantations in Tiquisate during the 1920's and 1930's. Investments were made by the company and the government in roads and other transportation facilities, which made the region more attractive to outside investors. Guatemalans also began to view the success of foreign entrepreneurs with some excitement. Coffee had already been introduced to the piedmont and highlands in the latter phases of the nineteenth century where it became the main crop in a monocrop economy. In the early twentieth century, largely because of the United Fruit Company and a limited number of German owned plantations, other export commodities such as sugar cane, cotton, and coffee began to be grown on coastal lands, but only in small amounts. Most coastal estates were treated with a certain amount of healthy inefficiency.

After World War II, the expansion of the economies of core countries brought a new and increased demand for tropical export products. The new demand caused a change in the coastal "environment" as land became increasingly more valuable. Of particular importance was the construction of a coastal highway in 1944, which later became part of the Pan American highway. The new road opened the region to economic development and to agricultural entrepreneurs. A more recent event that was to have powerful repercussions was the shifting of Cuba's sugar quota by American policy makers in favor of the Central American republics. This, then, was the new environmental setting for Guatemalan agricultural entrepreneurs alluded to earlier which had such tremendous potential for future economic development. The preceding events established the setting for the transformation of coastal agriculture by entrepreneurs.

Entrepreneurs and the New Combination

Up until 1960, the history of land use in coastal Guatemala is hazy. It is clear, however, that there has been a dramatic transformation of the coast since the 1950's, but perhaps in directions no one could have foreseen. From the turn of the century up until the late 1950's and early 1960's, there were only a few large coastal plantations exporting tropical and subtropical agricultural goods. Since that time, the coast has been transformed so that corn, beans, squash, and other traditional staples are presently only grown on a few scattered subsistence oriented minifundios. Today, as far as one can see, almost all of the land is in cotton, sugar cane, or coffee.

The attitude of Guatemala's commercial elite towards agricultural entrepreneurs is graphically displayed on a day to day basis in the national newspaper El Imparcial. Editorials praise entrepreneurs as Guatemala's modern saviors. Detailed analyses of cotton, sugar cane, and coffee markets, national profit and loss statements, international debts and loans and international economic arrangements are published which clearly extol the need to back the agricultural entrepreneurs. Successful entrepreneurs are recognized by being given honorific titles in the voluntary associations they belong to like the Rotary and the Chamber of Commerce. Clearly, given the international world economy as presently organized, agriculturalists are the heroes of Guatemala's growing economy.

The changes that have occurred on the coast can be seen on the two maps of Siquinala contrasting 1900 to 1966. On the maps, C stands for cosmopolite or national elite, F for foreign (mostly German), L.U.C. for local upper class, and E.M.C. stands for emerging middle class and refers to entrepreneurial agriculturalists who have only recently begun to operate in the region. The distinctions between local upper class and the other three categories are fairly clear. L.U.C. are not wealthy and they tend to be tied into the local social structure. At one time, they controlled much of the local and regional power and primarily grew food for local towns and cities. Since the turn of the century, their lands have fragmented through inheritance. Many of their lands have been purchased by members of the E.M.C. and turned over to the production of export commodities. The remaining L.U.C. tends to grow a wide variety of goods, mostly foodstuffs, which are marketed locally. The average size of their properties is considerably smaller than it was in the 1900, averaging twenty acres.

The distinctions between cosmopolites and members of the emerging middle class are much less clear. In very general terms, and there are many exceptions, the cosmopolites represent the old wealth of the aristocracy. Their estates, like those of the local elite, were consolidated at the turn of the century, with a few exceptions. The estates tend to be quite large ranging from a few thousand acres to twenty thousand acres. Furthermore, cosmopolite estates tend not to be the only properties owned by their owners' families. For example, the owner of the plantation Magdalena had a brother with an extensive coffee plantation in Alta Verapaz. Cosmopolites also tend to be involved in international industrial investments abroad. They do not invest in the economy of Siquinala. However, since their estates tend not to be their only source of wealth, the intensity with which they work their lands and laborers is less than that of the E.M.C.

It is with the E.M.C. estates that real behavioral differences can be noted in terms of the treatment of land and labor. In every case investigated, the owners of the E.M.C. estates were either small businessmen, middle level bureaucrats, middle level managers of corporations (one manager worked for the Coca Cola Company), or members of the Guatemalan military (one owner was a corporal in the Guatemalan army who was married to a woman who ran a beauty shop in Guatemala City). The properties of the E.M.C. tend to be smaller than those of the cosmopolites and larger than the L.U.C. ranging between two hundred acres to a few thousand. However, like the cosmopolites, they are all absentee land owners who, for the most part, live in Guatemala City. They usually visit their estates once every one or two weeks, and then only stay a few hours to check their books and discuss business operations with the administrators. Administrators range in background from illiterate workers to members of the E.M.C. The larger the estate, the higher the status and education of the administrators. The preceding forms the

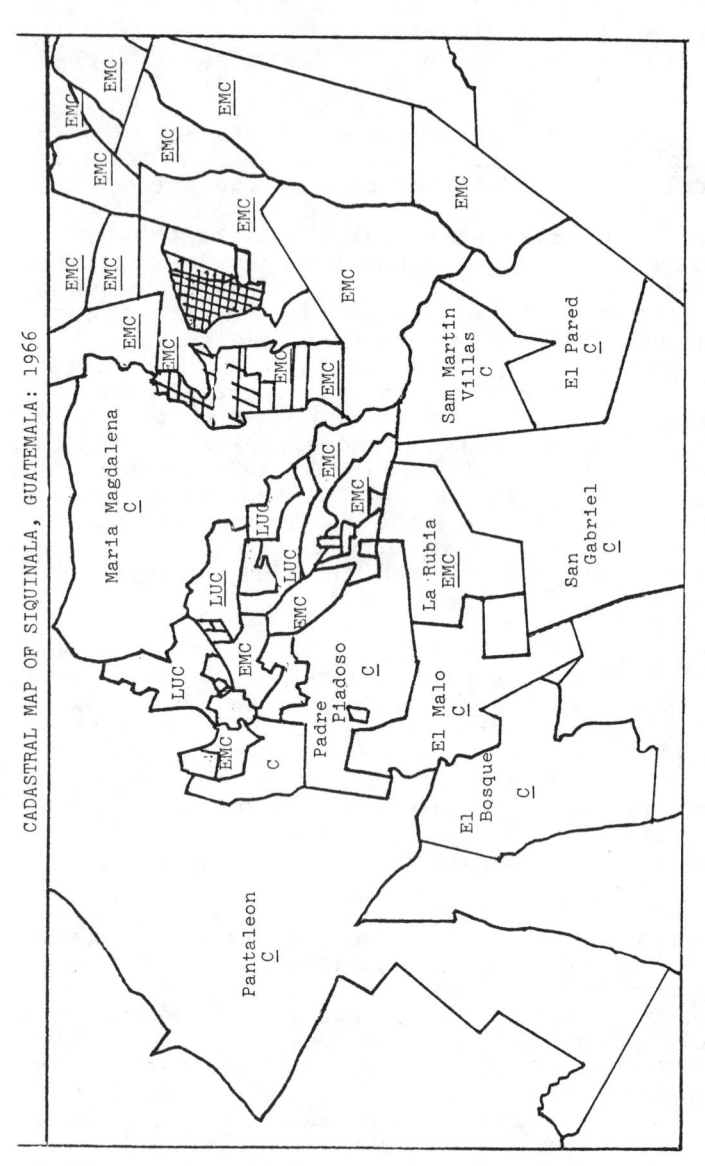

CADASTRAL MAP OF SIQUINALA, GUATEMALA: 1966   Map No. 2

C = Cosmopolite
EMC = Emerging Middle Class
LUC = Local Upper Class
F = Foreigner or Foreign Owned

descriptive backdrop for the following analysis of what I call the central-satellite plantation system.

Schumpeter, in his discussion of entrepreneurs, used the term "swarm" in reference to those individuals who follow and imitate successful entrepreneurs (Schumpeter 1961). In the case of south coast Guatemala, the "swarm" was made up of businessmen speculating on plantation agriculture. The new entrepreneurs bought up coastal properties and attempted to turn them into profitable economic enterprises. In so doing, they not only transformed the economic organization of their own individual properties, but they brought into existence an entirely new region economy, which I have given the name of the central-satellite plantation system (Smith 1975, 1982). Central satellite plantation systems have been recorded for other world regions, such as coastal Cuba, Puerto Rico, and the Philippines, but they tend to be transformed into large factories in the field as satellite plantations are swallowed up by the centrales (see the case studies in Steward's Peoples of Puerto Rico). This has not happened in Guatemala due to the relative political and economic power of satellite owners, an issue examined elsewhere (Smith 1982: 14-16).

The central-satellite plantation system is part of a larger pattern of evolving export agriculture described for world regions by Lappe and Collins (Lappe and Collins 1977). It is not restricted to the Guatemalan coast but has been reported for the Cauca Valley of Colombia and is no doubt widespread (Knight 1968, 1972).

Siquinala is representative of the pattern of landownership on the coast of Guatemala shown on the cadastral map of land ownership. The map shows a pattern of small to medium size estates surrounding giant latifundia which are corporately owned (factories-in-the-field). The smaller plantations occur next to major towns and are composed of lands once owned by members of the local upper class and have, to a great extent, been taken over by entrepreneurial agriculturalists. Extremely large units of land measured in square kilometers are not represented on the map and occur to the east of Escuintla (El Salto) and to the west of Siquinala (Pantaleon). The dimensions of these corporately owned estates are not available. The factories-in-the-field are linked to transnational corporations through marketing associations, such as the Guatemalan Sugar Association, which they tend to dominate (the president of El Salto, one of the largest plantations in Guatemala, was an Englishman who was also president of the sugar association). Other smaller plantation owners may or may not belong, but they do not have much voice in the decision-making process. The small entrepreneurial group and cosmopolite owners should not be viewed as automatically linked to the transnationals. They are often very independent and hostile to the power of the giant corporations. One powerful entrepreneur from the region in which I worked, who was machine gunned to death in the early 1970's (probably by guerrillas), was well known for editorials he wrote for El Imparcial demanding legislation to control the ingenios (another name for centrales). The capacities of these new finqueros to hold their own may be the result of a growth in power of the Guatemalan national middle class (Smith 1982).

In the region of Siquinala, the dominant crop is sugar cane, which is trucked to large centrales. Sugar mills are usually located within relatively short distances of smaller plantations. Transportation costs are low and owners often have between four to five ingenios from which to chose.

While the term central-satellite fits the Siquinala situation, it may not be appropriate further south where cotton is dominant. South of La Democracia, the lands of the coast have been increasingly put into cotton agriculture. Large landowners control the cotton associations but, as is true for Siquinala, smaller owners are not particularly intimidated by the associations. While a central-satellite pattern may not characterize the region south of La Democracia, as the map shows, the pattern of land ownership is the same, a mix of large and small properties, almost all involved in speculative plantation agriculture. In the central-satellite plantation system, small to medium and large size plantations belonging to members of upwardly mobile middle class, local upper, and national upper classes supply huge corporate factories in the field with raw sugar cane which is then processed by them. Prior to the 1960's, smaller plantations processed their own sugar through the use of trapiches to produce panela or brown sugar and molasses. Suppliers have some choice in terms of which central the cane will be sent, but associations set monopoly prices on sugar purchased. More importantly, supplier plantation owners have sufficient political and economic power to prevent their lands from being absorbed by the factories-in-the-field, something which was not true in many other parts of the world, such as Puerto Rico, the Philippines, or Cuba when a conversion towards sugar production occurred at the turn of the century. Small holders were absorbed by internationally owned sugar corporations. It appears that the political and economic changes in Guatemala, particularly the rise of a powerful middle class, explains the fact that the smaller plantations are not being gobbled by the larger ones, although attempts have been made by centrales like Pantaleon to absorb neighboring plantations, particularly those of the old local elite. These attempts have created considerable animosity and have added to the political tensions of the region.

Rolf Knight (1968, 1972) has pointed out another characteristic of this system, which is largely in agreement with my own assessment, and that is the function of the central-satellite system is specifically to destabilize the working population. Carol Smith's recent paper (1981) has described how Guatemala's elite (which would include my middle class) and the government maintains the working class in a continued state of poverty and disorganization in order to insure low wages for plantation workers. Paul Diener has recently shown how the highland Indians' cargo fiesta system has been incorporated into the migratory labor system by placing cargo holders in debt relationships to Ladino tienda (shop) owners (Diener 1978). Debts are worked off by migrating to the lowlands and working on plantations. Furthermore, the enganche system of the colonial period is still in operation (this is an illegal, forced contracting of laborers through a variety of means, including debt peonage). In the central-satellite system, the standard of living is low as to force laborers to constantly struggle to survive, and, consequently, to accept the low standard of living characteristic of plantation villages. Workers on small plantations cannot organize themselves to improve their situations and outside organizers are considered outside agitators, with well-known consequences. Whether or not the system has been consciously worked out, the fact is that this is a system which, once in place, has brought about such a state of labor instability that labor exploitation has become a relatively easy matter and the system is to the advantage of exploitative entrepreneurs. The profits in plantation agriculture are high when international demand is high. Several plantation owners and administrators admitted to making profits of about 50 percent.

In Siquinala, for the last 30 years or so, there has emerged a combination of extremely large and somewhat smaller plantations organized to grow and sell sugar cane to large corporately owned centrales. While cosmopolite plantations date back to the turn of the century, the plantations of the emerging middle class are much more recent. For the most part, they were developed between 1950 and the present. In a large number of cases, the new entrepreneurs are Guatemalan businessmen looking for a place to invest their money and to make higher profits. They buy up plots of land that are too small to support members of the old local elite and they consolidate them into new plantations. In this way, Guatemalan businessmen conform to a common Latin American cultural pattern. Land is more than just an investment, it is a cultural value and to own land is an end in itself. But the land is not worked by its owner who may only travel to it a few times a month. The entrepreneurial owners differ from other "locals", however, in that they have access to credit which is not available to other local farmers. They are able to use modern technology, such as planes, to dust their crops, and they can afford to buy such items as tractors. They perceive themselves to be businessmen, not farmers. As businessmen, they usually have investments elsewhere, such as in the growing industries of Guatemala.

The development of this system is largely a response to world demand for sugar and other export commodities. It is also the result of a social structure in which a small elite has political and economic control of the land. In several instances, members of the old elite and smaller farmers of the region have sold out to outside businessmen after being threatened and have left Siquinala. There were also several instances in which plantation ownership was nominally held by one individual who represented another businessman (in one case, an ex-presidential candidate known for his right wing views and for having helped overthrow the Arbenz government in 1954). While cosmopolites have been involved in the entrepreneurial development of plantation agriculture, it is the members of the emerging middle class that give the system its characteristics. On the older and more traditional plantations of both the local elite and the cosmopolites, paternalistic relations between owners and workers still survive and there is some pride in their maintenance. The owner of finca Maria Magdalena (the names of all the properties are fictitious) was particularly proud of his relationship with his workers and recounted a story of how his father had been one of the few large landowners whose property was not threatened during the revolutionary period of 1944 to 1954 due to mutual feelings of goodwill. The owner had made considerable improvements in housing, building a large number of units out of cinder block. He has also tried to assure that workers had an adequate diet and medical attention. However, he paid no more than the local minimum wage, about one dollar a day.

The finca La Rubia is an example of a plantation owned by a middle class entrepeneur. Originally owned by a wealthy businessman/landowner who owned other land in Guatemala and had it worked on a sharecropping basis, the plantation in question was sold to Alvaro Lopez, a highly aggressive businessman. Lopez owns a large grocery business in Guatemala City with two brothers and La Rubia is one of his speculative investments. The contrast between life on the upper class owned Maria Magdelena and the speculatively owned La Rubia is dramatic. Whereas most of the workers of Maria Magdelena have homes of either wood or "bloque" (cinder block), a majority of the buildings on La Rubia were pole and thatch affairs. Workers on Maria Magdelena had access to about an acre of land on which to grow food, but on La Rubia, all of the milpa plots had been taken away from the workers and planted with sugar cane. Workers did not have access to medical facilities. A household census showed much greater poverty on the speculative plantation where workers stayed an average of 6.3 years as opposed to 17.3 years on the elite owned plantation. The two plantations are about a mile apart.

To the east is the finca Mi Juanita which has a history similar to that of La Rubia. Originally it was owned by a cosmopolite family which decided to pull out of the region after the violent takeovers of local plantations during the early 1950's. They sold out to Don Robles, a supervisor of the American owned Coca Cola Company. The property was originally a cattle operation but its owner has progressively placed all of the land into sugar production. The social and habitat conditions of the workers are identical to those of workers on La Rubia.

In strong contrast to La Rubia and Mi Juanita is the finca Dios Bendiga. It is owned by a member of the local elite and represents conditions found on properties owned by local landowners who reside on their fincas. Originally, the property was a zone of minifundios owned by Indian families. The land was consolidated by Haremillo Vargas over a period of 20 to 30 years after the turn of the century and then purchased by Don Guido, its present owner, in 1946. Don Guido, who was of Italian descent, was the governor of one of the northern provinces from 1918 to 1920. His brother was a presidential candidate during the elections of 1920. Guido exiled himself to the United States for a decade after Orellana won the presidency. He returned to work for the United Fruit Company in Tiquisate until buying Dios Bendiga in 1946. Unlike cosmopolite and emerging middle class plantation owners, Don Guido lived on his plantation. He graciously let me stay there for a week. Although, at the time, he was 80 years old, he worked the land with his hired help, most of whom lived in houses which, while smaller, were the equivalent of the house he lived in. He was proud of his egalitarian treatment of his workers and scathing in his denunciation of the treatment of workers by absentee landowners. Although at the time rural violence was becoming endemic, he went around unarmed, unlike the absentee landowners who usually carried loaded handguns when visiting their plantations. Don Guido was fairly representative of other local landowners, both in his treatment of workers and in his lack of fear of local guerrillas. Almost all of the attacks against finca owners were aimed at absentee landowners. Guido did not feel anyone would threaten him since he felt he was a member of the local community. He did voice a fear that increases in the numbers of absentee, entrepreneurial style fincas would have a destabilizing effect on Siquinala. At the time, several migrant workers in Escuintla had been killed by right wing hit squads and it was Don Guido's opinion that the killers had been hired by absentee landowners to take care of "trouble makers."

The Social Consequences of the New Combination

The differences between the treatment of the land and of labor by the cosmopolites and local elite on the one hand, and speculative buisinessmen on the other is very clear. While cosmopolites and local elites are part of the agricultural system described in this paper, they are much less intense in their search for profits and tend to observe traditional social moves in the treatment of laborers. The new entrepreneurs, however, are using both land and labor as aggressively as they can in order to make the highest profits in a short period of time. They bring in and use chemical herbecides and pesticides along with the petroleum-based fertilizers with little regard for the health of workers. There are reports of rented crop dusters being flown over the plantation lands of speculative land owners and spraying both crops and workers with lethal mixtures of chemicals with little regard for human health (Lappé and Collins 1977: 48). It is perhaps in response to this spraying that a group of guerrillas blew up several crop dusters in the late 1970's (for this act they were accused of destroying Guatemala's potential for economic development by national newspapers).

The destabilizing influence of the agricultural entrepreneurs is largely disregarded by the national media of Guatemala. The two major newspapers, El Imparcial and El Grafico portray the modern agriculturalist as the cutting edge of modernization. These modern heroes are viewed as the leaders of economic development and transformers of the national economy. As far as the country's elite are concerned, any turning away from export agriculture would be a national disaster since it would be increasingly difficult to pay off already expensive international debts and balance of payments deficits. This cutting edge, however, has had the real effect of creating increased poverty in the countryside. Wages have not kept up with inflation and many workers have lost access to traditional milpa plots where they once grew subsistence crops.

There is considerable reason to think that the activities of speculative agricultural entrepreneurs contribute directly to the revolutionary violence of the left. Allan Nairn, a journalist, recently spent four months in Guatemala studying the activities of the military, particularly one squad attached to the finca La Perla. He writes:

> When the army began killing peasants whom speculators were evicting from the land, the guerrillas were ready to take advantage of the resulting popular resentment (Nairn 1983:21).

It is not difficult to understand that colonos, voluntarios (migrant laborers), and small landowners may become the recruits of guerrilla activists. Data I collected in the 1960's showed that many colonos working on plantations in Siquinala had been actively involved in the revolutionary activities of the 1950's. Several of these had attempted to take over plantation lands and were subsequently thrown off of the land and were forced to become voluntarios. Their activities were monitored by local officials.

It is meaningful in this context to remember that Eric Wolf in his Peasant Wars of the 20th Century attributes much of the revolutionary violence of the 1950's in the Cuba to peasant farmers who had been evicted from their lands by plantation owners who were trying to expand the production of their sugar cane plantations (Wolf 1968).

While the national press may laud the landowners, it is obvious that their activities make them the focus of revolutionary violence. When I was in Guatemala, one of my informants, a colonel in the army, as well as a plantation owner, was machine gunned to death while coming into the town of Escuintla for an interview with me. The same week, the son of another wealthy landowner whom I had interviewed was kidnapped and held ransom for $125,000 (he was later found and freed by the police on the basis of an anonymous tip). After I left Guatemala, I received reports and ran across newspaper articles reporting the deaths of other prominent landowners who had been a part of my study. In several instances, the landowners in question were also prominent right wing politicians, including one who was reported to have loaned the use of one of his fincas (not in Siquinala) for the training of counter-revolutionaries by the C.I.A. prior to the 1954 coup.

While events in Guatemala are difficult to cover at this distance, and only fragments of information are available on events in Siquinala, what evidence there is indicates that the involutionary processes described in this paper have become increasingly intensified and are central to the revolution occurring in that country.

Involution and Revolution

At the beginning of this paper, I made the point of questioning the developmental theories of both traditional economists and "dependistas". Recently, leaders of these two traditions questioned their own theories and moved more closely to each others' perspectives. Raul Prebisch, in his Capitalismo Periferico: Crisis y Transformacion (1981), altered his dependency argument by placing less weight on international economic forces and more weight on indigenous factors inherent in Latin American social structures which prevent economic development. A few years earlier, W. Arthur Lewis, the dean of the diffusionist school, published his The Evolution of the International Economic Order (1978) in which he argued that no matter what investments developed countries make in third world countries, whether private or public, the chances for economic development at the level of "take-off" (Rostow 1962) occurring are remote unless their agricultural systems are given priority in the modernization process. His argument, then, is that food comes first, and by implication, that countries like Guatemala are doomed to economic underdevelopment, not because of the transnational corporations, but because of export oriented plantation agriculture (although transnationals are involved in plantation agriculture at the international level of marketing and distribution).

Both W. Arthur Lewis and Paul Prebisch, then, are finding the roots of Latin American economic underdevelopment in social structure. Here it is possible to move beyond the static description of social class and towards the dynamics of the interrelationship between both social classes and regions. Earlier, Geertz' concept of "involution" was defined in terms of pattern and style. Another way of looking at the same concept is to define it in terms of energy and structure borrowing from Leslie White (1959) and R. N. Adams (1975). According to these two theorists, evolution is a process whereby an evolving organic or cultural system captures increased amounts of energy from its environment while undergoing negative entropy (increased organization). Devolution would be the opposite, a process of energy loss and entropy. Involution can now be redefined without losing its original meaning. Involution can be viewed as a process whereby the upper ranks of an evolving but hierarchically organized system evolves (in the above sense) by drawing increased amounts of energy not only from its environment, but from its own lower ranks enducing entropy in the lower levels of hierarchy. What from a global or national perspective may appear to be a totally evolving system (the G.N.P. as seen from Washington, D.C.) linked in a positive fashion to national and transnational socioeconomic systems, when looked at in terms of social class and region turns out to be an evolving system which is partially feeding on itself, a form of class cannibalism.

In Guatemala, and elsewhere in the Americas, what looks like economic growth and development is the result of the exploitation of regions like Siquinala. While there has been continued hope that Guatemala will someday "evolve" to a point where it will "take off" (Rostow 1962), there is good reason to believe that the current relationship between energy (wealth) and social structure (plantation land tenure) condemns that country to continued economic underdevelopment of the kind it has suffered historically for over a century. As long as a country is dominated by plantation/export agriculture, it will be necessary to keep labor cheap. It is only with cheap labor that such systems make sense, and that is why the central-satellite plantation system makes economic, though not human, sense. But cheap labor requires certain types of national policy by governments in order to insure a cheap labor pool, and that is just another way of saying human rights violations. With such social structures and policies in place, neither democracy nor economic take-off are possible. Instead, it is possible to argue that such combinations of policies and structures lead to involution and disintegration "from the bottom up" as occurred in Cuba, Nicaragua, and presently in El Salvador. While elites attempt to maintain dominance and control, assuming some kind of creeping communistic mennace, the countryside slowly slides into disequilibrium and violence. Violence is directed against elite landowners. Landowners counterattack with right wing hit squads and the military, who are then attacked in return by organized guerrilla units. The guerrilla units are partially made up of disgruntled landless laborers and peasants who have been dispossessed of their lands.

To those familiar with the history of Latin America, revolutions and counter-revolutions are processes as natural as American elections. But attempting to understand the politics of Latin America without examining the organization of land and labor can lead the observer to simplistic ideological explanations such as "subersive communism" or "international imperialism" or "fascism". This paper is an attempt to shed some light on the violence in Central America by studying plantation economics from the ground up in one small municipio on the coast of Guatemala. I do not wish to hint that one can view all of Central America from Siquinala, but Siquinala does help us to understand the linkages between a form of entrepreneurship, plantation social organization, involution, and revolution.

REFERENCES

ADAMS, Richard N. 1975. Energy and Structure. University of Texas Press: Austin.

BARTH, Fredrik. 1972. The Role of the Entrepreneur in Social Change in Northern Norway. Universitetsforlaget: Bergen.

BENNETT, John, W. 1968. Northern Plainsmen. Aldine: Chicago.

_____. 1980. "Natural and social science: historical background." In E. Zube (Ed) Social Sciences, Interdisciplinary Research and the U.S. Man and the Biosphere Program. United States Man and the Biosphere Secretariat, Department of State.

BERGER, Peter. 1974. Pyramids of Sacrifice. Anchor Books: New York.

BODENHEIMER, Suzanne. 1970. Dependency and imperialism. N.A.C.L.A. Newsletter IV: 18-22.

CHILCOTE, Ronald and J. C. Edelstein. 1974. Latin America: the Struggle with Dependency. John Wiley and Sons: New York.

CHIROT, Daniel. 1978. Social Change in the Twentieth Century. Harcort Brace Jovanovich: New York.

COATSWORTH, John. 1974. "Railroads, landholdings, and agrarian protest in the early Porfiorato." Hispanic American Review. V. 54, no. 1: 48-71.

_____. 1979. "Obstacles to economic growth in nineteenth century Mexico." American Historial Review. V. 39: 939-960.

DEAN, Warren. 1969. The Industrialization of Sao Palo, 1880-1945. University of Texas Press: Austin and London.

DIENER, Paul. 1978. "The tears of St. Anthony: ritual and revolution in eastern Guatemala." Latin American Perspective. V. 5: 92-116.

DOS SANTOS, Teodosius. 1970. "The structure of dependence." American Economic Review. V. 60, No. 2: 230-232.

DUNCAN, Kenneth and I. Rutledge. 1977. Land and Labor in Latin America. Cambridge University Press: Cambridge.

FISHLOW, Albert. n.d. "The rise of Brazilian industrialization before the Second World War." Unpublished paper used at N.E.H. Summer Seminar on the economic history of Latin America, University of Chicago, Department of History.

FLETCHER, L., and E. Graber, W. C. Merrill, E. Thorbecke. 1970. Guatemala's Economic Development: The Role of Agriculture. The Iowa State University Press: Ames.

FRANK, Andre G. 1968. Capitalism and Underdevelopment in Latin America. Monthly Review Press.

FURTADO, Celso. 1965. Diagnosis of the Brazilian Crisis. University of California Press: Berkeley.

GEERTZ, Clifford. 1963. Agricultural Involution. University of California Press: Berkeley.

GREENFIELD, Sidney and A. Strickon. 1981. "A new paradigm for the study of entrepreneurship and social change." Economic Development and Cultural Change. V. 29, No. 3: 467-500.

HOLLOWAY, Thomas. 1977. "The coffee colonos of Sao Paulo Brazil: migration and mobility." In Duncan, K. and I. Rutledge (Eds.) Land and Labor in Latin America. Cambridge University Press: Cambridge.

HOSELITZ, B. F. 1952. The Progress of Underdeveloped Areas. University of California Press: Berkeley.

HUNT, Shane. 1973. "Growth and guano in nineteenth century Peru". Discussion Paper No. 34. Princeton.

KNIGHT, Rolf. 1968. "Why don't work the way other men do: the central-colono plantation system of the Cauca Valley." Unpublished Ph.D. thesis, Columbia University.

_____. 1972. "Sugar plantations and labor patterns in the Cauca Valley University of Toronto," Anthropology Series, V. 1952.

LAPPE, Thomas and J. Collins. 1977. Food First: the Myth of Scarcity. Houghton Mifflin: Boston.

LA BEAU, Francis. 1956. "Agricola de Guatemala." In Jorge L. Arriola (Ed.) Ingracion Social en Guatemala. Guatemala: Seminario de Ingrecion Social Guatemalteca, V. 3: 267-312.

LEFF, Nathaniel. 1969. "Long term Brazilian development." Journal of Economic History. V. 29, no. 3: 473-93.

LEVY, Marion. 1972. Modernization and the Structure of Society. Princeton University Press: Princeton.

LEWIS, W. Arthur. 1955. The Theory of Economic Growth. R. D. Irwin: Homewood, Ill.

_____. 1977. The Evolution of the International Economic Order. Princeton University Press: Princeton.

MC GREEVY, William. 1971. The Economic History of Columbia, 1845-1930. Cambridge University Press: Cambridge.

NAIRN, Allan. 1983. The guns of Guatemala. The New Republic, April.

PARSONS, James. 1968. Antioqueno Colonization in Western Colombia. University of California Press: Berkeley.

PETRAS, James. 1973. Latin America: from Dependency to Revolution. John Wiley and Sons: New York.

POLYANI, Karl. 1944. The Great Transformation. Rinehart: New York.

PREBISCH, Raul. 1981. *Capitalismo Periferico: Crisis y Transformacion.* Fondo de Cultura Economica: Mexico City.

ROSTOW, W. W. 1962. *Stages of Economic Growth: A Non-communist Manifesto.* Cambridge University Press: London.

SCHUMPETER, Joseph. 1961. *The Theory of Economic Development.* Oxford University Press: New York.

SMITH, Carol. 1981. "Local response to global processes: social and economic transactions in Western Guatemala." Paper presented for the Plenary Session, Micro-level, Macro-level Articulation in Anthropological Theory and Method. American Anthropological Association meeting, Washington, D. C., Dec.

SMITH, Sheldon. 1982. "Human ecology, socionatural systems, and the central-satellite plantation system of Guatemala and Columbia." *Studies in Comparative International Development,* V. 17, no. 1: 3-21.

SPAULDING, Karen. 1980. "Class structures in the southern Peruvian highlands, 1750-1920." In B. Orlove and G. Custred (Eds.) *Land and Power in Latin America,* pp. 1750-1920. University of California Press: Berkeley.

STONE, Irving. 1977. "British direct and portfolio investment in Latin America before 1914." *Journal of Economic History,* V. 37, No. 3, pp. 690-722.

VERSIANA, Flavio Rabelo. 1979. "Industrial investment in an "export" economy: the Brazilian experience before 1914." Working paper #2, University of London.

WALLERSTEIN, Immanual. 1972. *The Modern World System.* Academic Press: New York.

WHITE, Leslie. 1959. *The Evolution of Culture.* McGraw Hill: New York.

WOLF, Eric. 1968. *Peasant Wars of the 20th Century.* Harper and Row: New York.

V. FAMILY ENTERPRISE AND THE PROCESS OF INDUSTRIALIZATION IN MEXICO

Larissa Lomnitz and Marisol Perez-Lizaur

The Latin American entrepreneur depends to a considerable extent on social resources for economic ends (Long 1977; Aubey 1977, Lipset 1967; Strickon 1965). As Greenfield and Strickon (1979) have pointed out, "social relationships that engender confidence and trust are critical resources in the entrepreneurial venture." In this paper we describe a period of over 100 years in the evolution of a Mexican urban kinship set which we call the "Gomez Family" and which produced a series of prominent entrepreneurs and businessmen. The purpose of this paper is to relate the events of Mexican economic history since about 1850 with the evolution of the Gomez Family in terms of origins of capital, economic decisions, and the fate of family enterprise in Mexico in general. Most particularly, we want to show the importance that social networks have had in the development of the industrial enterprise.

Mexican economic history during the historical period of interest may be divided into three periods, as follows:

(a) <u>1850-1910</u>. This period corresponds to the Reform, the Empire, the Restoration of the Republic and the administration of Porfirio Diaz: a time of deep crisis followed by thirty years of stability and emergence of the modern state.

(b) <u>1925-1960</u>. After the Mexican Revolution, the period of 35 years which followed was a period of national reconstruction and modernization: policies of protectionism of national capitalism, import substitution and "the Mexican Miracle," stimulated by the Second World War.

(c) <u>1960 to the present</u>. In the present stage of Mexican history a marked change has occurred, because of the inability of Mexican business to resist the penetration of technically more advanced foreign and multinational corporations. Local industry looks increasingly to foreign business and the state for guidance and protection. Serious weaknesses appear in the structure of family enterprise.

The early days, 1850 - 1910.

Our data on the Gomez Family includes five generations of descendants from a common ancestor. Carlos Gomez (+1876). At present the family includes five main branches (one upper-class entrepreneurial branch and four middle-class branches), numbering about 360 living members plus their spouses, if any. Practically all live in Mexico City.

Carlos Gomez was a rural criollo of modest means. His first wife, a Spaniard, died after giving birth to her third son. Don Carlos then married his Indian housekeeper, Mama Ines, who raised his three sons and gave him seven more sons and daughters. After the death of Don Carlos, Mama Ines was left nearly destitute. Her three stepsons by then were old enough to fend for themsleves; her eldest son, Leopoldo (1862-1925) age 14, was sent to a relative in the state capital, Puebla, where he became a store attendant.

Leopoldo Gomez eventually moved to Mexico City with the store he helped to buildup into a prosperous commercial venture. The owner, a cousin's husband, died in 1887 and by that time, Leopoldo was in charge of all his business and family interests. By 1906 Leopoldo had brought his mother and siblings to Mexico City. He had become a major entrepreneur. According to the records of business transactions found in notarial archives he owned textile factories, lumber mills, tobacco manufactures, mines, clothing industries and retail stores. He was also a shareholder of banks, finance corporations and insurance firms. In spite of being a mestizo he had been admitted into the exclusive preserves of Mexican high society.

How did Leopoldo Gomez become the first in the line of Gomez entrepreneurs almost overnight? According to Gomez family lore, he was exceptionally shrewd, thrifty and hard working. Even so, the capital he had to invest can hardly have originated from personal savings. His only resource was of a more personal kind: social contacts.

We can only speculate as to what these contacts may have been. It is a fact, however, that Gomez family members were exceptionally devout Catholics even for those days. Leopoldo and his descendants have since been closely identified with the Church: during the religious persecution (1927-1930) they harbored priests and nuns and had services conducted secretly in their homes. The major Gomez entrepreneurs have been prominent benefactors of Church-sponsored causes, such as the shrine of Our Lady of Guadalupe. It is also a well-known fact that the church, once the major landowner and banker in Mexico, developed new strategies after the 1857 Reform Laws had divested it of legal status (Bailey 1974:5-13; Knowlton 1976; Quirk 1973). The Church properties were forcibly sold on the open market; but vast amounts of Church capital remained and eventually seemed to have surfaced in the enterprises of trusted members of the new Mexican bourgeoisie who consented to act as informal partners of the Church. We surmise that Leopoldo Gomez may have derived his capital in this fashion.

At the same time a tight network of kinship relations developed into the management group of the Gomez enterprises. Trust was of the essence. Mama Ines (+1927) became the central symbolic figure who held together the evolving branches of the family network. All major family reunions were held at her home. Leopoldo faithfully visited her every day in the company of his children. He helped establish his brother-in-law, nephews and other relatives in business positions under his direct protection; and he contributed partially or totally toward the economic support of a number of related households. In this fashion, the status of each household and eventually, the economic positions of the present branches of the Gomez family were established at that time.

The Miracle Years: 1925 - 1960

Leopoldo Gomez had two sons and five daughters. At his death (1925) the sons inherited the industrial enterprises, while the daughters received rent-producing properties and shares in other ventures. This policy became traditionally instituted among all subsequent generations.

Control of family capital by the male descent lines of the entrepreneurial branch (i.e. by the descendants of Leopoldo Gomez) meant that the female descendants tended generally to marry non-entrepreneurs; foreigners, or middle-class professional people of good Catholic stock, who could become integrated into the family business, became preferred partners. The male descendants, on the other hand, should ideally marry wealthy heiresses since this involved no dependence of family capital on outside economic interests.

Leopoldo Jr., eldest son of Leopoldo Gomez, inherited the old textile mills and never strayed from the textile industry. He eventually became the family patriarch and his lifelong pre-occupation was family prestige and legitimization in high society. He instituted the Gomez taste for aristocratic country life and the studious identification with Spanish traditions. This seemed all the more desirable as grandmother Ines had been an Indian.

Pablo Gomez (1900-1960), Leopoldo Jr's younger brother, became the most successful of all Gomez entrepreneurs. The administration of Lazaro Cardenas (1934-1940) had been nationalistic with strong socialistic overtones; but his far-reaching reforms opened the way for industrial development (Hansen 1971:49-50; Nafinsa 1971:213-214). With the Second World war and throughout the successive administrations of Avila Camacho (1940-1946), Aleman (1946-1952) and Ruiz Cortinez (1952-1958), there prevailed an atmosphere of cordiality between business, labor and state. Nationalism was synonymous with economic achievement, and social justice with negotiation and the avoidance of direct confrontations. The Mexican political system concurrently developed methods based on co-optation as an alternative to armed repression (Glade and Anderson 1963; Godau and Marquez 1981:49-53; Purcell and Purcell 1977:191-227).

Much of the industrial infrastructure (oil, transporation, irrigation, finance, labor, education and import-substitution policies) had been organized in the preceding decade. Now the war produced not only a captive, growing internal market, but new export opportunities, as well. The Mexican economy began to grow: 6.7% during 1940-1950 and 5.8% through 1970. This was the so-called "Mexican Miracle."

Unlike his older brother, Pablo Gomez was unencumbered by social prejudice. He befriended the new political elite born of the Revolution. His enormous mansion, on the most elegant residential avenue of Mexico City, became the symbol of the new prosperity. Top politicians, cardinals and movie stars congregated at his well-publicized parties; and he was a personal friend of the President of the Republic. Pablo Gomez remained observant of the family traditions, even as he adapted to the new realities of business and politics. Family, nationalism and the War, all provided means and opportunities toward increased gain and power.

Thus Pablo Gomez was an innovator in the entrepreneurial sense. He had an original and ultimately more profitable use of his social resources, this time with the post-revolutionary political elites. He became president of one of the Mexican chambers of industry, as well as of service clubs and major Church charities. He also was the originator of the so-called "Gomez lifestyle"; a large-luxurious home, ownership of prestige cars, conspicuous consumption, foreign travel, colonial art, country estates, and above all, money and power.

The increasingly complex family tree was unified by ritual; an endless round of weddings, christenings, coming-out parties, birthday parties, and funerals, not to mention the weekly dinner parties at the home of one's parents, and the ephemerides of the Catholic calendar. Communications between the branches at different socio-economic levels was efficiently maintained by half a dozen "centralizing women" (cf. Lomnitz and Perez-Lizaur 1978:398) who circulated the gossip and alerted the entrepreneurs to the special needs of less fortunate members of the family. Eventually, Pablo Gomez had 22 members of the Gomez family on his payroll, including his three sons and most of his direct relatives. He created new business ventures for the sole purpose of providing opportunities for relatives. The Gomez business empire thus came to resemble the kinship network in structure. Firms were set up to cater to the needs of other firms: jobbing companies, trucking firms, finance corporations, contractors, law firms, and so on. At his death, Pablo Gomez was a member of the board of directors of public corporations as well as countless other businesses in which he had a controlling interest.

Winds of Change: 1960 to Present.

Pablo Gomez died a national personality. He was mourned publically on the front pages of the daily press. But soon the political climate would change, as investment came to be synonymous with foreign penetration in Mexico.

After 1960 the United States, Europe and Japan had recovered from the effects of the war and had developed new technologies and consumer goods. The impact of synthetic fibers for example, was felt throughout the textile industry. But the Gomez family, like many Latin American entrepreneurs, were disdainful of technology. They saw themselves as plain-spoken men of action who had no use for bookishness; besides, they had worked since adolescence and most of them had barely finished secondary school. Technicians in their enterprises were people who took their instructions from the boss, and who were hired and fired according to needs.

During 1950-1960 the main textile enterprises of Pablo Gomez had been managed by a cousin, Pedro Jimenez, since Pablo's three sons were not yet of age. Pedro became a major entrepreneur in his own right;he not only had close friendships among the political elite and the clergy, but he opened up new avenues of social contacts among the resident Spanish community, including important banking interests.

On Pablo's death, however, Pedro was unable to reach a compromise with Pablo's sons. He withdrew to manage his own financial interests, at a time when consolidation of the Gomez enterprises into a single conglomerate might have improved their capacity to resist the loss of foreign markets and the invasion of high-technology corporations. Eventually Pedro's textile products were outsold by the new synthetics and he had to acknowledge defeat.

After the loss of his major enterprises, Pedro withdrew to his ranch in the country. Slowly he built up a good-producing business, and in a matter of ten years (and with the help of his friends in the financial community) he managed a moderate comeback. By that time, however, multinational corporations were in control, and he reluctantly agreed to a partnership with a large American-based firm in order to remain competitive.

Meanwhile, Pablo's sons had managed to hold on to their father's business interests by diversifying into areas of consumer goods which had been spared by the penetration of the multinationals. These were mostly products which could not be mass-produced for technical reasons (relatively low demand, diveristy of items, etc.).

At present, the strength of the Gomez enterprises is based largely on construction and land development. These fields require excellent contacts with politicians and bankers: the social resources of the Gomez family are proving essential to business once again. Another field which has become lucrative is the small or medium-sized industry supplying semi-manufactured goods or parts for industrial use (e.g. spare pieces of automobiles). These specialized industries thrive on government protection in the form of import restrictions, a result of lobbying activities. Finally, a few fourth-generation Gomez had actually become technocrats for the government in defiance of family ideology, thus opening up new networks among fellow graduate students with connections in the developing class of the educated bureaucracy.

Discussion

Social relations among Mexican entrepreneurs have acquired an economic relevance which is generally unrecognized in the structure on the business communities of the developed world. Three major aspects of the economic utilization of social resources may be singled out: action groups, social networks for the circulation of information, and social networks for facilitating access to economic resources.

(a) Action groups.

The role of small corporate groups centered around an entrepreneur has often been described in the anthropological literature, starting with Barth (1963). In Mexico, these action groups are constituted primarily by relatives.

Initially the Gomez entrepreneurs attended their business personally in all aspects. With growth and diversification they placed cousins and brothers-in-laws in positions of trust. They became brokers between the family enterprise and the national system, without relinquishing absolute control of the enterprise. Potential role conflicts as between brothers or cousins, are avoided by providing or encouraging independent enterprises related to the leading Gomez entrepreneur by patron-client connections. In order for brothers-in-law to be trusted members of the group it is more convenient for the entrepreneur's sisters to marry talented men without money. This trend is not explicit and we cannot tell how it became established among the Gomez; but it persists as a statistical fact.

Hiring a relative is called "helping out". Leopoldo Gomez, the first of the Gomez entrepreneurs, "helped out" -- relatives, and Pablo Gomez is said to have "helped out" -- relatives. Nephews or sons-in-laws holding key managerial positions are expected to step down when the sons of the entrepreneur are old enough to take their place. Instead, they are often provided with a business opportunity as subcontractor, trucking or manager of a retail outlet.

The ideology of the Gomez kin provides support for this system of action groups. Loyalty and cooperation are expected (and expected only) from relatives. The entrepreneur (self-made, independent, powerful) is the ideal of masculinity. Relatives who remain employees in the firm all their lives are esteemed in a pitying sort of way ("the darling man"); but a true man is his own boss.

Looked at in terms of their position in the economy, the Mexican Bourgeoise includes only the owners of the means of production and their business confederates. When looked at as social groups, however, the entire kinship network of each entrepreneur, which represents the pool of their managerial personal and the cluster of small businessmen and liberal professionals who cater to their needs, must be included in the social class. Each kinship network is an intricate weave of patron-client relations. Class, then, would not necessarily be defined as the basis of a shared scale-economic level; the kinship networks of the entrepreneurs embrace the full spectrum from lower middle class to upper class. They represent a ranked system of economic solidarity with the bourgeoisie.

(b) <u>Access to information</u>.

Economically valuable information is circulated primarily among the Gomez kinship network and their allied networks beyond the family boundary. Occasions are provided by innumerable family gatherings (birthdays, christenings, funerals and so on), at which relatives are expected to attend. The prominence of family ritual is supported by an ostentatious lifestyle among the wealthy entrepreneurs; this is justified on grounds of family prestige and solidarity; but it also makes good business sense.

Information is a prime resource in Latin American economies (Aubey, Kyle and Strickon 1974:73-95). The markets are thin and public information is scarce and unreliable. Networks of relatives and friends represent the main source of business intelligence. Family parties and gatherings among the Gomez contrast with similar gatherings in Anglo Saxon countries in that business conversation is quite active, even (to a surprising extent) among the ladies. Hardly an occasion goes by without a new business deal being made. For this reason alone, family affairs are not to be missed. Relatives who stay away from such gatherings for a prolonged period of time are eventually dropped from the unwritten role of the kinship network.

The unit of solidarity among the Gomez (as throughout Mexico) is the three-generational grand-family (Lomnitz and Perez-Lizaur, in press). Each grand-family represents a corporative unit sharing social resources often including information. Dinner parties bring the grand-families together at the home of each set of grandparents, once a week. Participation in rituals is normally by grand-families, plus other branches according to social distance and the occasion being celebrated.

(c) <u>Access to economic resources and power</u>.

An entrepreneur is a businessman who is also an innovator (Schumpeter 1976). Usually the innovations introduced by the entrepreneur consist in introducing new technology, developing new products or opening up new markets; but in the case of Mexican entrepreneurs such as the Gomez, the most remarkable innovative aspect refers to their development and use of social networks for tapping economic resources.(Barth)

Mexico came late to industrialization, under adverse conditions including a scarcity of capital and a feeble market. There was no modern skilled labor force and no local technology which could readily be adapted for industry. Initially, the Gomez proved innovative in tapping hidden financial resources, at a critical historical juncture, for industrial development. We assume that this was possible because of their social relations with the Church hierarchy.

At a later stage, when a new revolutionary elite had consolidated its political and economic power in Mexico, the Gomez succeeded in making valuable contacts at the top of the government hierarchy. Pablo Gomez was the innovator who opened the way for others to follow. At the same time, Pedro Jimenez diversified the banking and business connections of the family through his contacts with the resident Spanish colony, while Leopoldo Gomez Junior (Pablo's eldest brother) continued to nurture the connections with the Church. Finally, the present generation of Gomez entrepreneurs has succeeded in gaining a foothold in the new economy dominated by big banks, multinational corporations and the state.

The use and development of the family network and of other social connections as a resource for capital and power is by no means an exclusive innovation of the Gomez. It is a distinguishing feature of entrepreneurship in Mexico, and probably elsewhere in Latin America, as well (Glade 1979, Greenfield and Strickon 1977, Long 1979, Aubey, Kyle and Strickon 1974).

Conclusion

Social relations represent an essential resource in family enterprise in Mexico. Family enterprise has been a feature of the early stages of industrial development everywhere (Benedict 1968, Barth 1963); but given the nature of the kinship system and unstable conditions of Latin American economies it has been uncommonly persistent. This is because family business provides for diversification as relatives develop business opportunities where they find them: manufacturing, commerce, land development, ranching or services. Delegation of management responsibilities to relatives assures that financial control will remain with the family. The kinship network becomes an extensive managerial pool in which a high level of solidarity is maintained through rituals of conspicuous consumption.

Social networks played a key role in securing the smooth transition of family fortunes over historical crises such as the liberal Reform, the Revolution, and the present contingency where private enterprise sees itself as increasingly isolated and holding out against the invasion of national and foreign corporations and the encroachments of the Mexican state.

Social networks cannot solve all problems however. Family enterprise embodies a basic weakness in that it tends to put loyalty before efficiency in management. Many cases could be cited in the history of Gomez enterprises. Eventually, some of the major Gomez industries proved no match against the superior efficiency of modern corporations using hired professional management.

Social networks can absorb the shocks of a bumpy historical road but they cannot replace technology or mobilize resources on a scale comparable with the large multinational corporations or the state. In other words, family business has limitations of growth, and its paternalistic structure adapts poorly to the corporative organization of modern business. Its share of the more lucrative modern fields (high-technology industries, banking and finance) remains relatively modest.

It appears that social resources are most valuable now as a source of security, rather than as a means of creating new economic wealth. In a completely different social setting, the Mexican shantytown people use their kinship networks as a form of social security; but they cannot use them to replace their lack of participation in the market economy (Lomnitz 1977).

Finally, the economic decisions of family-style entrepreneurs are often guided by symbolic-cultural or ideological beliefs rather than by strictly economic motives. Thus, the Gomez missed an opportunity of consolidating their economic resources after 1960, because of their reluctance to resign their personal power and consign it into the impersonal hands of a modern corporation. If a capacity for postponing power gratifications in exchange for economic security is a common denominator of today's urban elites, the Gomez and their likes may be at a disadvantage in terms of adaptability to corporate designs of living.

REFERENCES

AUBEY, Robert T. 1979. "Capital mobilization and patterns of business ownership and control in Latin America: the case of Mexico". In *Entrepreneurs in cultural context*, Greenfield S., A. Strickon and R. Aubey eds., Albuquerque: University of New Mexico Press. Pp. 225-242.

_____, Kyle and A. Strickon. 1974. "Investment behavior and elite social structures in Latin America". *Journal of Interamerican Studies and World Affairs*, 16(1):73-95.

BAILEY, David. 1974. *Viva Cristo Rey! The Cristero rebellion and the Church-State conflict in Mexico*. Univ. of Texas Press.

BARTH, Frederick. 1963. *The role of the entrepreneur in social change in nothern Norway*. Oslo, Beergen, Tromso: Scandinavian University Books.

GLADE, W. P. Jr., and Ch. W. Anderson. 1963. *The political economy of Mexico*. The University of Wisconsin Press.

_____. 1979. "Entrepreneurship in the state sector: CONASUPO of Mexico". In *Entrepreneurs in cultural context*, Greenfield S., A. Strickon and R. Aubey eds., op. cit.:191-222.

GODAU, Rainer and Viviane B. de Marquez. 1981. "Burocracia publica y empresa privada: el caso de la industrializacion mexicana". El Colegio de Mexico. Mimeographed.

GREENFIELD, S. M. and A. Strickon. 1979. "Entrepreneurship and social change: toward a populational, decision-making approach." In *Entrepreneurs in cultural context*, Greenfield S., R. Strickon and R. Aubey, eds., op. cit.:329-350.

HANSEN, Roger D. 1972. *The politics of Mexican development*. Baltimore: The Johns Hopkins University Press.

KNOWLTON, Robert J. 1976. *Church property and the Mexican Reform 1856-1910*. De Kalb: Northern Illinois Press.

LIPSET, Seymour. 1967.

LOMNITZ, Larissa. 1977. Networks and marginality: life in a Mexican shanty town. San Francisco/New York: Academic Press.

---------- and M. Perez-Lizaur. 1978. "The history of a Mexican urban family." Journal of Family History, 3(4) Winter:392-409.

----------. 1982. Family and enterprise: the history of a Mexican elite kinship group.

NAFINSA. 1971. "Comision Economica para America Latina." La politica industrial en el desarrollo economico de Mexico. Mexico.

PURCELL, J. F. H. and S. K. Purcell. 1977. "Mexican business and public policy." In Authoritarianism and corporatism in Latin America. J. Malloy ed. University of Pittsburgh Press: 191-227.

QUIRK, Robert E. 1973. The Mexican Revolution and the Catholic Church 1910-1929. Bloomington and London: Indiana Univ. Press.

SCHUMPETER, Joseph. 1976. Teoria del desenvolvimiento economico. Mexico F.C.E. (1st pub. in German 1912).

STRICKON, A. 1965. "Class and kinship in Argentina." In Contemporary cultures and societies of Latin America. Heath and Adams eds. New York: Randon House. Pp. 324-341.

LONG, Norman. 1977. "Commerce and kinship in the Peruvian highlands." In Andean kinship and marriage. R. Bolton & E.Mayer eds. Washington: American Anthropological Association (7):153-176.

----------. 1979. "Multiple enterprise in the central highlands of Peru." In Entrepreneurs in cultural context. Greenfield, Strickon and Aubey, eds., op. cit.:123-158.

VI. THE IMPRESSARIO AS ENTREPRENEUR

Erwin H. Johnson

My Oxford English Dictionary indicates an etymological likelihood that the "impres" of "impressario" and the "enterprise" of "enterpriser" and thus, entrepreneur (had it been an Oxford French Dictionary) are cognates. This is fitting because nothing characterizes the activity of the opera company general manager (whatever his or her specific title in a given company) so much as the assembly of the disparate components of an enterprise - an opera production - and the fiscal wherewithal for their employment, generally in unique combination, several times each season.

This paper is the first product of an attempt to do an ethnographic study of professional opera, a broadly spread out social system, which, while lacking a central coordinating agency, has persisted over the centuries and throughout much of the world. In North America it is a system which services a constituency in most of the large and medium sized cities, but one in which the majority of those providing the service are not of those cities. In short, it is a system which would, were it not for its visibility and saliency, defy an ethnographic approach. It does persist, however, and it is indeed structured. It is a viable ethnographic unit, and studying it has not only been a methodological revelation, it has been fun as well.[1]

In this paper, I focus on an important status position within that system. The general manager, or "impressario" is a pivotal position without whom the system might not work at all, and without whom an ethnography of the national system would be almost impossible. Putting the position of the general manager into perspective in the system of "professional" opera has allowed me to draw on some ideas important to ethnography, but previously applied by anthropologists mainly to small and encapsulated populations, either village communities, or ghettoized populations in the urban milieu.[2] Important among them are Barth's ideas of inclusion and exclusion as he applies them to "ethnic" groups (Barth 1969) and the ideas on reciprocity, summarized by Sahlens (1965). I hope to show that an ethnographic approach is not only possible, but fruitful, even when employed well beyond the "atoll" community of classical ethnography.

For the purpose of our presentation, professional opera will be viewed as consisting of two levels of interfacing social systems. The first is national and, for some purposes, international in scope, and is comprised of those full-time and almost full-time performing and production personnel who make their service available on the market. This is a relatively small professional group, numbering in the thousands for North America, but not in the tens of thousands. To a surprising degree they are known to each other, aware of each other's skills and weak points, and secure in the knowledge that they are professionals in opera.

The second level consists of the opera companies themselves, and the community infra-structure supporting them. There are well over one hundred professional companies with budgets over $100,000 a year in the United States and Canada, and over a thousand production units of all sorts. The 133 companies designated as "major" by Opera News gave just over 3500 performances during the 1981-1982 season and had budgets totalling $191 million (Rich 1982, 20). Despite national economic problems, these figures are all up slightly from the 1980-81 season (see Rich 1981).

The national and local levels come into direct contact through the production of opera in any particular city. The national level provides the professional expertise and personnel for the production, and the local level provides technical support, administrative backup, the audience, the theater, and the funding. The individual who stands at the interface between the two systems is the company general manager, the impressario. He or she is at the same time the professional who represents local interests and the local person who deals with the professionals. In both systems, this position is defined substantially in terms of this interface function, and therein lies the unique and strategic character of the impressario.[3]

THE NATIONAL LEVEL

The national level of professionals in opera is quite complex in its structure, and is the proper subject of a separate analysis. However, a brief discussion of its major elements will provide the background for the general manager's participation in the system.

The system can be bounded at several points. For the purposes of this discussion, it can be limited to those persons involved in production, and those who secure employment for them - their agents, publicists, etc. - although it could be expanded to include also those persons who help train the performers - conservatory personnel, teachers, coaches, etc. The latter frequently are also performers, or were before their retirement. They often help significantly in securing employment, especially for young production personnel.

New York is the single most important city in North America, within which the dynamics of the system are played out. While there are other regional foci, most serious aspirants to the world of professional opera move to New York in order to "break in". Almost all artists' representatives (agents) maintain their offices there. Large numbers of regional operas also are cast in the city. The largest New York based company, The Metropolitan Opera, casts from an international pool of artists. New York City Opera, however, holds auditions in the city as do a number of much smaller companies. These do not, however, equal in number or in scale the regional companies that draw on the pool of performers in the city.

Each regional company may have from one to six or seven performances of each production, with most having two or three. Rehearsals run from one to three weeks, with two weeks being both the median and the mode. Thus, including performances, a regional engagement may be from two to five or six weeks. To be moderately successful as a professional, a singer should probably be in six productions a year.

There is no central casting office or uniformly used clearing house for casting. The Central Opera Service, an organization supported by the Metropolitan Opera National Committee does provide an employment information service to members and publishes a quarterly Bulletin, plus a number of informational volumes. Among these is an up-to-date listing of regional opera companies with the names of their general managers (Central Opera Service 1978). The Central Opera Service, however, is not an employment agency.

Opera America, an organization of major professional opera companies, serves as an umbrella under which professional general managers may regularly communicate. Not only does it have annual meetings, but also ongoing standing committees that serve effectively to put managers in regular face to face contact with each other. Opera America also makes available to its membership important information, drawn from its own surveys, on the condition of professional opera in the United States and Canada.

Unlike other professions there is no self-regulating professional association in opera that sets minimum standards for entry into the field. Formal degrees and credentials are not required. All aspiring performers who are admitted to an audition need is a resume listing roles sung, companies worked for, prizes won, and an abstract of favorable reviews.

There are numerous vocal competitions at the regional and national level which carry both prize money and prestige. Prize money from regional competition is often used to send a singer to New York, while that from New York competitions is used to support the singer while there. Occasionally, a competition will carry with it as a prize the opportunity to perform with a particular company. Most parts, however, are gained through auditions.

A number of small, marginally funded "showcase" companies are to be found in the New York Metropolitan Area. Singers are not only willing to perform in these productions for a minimum fee, or no fee at all, but, in some cases, will contribute to production costs for the opportunity to sing. These companies often do rarely performed operas, thereby increasing the chance that they will be reviewed by the New York daily newspapers, especially The New York Times, and occasionally by national magazines.

Success in the field of opera is almost always the major goal of professionally trained singers. The selection process at each stage in a singer's career, from finding the first voice teacher through auditioning for a lead role with a professional company carries with it the constant potential for rejection. The training and recruitment system is such that it produces many times the number of qualified aspirants needed to fill available positions. Thus, there are many more qualified persons for the available roles in regional companies than there are opportunities. This has set the stage for a basic perception within the field that success results from some mix of talent and luck.

There is, of course, a star system, and a complex and informal system by which both performers and companies are ranked. In general, performance fees reflect the position of a particular house, but it is possible for a company to trade on its name, attracting performers for less than they might make in a comparable house. On the whole, though, the prestige level of both performer and house may be seen as reflected in the market. The market, then, would be seen as comprising the thousands of contract negotiations that occur in the course of casting the hundreds of productions which take place annually.[4] The fees and salaries from these productions are the main source of income for the professional system. They are paid to the performers, who in turn must pay a part of what they receive to agents, teachers, coaches, publicists, etc. Except for these payments for personal services, little money is exchanged within the national system.

What holds the national system together is a complex set of relationships organized around the flow of information and the exchange of favors.

New York City is the principal focus of these activities, but they also occur to a degree wherever professional opera is produced. The agents have their offices in New York, but they travel around the country, hearing singers, conferring with general managers, and "catching" their clients' performances. Artists expand their contracts with other "opera persons" by working with them in productions throughout the country. The skills and deficiencies of each performer are quickly noted by their co-workers in every production, and this information becomes a part of the inside evaluation system. It is a far-flung system, and New York is the symbolic center although not the only place where the action is.

THE LOCAL LEVEL

While it can be argued that the professional level of opera, complex and specialized as it may be, can be conceptualized as a single nation-wide system, it seems important to view the producing companies (excluding a very few specialized ones) as local phenomena, tied directly to local and/or regional social systems. In this paper, we will be dealing only with the category of companies referred to in the profession as "regional companies." This does not include the Metropolitan Opera, which is an "international house," and which receives support from a nationwide network of sponsors. Regional companies, as a minimum, employ professional orchestras, professional directors and conductors, and draw a significant portion of their lead singers from the national system. They are also characterized by professional management. As a category, they are contrasted to community companies where the production relies mainly on locally based talent, rather than professionals from the national system. There are other types of production units, the most numerous of which are university and college based opera theaters and workshops that will not be discussed here.

With few exceptions, regional companies have larger budgets than community companies. Regional company budgets range from a low of not much more than $100,000 to in excess of ten million dollars per year.

SUPPORT

Regardless of company-to-company variation in internal structuring, all companies share common problems. The company must be maintained as a fiscal and administrative entity from year to year, and it must produce and perform opera. The charter documents of all companies examined, where the company is an independent organization, assign the fiscal maintainance function to the board of directors and the production function to the general manager. The general manager proposes the budget and the board approves it. The general manager proposes a schedule, and the board must approve it. Solvency depends on how influential the board can be in attracting money from the local community, as well as to what extent they are willing to collectively underwrite the season.

While it is not always true that board members are opera lovers, continued participation on an active board requires that some benefits devolve on the members. Board participation may result from an interest in validating social position, in extending business contracts, and/or in a feeling of participation in a glamorous segment of the national scene. In short, participation on an opera board as on any civic board, may be looked upon as part of an overall local career strategy.

In addition to the board, most companies have other support groups, most commonly opera guilds. These are membership organizations devoted to the support of the opera, both through dues, and through a variety of fund raising events. Bake sales and auctions are more or less straight fund raisers. Receptions for visiting stars and annual opera balls combine fund raising with status validation. A frequent product of these events, aside from the funds raised, will be a photograph of a visiting celebrity, the general manager, the chairman of the board, and several prominent company patrons on the society page of the local newspaper(s).

ADMINISTRATION

In the table of organization of regional companies, a distinction is customarily made between production staff and administrative staff. Administrative functions include the maintenance of the company itself as an economic entity capable of producing an opera. The production functions include the actual production and performance of the operas. Specific personnel may not be as easily separated as the functions - a managing director might also be a tenor, but tenors cannot categorically be expected to manage. Some persons move from one category to the other. Still, the functional distinction between production and administration is made in every professional company we have encountered.

Only a few regional companies may maintain the nucleus of a production support staff year-round. The nucleus of the administrative staff, however, is almost always employed on an annual basis. This nucleus may, however, be quite small, and except for a few large companies, will be no more than five to ten employees. The junior administrative staff is frequently a local one with no previous experience in opera. In many regional companies, certain administrative functions are handled by local professionals on a part-time or contract basis, e.g. accounting, bulk mailing, etc. The administrative parts of companies may vary in scale and in internal efficiency but are, nonetheless, quite similar to each other in structure. Effective managment requires an effective working boss for the administrative staff.

PRODUCTION

Since few regional companies have production activities on a regular basis throughout the year, production staffs are likely to be assembled for each production. While nothing prevents the same persons from being employed for all the productions of a given season, they would still not be year round employees. Most companies have developed a cadre of reliable technical persons, generally from the nearby area, who can be contracted for each of the productions. Among the most important of these are a technical director, a stage manager, and a coach accompanist. Nearby universities with theater and opera staffs are a common reservoir for such persons. Some companies find it necessary, and others desirable to bring people in from the outside to perform any or all of these particular functions, and there are a number of full-time professionals available on the job market for these tasks. Other technical tasks are almost always handled by local residents who frequently are volunteers. Lighting and projections may be done by a local professional, although increasingly, they are done by full-time professionals who work throughout the country. Lighting design is included as part of the operatic conception, with the lighting person (now thought of more as a designer than a technician) sharing credit with the set and costume designers.

Companies almost always have a single chorus mistress or master employed from production to production, but who is rarely a full-time employee of the company. He or she is generally a specialist on choral music with experience in opera. It is his or her task to recruit a chorus, train it in the repertoire, and prepare it to the point at which the conductor can take over in rehearsal. Once established, the chorus remains an ongoing part of the company, although it is only activated in time to rehearse each opera which calls for a chorus. The chorus is recruited locally. Its members are part-time employees who earn their livelihood in other ways.

Serious production problems may develop if any of the specialized tasks are mishandled. The local company must be able to assure that all the behind-the-scenes activities are performed by capable persons. The orchestra is usually the professional organization of the community, arranged for through negotiations with its own management. Here, scheduling, and the acquisition of the musical scores present the greatest difficulties. If, as is the case in a few companies, the opera has its own orchestra, the task of assembling and maintaining it is an added burden to the management. Routinely, however, the orchestra is the one area of local production which does not require day to day involvement of management.

There are a number of elements in an opera production and performance which are considered "artistic" and are treated as such. They include both the conception of the work, and the realization of that concept in performance. While the overall quality of production, that for which the entire production staff is responsible, is considered important, high production standards are more and more taken for granted in regional presentations, and the artistic matters are focused on in evaluation. The important persons involved in these interpretive areas are the designers; set, costume and lighting and projection, the director, the conductor, and the principal singers. It is precisely this personnel who are brought to town in unique combination for each new production.

It is the conductor, the director, and the lead singers whose work is largely responsible for whether or not a particular production of a well organized regional company is a success or not. It is also these persons who will be full time professionals drawn from the national pool of available professionals, and specifically contracted for a particular opera for a particular company at a particular time. It is also these persons, along with the stage manager and the accompanist, who will spend intense periods rehearsing the production. While hundreds of persons must be coordinated for the total production, it is these half dozen or so artists, in rehearsal, who develop, in the two or three weeks prior to the performance, the timing, the momentum, and the elan which may make or break the production.

Thus, the very important rehearsal of the principals brings a number of artists, most or all from out of town, together in a hall which may not even be in the theater, to prepare for the performance of a regional opera company. During this crucial period of intense interaction, there need be hardly any contact with local elements of the opera production. One singer reported to me that he had to return to New York from a southwestern city where he had sung an oratorio with the regional city's symphony, to rehearse there in New York for an opera to be presented by the city's opera company. It was decided that since all of the principals, the conductor, and the director were from the New York area, that the rehearsals up to the point where the chorus and principals rehearse together, might just as well take place in a New York hall. This is not an isolated case. In fact, the nature of opera production is such that the preparation and performance of a given opera provides little opportunity and less need for close interaction between local production persons and the outside artists. The two systems remain quite discrete.

THE IMPRESSARIO

The roster of legendary impressarios is almost as long as the comparable lists of divas or tenors, and probably longer than that of legendary opera conductors. Yet they rarely appear on stage, are not subject to performance reviews, and what they do is largely not understood by the audience. They are the proto-typical "wheeler dealers," dynamic actors in a system where fast pace, theatrical spectacle and flamboyant behavior is commonplace.

We have outlined a number of major units in "the world of opera"; the national pool of professionals with its own intricate structure, the local administrative structures, and their support and governing bodies, the community base of the company. These units come into contact with each other almost exclusively in the process of operatic production, and then, almost exclusively through the activities of the general manager, the only person who by status designation is in contact with all.

In any city, a few patrons, often board members, may have established opera contacts outside the city, often through Metropolitan Opera activities. Only if the person is a retired opera professional, however, will these ties reach deeply into the professional network. Quite the reverse is true for the general manager, who is always extending his or her contacts.

As a manager at the local level, the impressario must be able to mediate the inevitable conflicts that occur between the administrative and production segments of the organization. He or she also must be able to work with a board of directors which, unlike boards in many other "not for profit" organizations, is a major source of locally derived revenue. Regional opera companies are "not for profit" organizations. A favorite statistic for comparing companies is the percentage of their annual operating budget realized through earned revenue. The difference between earned revenue and the operating budget is the amount of money which must be obtained through fund raising efforts, contributions, and private and public grants and donations. The task of assuming that the budget can be met rests with a board of directors, while that of preparing the schedule and determining the budget to implement it is that of the general manager. In practice, however, although this division of labor is recognized, the impressario also is expected to assist in fund raising activities, and many boards of directors take an active role in establishing the schedule. Where tensions exist between board and professional management, it is usually around the question of managerial autonomy in scheduling and casting. When companies have failed and then disappeared, the most immediate cause can usually be traced to a failure of these two components of the local level to work in support of each other (Rich, ed. 1981).

Since matters of artistic integrity and budget are played out before the board, the general manager should be able to function comfortably with the members. He must be comfortable interacting with persons of the local elite, but since, in a sense, he is their employee, he will never be a part of this elite.

In his or her capacity as representative of the local company and its interests to the national level of opera, the impressario has a task that distinguishes him or her from the managers of other public enterprises. The number of contracts which must be negotiated annually as a consequence of the frequency of new productions, if nothing else, accentuates this interface function of standing between the national and local systems. The fact that he or she is employer or employer's agent of a local company, rather than fellow employee, inevitably separates him or her from the national system out of which he or she may have come. The only real peers he or she has are other impressarios, and they are either in other cities, or in other art forms.

The adequate fulfillment of the functions outlined above will generally result in a successful company and successful entrepreneurship. A distinguished or outstanding career requires something more. One of the most important tasks a general manager has is to establish the character of his or her company, and to project this character, both to the people in the region, and to opera followers elsewhere in the country. Most boards, by their very nature as influential citizens concerned with opera, prefer that popular and proven operas be produced. Traviata, Boheme, and Carmen almost always sell well. Gilbert and Sullivan, The Merry Widow, and Die Fledermaus are also useful in balancing a budget. Furthermore, sets and costumes for this standard fare are usually available for rental, and there are a number of singers available who know the roles well. There is, however, little chance that such a production, no matter how well received locally, will be noted outside the region.

A company can gain rapid national visibility by experimental programming, thus leading to enhanced prestige for its general manager within the national system. It may, however, go broke in the process. The successful impressario is so, partly because she or he is able to balance the needs of the particular community for familiar productions, and his or her own perception of what is good for opera (and for his or her own career). Unusual repertory can be made to work for a city as well as for the connoisseurs and the impressario. If the board, the guild and other support groups, the local press, and local business leaders can be convinced that something out of the ordinary will be exciting to produce and will be beneficial to local interests, a producer can, in fact, satisfy both reference groups for different reasons. A U.S. premiere, or even better, a world premiere by a well-known opera composer is one route to take. Two Thea Musgrave premiers have put the Virginia Opera Association in the national spotlight.

An important revival, ideally with a select cast, is another way to gain recognition. Dallas Opera revived an important Handel work and combined it with a symposium on Handel, with invited scholars from around the world. Handel may not have appealed to Dallas' taste makers, but the coverage of the opera by Time, Newsweek, The New Yorker, and the New York Times certainly appealed. The Opera Theater of Saint Louis has established a strong reputation in but six years time. Important premieres and revivals have been the major vehicles, along with high quality productions with very good young casts. The company performs in a small theater and this almost guarantees close to capacity houses. It is heavily supported by wealthy citizens and locally based industry. It has one of the lowest ratios of earned income to operating budgets of any company in the country, 24%, and this would not have changed more than a point had the programming been nothing but popular opera. Its operating budget is approximately the same as the company in Kansas City and its attendance, although close to capacity, is less than half that of the other company. Its position in the national limelight is much more prominent. Both Missouri companies must be judged as successful, however. What works in St. Louis would probably never succeed in Kansas City.

A number of companies concentrate on major productions of standard repertory. Milwaukee's major company concentrates its efforts on two performances each, of three standard operas each year. The singers, while rarely international stars, are nonetheless, first rank American singers. Miami follows essentially the same format, although it has a longer season and invests proportionately more in its lead singers. The company in Miami features its tie-in with the local elite in a flamboyant fashion that the companies in Rochester, Cleveland, or Syracuse would probably dare not do.

Second companies in New York, Chicago, Boston and Philadelphia attempt to compliment the larger and well established houses, thus allowing them to develop a special image and tap resources not already co-opted by the larger houses.

There are many ways in which the visibility and support for opera may be expanded in a given community. The successful general manager must be familiar with these and capable of initiating those which show local promise. Many companies have, for example, succeeded in developing activities without casting them in major roles. This not only defuses attempts at competition for a loyal and committed following by a 'community' company, but also generates support from what is frequently a well organized musical segment of the city, one which might otherwise resent the presence of outside professionals in the city. One way of gaining support is through open auditions for local casting of supporting roles. Others include the development of local ensembles to perform for various audiences: the "shopping mall performances" prior to the major production. In these performances, the highlights of the coming production are performed as part of an effort to increase ticket sales, and to develop good will for the company.

Impressarios are managers, and they are initiators. Their contribution is their ability to bridge the national and local systems, and to successfully move resources from one to the other. Because of this unique role, if for no other reason, an impressario cannot remain a permanent part of either of the systems. This brokerage function which keeps the impressario marginal to both, however, is attractive, since the dynamics of opera production are glamorous, often spectacular, and very much in the public eye. Nonetheless, it seems likely that if we examine the condition of any successful entrepreneur, we will find a "marginal man," strategic to social systems which do not, and probably cannot completely accept him.

SUMMARY

Recognition that production personnel comprise a nationwide network of professionals and that there are a number of local systems, each held together by reciprocity and mutual advantages, puts the unique role of general manager, the impressario, into an understandable perspective. Money changes hands in important ways between these two systems, and the general manager is the conduit. It is he or she who understands enough of each system to effectively carry on negotiations. The general manager has a foot in each system and stands at the interface between them.

Each system functions with a dominant mode of interaction based on reciprocity. Anything other than that would and occasionally does lead to charges of impropriety, the "buying" of favors etc. With the contract between the company and the artist the only legitimate channel for "converting" the resources of one of these systems into one usable in the other, it follows that power rests with the general manager. This power to convert resources from one realm into those usable in another would diagram in the same way as Bohannon's example of "conversion" in his contrast between conversion and conveyance (1963:251ff). Each of these systems or levels can be thought of as a cultural sub-system, if not a sub-cultural system, and the anthropological literature on cultural brokerage and system gate-keepers, as well as that of "marginal man," would appear to be relevant.

In classical economic theory, the entrepreneur is the person who successfully assembles the parts, mainly capital and labor, for an economic enterprise. She or he is the antithesis of a bureaucrat in that she or he is self-starting and almost by definition inventive in the way in which she or he combines elements. We believe that by seeing this position, as exemplified in opera, as one which bridges two systems, moving resources between the two and converting information from one to useful information in the other, light is shed on the nature of this position.

Almost as though to validate that we had in fact discovered eternal verities in using the impressario to examine entrepreneurship, we found after this paper was fully drafted, that the Oxford English Dictionary referred to above had as its first definition (1935 ed.) for entrepreneur, "a manager of a public entertainment."

NOTES

(1) A number of persons in the opera world were kind enough to comment on an earlier draft of this paper, and must be acknowledged. While their remarks were extremely helpful in setting me straight on several matters, they are not responsible for any failings in this paper.

I wish to thank Mrs. Margo Binhardt, and especially Ms. Margaret Genovese of the Canadian Opera Company for their helpful comments. Ms. Genovese was an anthropology major at Brown University before entering opera administration and understood the paper from both professional sides. Ms. Maria Rich of Central Opera Service offered many helpful criticisms, most of which have been incorporated into the final version. I would also like to acknowledge the help of Ms. Jean Kemp of the COS. Among the "impressarios" who have been especially helpful and who deserve my public thanks are: Mr. Steven Thomas of Opera Hamilton, Ms. Ruth Rosenberg of the Opera Theater of Rochester, Mr. Robert Driver of the Opera Theater of Syracuse, Mr. David Midland, formerly of Artpark, Mr. Jean-Paul Jeannotte of L'Opera de Montreal, Mr. Peyton Hibbett of Tri-City Opera, Binghamton, N.Y. and Mr. Leonard Treash, now retired, the longtime director at Chautauqua.

Others in opera administration who have been very helpful include Ms. Ruth Slater of Opera Hamilton, Ms. Denise Monpetit of Festival Ottawa, Professor Edward Rhodes of the University of Waterloo and the Kitchener Oktoberfest, and Ms. Edwina Carson of the Guelph Spring Festival. Insight into the Canadian opera scene was gained from Ms. Ruby Mercer, editor of Opera Canada, and on the American scene from Mr. Melvin Novick, a performer with the New York City Opera. Both are also gratefully acknowledged.

Singers, directors, conductors and other artists too numerous to acknowledge individually contributed to my understanding of the system. Many of these will be acknowledged in other publications.

Thanks are also extended to Raoul Naroll, Frederick Gearing, and the late Richard Patch of my department for their helpful comments. They, too, are absolved from any blame.

(2) I am not suggesting that the role of reciprocity in American society is unrecognized. It is all too clear, for example, in Sahlins' choice of words to characterize various forms of reciprocity, e.g. "sharing," "help," "generosity," and a number of "dues," which makes one think, when dealing with a theatrical group of "paying one's dues," that the behaviors are not alien to Western thinking.

(3) There is no shortage of biographical and autobiographical material available on prominent participants in the "world of opera" and such material is as well represented for general managers as for any other group within the field. Biographies of three successive general managers at the Metropolitan Opera, Johnson (Mercer 1976), Bing (1972), and Chapin (1977), as well as that of a longtime intendant at London's Covent Garden, Webster (Haltrecht 1975), all clearly illustrate the general remoteness felt by them both from their respective boards (Chapin was of course dismissed by his), and from their artists, except where close friendships had been established earlier in their careers. Mansouri (Mansouri and Layton 1981) is still directing the Canadian Opera Company, and Sills (1976) the New York City Opera, and their biographies reflect no such problems, but are not, I am sure, their final words on the subject.

(4) In the three years or so since this research began, in addition to the interviews and rehearsal observations, I attended performances of 86 operas given by 18 different companies. I have recorded over 1300 cast credits from these performances. That is, 1300 listings important enough to have been in the program. They consist of records on 685 separate individuals, with some, of course, appearing or working in more than one of the productions I saw. These do not include chorus members, members of the orchestra, nor most of the persons who work backstage. I attended all six of the Canadian Opera Company's 1982 productions. For these I have 118 separate cast, conducting, directing, design, and stage

management assignments to 80 separate individuals, again, not including chorus, orchestra members, nor the technical or stage crew. While many of the contracts involved would entail little more than offering union minimums, many involved intricate negotiations. All entail careful calculations on the appropriateness of an artist to a particular role or function. Casting at the Canadian Opera Company ranges from young singers who are members of that company's "ensemble" group, used as much for training as for other purposes, to such reigning stars as Joan Sutherland, Martina Arroyo, Elizabeth Soederstrom, Tatiana Troyanos, and Louis Quilico.

BIBLIOGRAPHY

BANTON, M. ed. 1966. "The Social Anthropology of Complex Societies." London: Tavistock Publications. A.S.A. Monographs, 3.

BARTH, Frederik ed. 1969. Ethnic Groups and Boundaries. Oslo: Scandinavian University Books. Universitetsforlaget.

BING, Sir Rudolph. 1972. 5000 Nights at the Opera. Garden City. Doubleday Company, Inc.

CHAPIN, Schuyler. 1977. Musical Chairs: A Life in the Arts. New York. G. P. Putnam's Sons.

HALTRECHT, Montague. 1975. The Quiet Showman: Sir David Webster and the Royal Opera House. London: Collins.

MANSOURI, Lotfi with Aviva Layton. 1982. Lofti Mansouri: An Operatic Life. Oakville Toronto Ontario: Mosaic Press/Stoddart Publishing.

MERCER, Ruby. 1976. The Tenor of His Times: Edward Johnson of the Met. Toronto: Clarke, Irwin Company Limited.

RICH, Maria F. 1981. Expanding Horizons: U.S. Opera Survey, 1980-81. Opera News. 46,5 16-25. November, 1982.

_____. 1982. "Holding Pattern: U.S. Opera Survey, 1981-82." Opera News. 47,5 20-25. November, 1982.

_____. ed. 1981. "Gateway to Opera: The Regional Companies. A Guide for Opera Administrators, Boards of Directors, Trustees and Volunteers." Transcript of the COS National Conference., St. Louis, June 1981. COS Bull. 23, 2.

SAHLINS, Marshall D. 1965. "On the Sociology of Primitive Exchange." In Banton ed. The Relevance of Models...pp. 139-236.

SILLS, Beverly. 1976. Bubbles: A Self Portrait. Indianapolis/New York: Bobs-Merrill.

157

VII. ENTREPRENEURS IN PUBLIC ENTERPRISES

Alfred H. Saulniers

INTRODUCTION

I would like to skip the customary remarks about the papers actually presented at this panel. It appears more useful to assume that everyone in the audience has paid careful attention, that the presenters are at least semi-satisfied with their work, and that we can all turn our attention to the future. It is apparent from the titles, at least, of those that will be presented tomorrow, that much of the current scholarly thinking equates the locus of entrepreneurship with the private sector. While this may have strong intellectual roots in the literature, it ignores what appears to be one of the strongest trends of the post-war period - the creation of a substantial number of public enterpries in all countries of the world. The most striking example, so common as to pass unnoticed is that in the U.S. we've seen virtually the entire sector of municipal transport pass from private to public hands in a relatively short time without any major furor over nationalization. However, transportation is not the only sector in which public enterprises dominate. At present it has been estimated that the U.S. has more then 5000 statutory public corporations (Walsh, 1978:354)

The situation is even more striking in developing countries. There, almost invariably, the largest corporations are public. The major concern for those of us interested in entrepreneurship is that one of the most important reasons advanced for creating such firms in a developing nation is entrepreneurship's domestic absence. Public enterprises are seen as remedying the problems caused by the weakness of domestic capital markets, risk aversion by private investors, lack of experience and/or motivation by private businessmen, and such "extraneous" objectives of the private sector as the maintenance of family control and wealth protection. Government action through public enterprises is envisioned as a means of injecting capital resources, incorporating a greater ability to take risks, providing more technical expertise, and deleting "extraneous" variables from the social objective function.

Having set the framework for discussion, my remarks center on three areas. First, I sketch out the context for future development of a corpus of studies on public enterprise entrepreneurs, confining my remarks to the Latin American context with which I am most familiar. Second, I examine characteristics of public enterprises which make it difficult to study entrepreneurship within a more public environment. Third, I present special areas of study which may form the basis for future research.

THE CONTEXT

At present, more than 6000 public enterprises exist in Latin America according to the archives of the Office for Public Sector Studies of the University of Texas. Contrary to the popular wisdom, such firms are profitable. Using the data provided in the Fortune 500 survey of the largest industrial companies outside the United States for 1979, the ratio of net income to assets for multinationals in Latin America was 1.0 percent, for private national firms in Latin America it was 5.1 percent, and for public enterprises, it was 11.6 percent. While there was problems associated with the low number of firms and the weight of petroleum producers, the point nonetheless stands that popular wisdom needs to be adjusted to the new realities of public enterprises.

A further issue is that public enterprises generally figure among the top firms in each country. In Argentina in 1977, 17 of the top 100 firms were public, while the comparable figures for Brazil and Chile were 24 and 25 respectively. As a rule, such firms have more sales, net income, assets and employment than their numbers would indicate.

However, not all public firms are the giants in each country. They range in size from the largest companies to small authorities employing only one or two individuals, and they range in scope of activities from abattoirs to zinc mines.

The main question is whether entrepreneurs can exist in such firms. If we consider a few of the commonly accepted characteristics of such individuals as having a will to power, being a creative problem solver, and showing a willingness to take risks, then all can be found in public enterprises. Further, if we examine Kilby's thirteen possible entrepreneurial tasks in an underdeveloped economy, they all mark public as well as private enterprises (Kilby, 1971:27-28). This even holds for the company executive's needs to deal with the public bureaucracy, as mentioned below.

Given such an incredibly rich contextual basis for examining entrepreneurship in the public enterprises, and given my assertions that the people are out there waiting to be studied, why has this field been neglected? The next section hazards some rather tentative thoughts on the matter.

PROBLEMS IN STUDYING PUBLIC FIRM ENTREPRENEURS

The first major obstacle to studying entrepreneurship in public enterprises is a crucial one, that of image. Public firms have the image of being inefficient, ineffective and corrupt. With such a view prevailing, one hesitates to even hazard a proposal to study entrepreneurship for fear of being laughed out of the profession. However, this is not so great an obstacle as may be surmised at first glance. A sufficient number of studies have shown that organizational slack and technical inefficiency are common phenomena in private firms in developing countries. Further, a quantity of contrary evidence has arisen in recent years, in the form of studies of rates of return, indicates that, as mentioned above, under certain conditions, public enterprises can be quite profitable (Saulniers 1980).

This negative image, which is common in the countries where the enterprises are located, gives rise to a subsidiary phenomenon which inhibits the development of entrepreneurship, considerably narrowing the field of potential study. This second issue is the constraint field within which public firm entrepreneurs must operate. Stringent laws oversee pricing policies, personnel policies, wage structures, administrative clearances, disposition of profits and external supervision, and restrict the scope of possible actions for the executive in a government-owned firm to a more limited set than those available to his counterpart in a private company. On a recent field trip to Peru, top managers of public enterprises cited the excessive control that severely constrained actions as the major problem affecting profitability (Saulniers, field notes, 1981).

In fact, it may be possible to distinguish two different effects of the constraint field on entrepreneurial behavior. The first, and most common, is that control which is too strong weakens or does away with the possible entrepreneurial response to a market situation. The second, found by Warwick in Indonesia, is almost the opposite. There, with firms operating in an environment of virtually no control, the uncertainty about when and how controls would be applied acted as a damper on entrepreneurship (Warwick, 1980:27).

A third barrier to conducting effective studies of entrepreneurship in public enterprises is time. Most top executives hold their positions only for a limited period. A common pattern found in many nations is that public enterprises are organized under the relevant sectoral ministry. This usually means that the power to name top company executives is vested in the minister. With each cabinet change, the entire team of top managers is also subject to change. I found turnover rates of up to 100 percent of top management in a recent study of public enterprises in Peru (Saulniers, field notes, 1981). Thus, public enterprise entrepreneurship is often a transitory phenomenon.

This must be contrasted to the private sector in many countries where rotation is by no means as frequent, and personal identification of the entrepreneur with the company is usually associated with a long and productive stay.

A fourth issue is that of self-selection. The literature of entrepreneurship abounds with explanations of why individuals choose to become entrepreneurs. With the overall negative image of public enterprises, it is not surprising that few individuals would consider management positions in such firms as a career objective from childhood.

The fifth issue is tied in with the objectives of the firms. The goal structures of public enterprises tend to be ill defined. The government is often unable to give firms a clear plan of action or complete autonomy to define the plan of action internally. It must be noted that conceiving a clear a priori plan is often not desirable since it can lead to missed business opportunities (Murthy, 1980:5). Further, communicating a plan, once conceived outside the firm, is costly (Ibid: 6).

A reason for which governments at times are unable to communicate even the semblance of a plan is that policy may be the outcome of a complex struggle for power among different agents of the state. These may include the managers themselves, members of a legislative body, ministers or their representatives, or other individuals in the government. This leads to a channeling of possible entrepreneurial effort to managing the political environment in attempts to coopt the controlling agencies or assuring their allegiances. Managers of public enterprises tend to spend more time in these activities than do their counterparts in private firms (Aharoni, 1980:5).

Even though the very goals of a public enterprise may not be well defined, a sixth aspect, related to the nature of such firms, makes the study of entrepreneurship difficult. Public enterprises have a public purpose. This purpose may be expressed in a wide variety of manners, but often leads to profit-making being assigned a low rank in the possible hierarchy of objectives. In more than one country, public enterprises have been criticized on the grounds that high profits were not compatible with a social purpose, or that use of standard management tools such as advertising was incompatible with that purpose. If one of the quick ways of sniffing out hidden pockets of entrepreneurship is to look for high and steady profits over time, then the public enterprises entrepreneurs will remain hidden.

Having a social purpose is also linked to the point mentioned earlier, that of control systems. Much of the literature on the management of public enterprises has centered on the design and programs for implementation of adequate control systems, not on developing entrepreneurial skills among company managers.

BASES FOR ACTION

This section briefly covers four promising areas which may be taken as starting points to develop a theory of public firm entrepreneurship, particularly with reference to Latin America. This first is the study of the role of the military in public enterprises. Large enterprises often linked to "strategic" considerations such as natural resources or petroleum have long been associated with the military in Latin America. Bibliographical and/or historical materials may productively be reexamined in the light of concern over entrepreneurship in public firms. This would be the case for the association of General Enrique Mosconi with the Argentinian firm YPF (Solberg, 1981) and the tenure of General Julio Caetano Horta Barbosa with the CNP, the precursor of Brazil's PETROBRAS (Wirth 1981).

A second related field is the extensive literature on "tecnicos," "technocrats," "engineers", or "professionals," particularly for Mexico and Brazil, two countries which have large corps of individuals falling into those categories. While much of the material until now has dealt with the positions of these tecnicos in the general government administration (Bianchi and Johnson: 1977), it was reexamined within the context of public enterprises (Kelley: 1981 and Kelly de Escobar: 1980).

A third starting point is the new literature on state bureaucracies. Here, some attempt has been made to focus on the comparison between top-level managers in the organs of central government, the public enterprises, and private firms. It is a fruitful field for research, and would benefit from the incorporation of an entrepreneurial perspective (Martins: 1974, 1977; Garcia and Nieto: 1979; Barletti and Fernandez: 1976).

The last focus is on attitudes, risk and entrepreneurship in public enterprises. This is, by its very nature, the most promising of the fields, but also the least developed. It is explicitly concerned with a detailed testing of whether some of the characteristics of entrepreneurs are, in fact, applicable to public enterprises and with a comparison of the public managers to their private counterparts (Adar and Aharoni: 1980; Tandon: 1980; Glade: 1979; Warwick: 1980).

REFERENCES

ADAR, Z., and Y. Aharoni. 1980. "Risk Sharing by Managers of State Owned Enterprises," Paper presented at the Second B.A.P.E.G. Conference, Public Enterprises in Mixed Economy LDCs, April.

AHARONI, Y. 1980. "The State-Owned Enterprise: An Agent Without a Principle," Paper presented at the Second B.A.P.E.G. Conference, Public Enterprises in Mixed Economy LDCs, April.

BARLETTI, B., and L. Fernandez. 1976. "Empresas Publicas y Burocracia Empresarial del Estado," Lima: Instituto Nacional de Administracion Publica.

BIANCHI, A., and J. Johnson. 1977. "In Search of the Tecnico: Two Countries, Two Perspectives," Paper presented at the 1977 meeting of the Latin American Studies Association.

GARCIA de Enterria, E., and A. Nieto. 1979. "La Burocracia de las Empresas Publicas," Paper presented at the International Seminar on Regulation of the Public Enterprise, Mexico City.

GLADE, W. 1979. "Entrepreneurship in the State Sector: CONASUPO of Mexico," in Entrepreneurs in Cultural Context, edited by S. Greenfield, A. Strickon, and R. Aubey, Albuquerque: University of New Mexico Press.

KILBY, P. 1971. "Hunting the Heffalump," in Entrepreneurship and Economic Development, edited by P. Kilby, New York: The Free Press.

KELLEY, G. 1981. "Politics and Administration in Mexico: Recruitment and Promotion of the Politico-Administrative Class," Technical Papers Series No. 33, Austin: Office for Public Sector Studies.

MURTHY, K. 1980. "Strategic Management of Public Enterprise: A Framework for Analysis," Paper presented at the Second B.A.P.E.G. Conference, Public Enterprises in Mixed Economy LDCs, April.

SAULNIERS, A. 1980. "Public Enterprises in Latin America: An Overview," Paper presented as the Conference entitled "Preparing the University Community for International Development," College Station.

SOLBERG, C. 1981. "The Politics of Energy in Argentina: Mosconi's Career Re-examined," Paper presented at the American Historical Association Meeting.

TANDON, P. 1980. "Hierarchical Structure and Attitudes to Risk in State-Owned Enterprises," Paper presented at the Second B.A.P.E.G. Conference, "Public Enterprises in Mixed Economy LDCs," April, 1980.

WALSH, A. H. 1978. The Public's Business: The Politics and Practices of Government Corporations, Cambridge, Mass.: The MIT Press.

WARWICK, D. 1980. "A Transactional Approach to the Public Enterprise," Paper presented at the Second B.A.P.E.G. Conference, Public Enterprises in Mixed Economy LDSc, April.

WIRTH, J. 1981. "The Politics of Energy in Brazil: Another Look at the Formative Early Years Under General Horta Barbosa, 1936-1943," Paper presented at the American Historical Association Meeting.

VIII. CLASS, POLITICAL CONSTRAINTS, AND ENTREPRENEURAL STRATEGIES: ELITES AND PETTY MARKET TRADERS IN NORTHERN LUZON

William G. Davis

I. INTRODUCTION

Although the concept of the entrepreneur has been a popular one in anthropological studies of social change, its use has not produced a major theoretical formulation of the change process. One basic reason for that situation, according to one prominent critic, is the failure of anthropological approaches to entrepreneurship "to link the detailed study of microprocesses to a consideration of macro-structures" (Long 1977:142). In the discussion that follows I attempt to overcome that criticism, and to render the notion of the entrepreneur more generally useful by combining structural and rational-choice levels of analysis in a common framework. That framework is intended to focus on the ways in which regional political-economic structures affect entrepreneurial activities, while preserving the potential for fine-grained analysis that choice models promise. The specific problem that I pose is to account for a set of observed behavioral patterns that occur between petty market operators and political elites in a Philippine municipality that I refer to as Benguet City. I will argue that those patterns developed as the result of innovation and expansive management efforts (i.e., entrepreneurial activity) on the part of both the elites and marketplace sellers as the parties involved have sought life goals to which they each attach high priority. To explain the behavior involved a model of "constrained choice" will be presented. The model is an attempt to incorporate both the constraints that rise from a specified pattern of resource distribution that characterizes the region described and the interaction of those constraints with the strategic choices made by actors. Finally, I will provide brief attention to some of the consequences of the relationship between constraints and choices for certain aspects of social change, including some of the consequences for class relations that are unintended by the participants. It is my position that neither a class analysis nor a decision-making approach, taken separately, would render a similarly complete model of the processes that I will consider.

II. <u>Political</u> <u>Economy</u> <u>and</u> <u>the</u> <u>Entrepreneur</u>

The fundamental problem to which Long's comments are directed is one that has divided economic antropologists for more than two decades. It involves the controversies that have risen between those antropologists who espouse one variety or another of a "superorganic" viewpoint and the adherents of methodological individualism, or "actor-oriented" models. It is not appropriate here to discuss the many dimensions of this controversy in detail, but a few general remarks are called for in order to provide a context for the discussion.

The basic issue in the controversy is the level of organization that provides the main locus of social processes. Individualists, of course, hold that individual persons are the principal concrete elements in social dynamics. Thus, social structure, cultural values and symbols, and normative rules are viewed as the aggregated outcomes of past decisions, actions, and agreements by individuals that persist because they have been successful in some sense. In turn, these products of previous actions influence and channel decisions, choices, and actions by contemporary persons. Expressions of this general position in economic anthropology include interactionist and transactional analyses, but most commonly appear as actor-oriented decision-making models that draw heavily on micro-economics. In the latter case, the usual model components are individual actors, the many goals they desire, a set of scarce resources, a plan of inter-connected decisions (a strategy), and a set of external conditions in terms of which some choices may be judged to be more successful than others.

In the actor-oriented view external conditions, or "constraints," are understood to include social groups and political arrangements of the sort that are focal elements in superorganic analyses (e.g., social classes), but their formation is assumed to be the consequence of individual action rather than the result of some supra-individual process. For instance, in the logic of actor-oriented analysis a social class is a collection of persons bound together by the benefits to be obtained through cooperative effort. However, the same logic predicts that on another level co-members of a class also are likely to compete with each other, for they seek the same goals and employ the same means to attain them. Thus, the solidarity of the association always is contingent and "class interest" is an empirical problem.

In this polemical portrayal superorganicists argue that individual persons cannot be the loci of process for they are themselves constituted by specifically social processes that do not exist at the individual level. Individuals desire the goals they seek, have the means they command, and make the decisions they express primarily as a result of the imposition on them of processes that are inherent in the external constraints themselves; e.g., principles of ecological systems (e.g., Rappaport 1968), socio-cultural norms (e.g., Polanyi 1957, Sahlins 1977), or the logic of modes of production and their articulation (e.g., Dupre and Rey 1973; Taylor 1979). Ecological systems, substantivist, and marxist approaches differ widely among themselves, but they all reject the view that social action is essentially the outcome of a multitude of self-interested choices by individuals.

The individualist perspective was introduced into anthropology primarily through Raymond Firth's efforts to correct the difficulties that classical functionalism had experienced dealing with social change. Firth's notion of "social organization" was particularly important in this regard (Firth 1954). From that time its use has been especially prominent in studies of economic action (e.g., Salisbury 1962, 1970; Schneider 1964, 1973; Ortiz 1967, 1978; Davis 1973); but it also has provided the ideas that organized some of the classic anthropological work that connected economics and politics, most notably studies by Fredrik Barth (1959, 1963, 1966).

However, superorganicists have been quite critical of individualist analytical strategies. Substantivists, such as Dalton (1969) and Halperin (1977), have rejected individualist propositions for years; but contemporarily it has been scholars influenced by Marx's ideas, especially the theoretical priority afforded production and related class structures, who have been most systematic and vocal in their criticism. They have pointed out that the empirical cases in which individualists have claimed to show how social aggregates are generated from individual interests have been limited to very small-scale situations (e.g., Homans 1958, 1961), not whole social systems. Furthermore, it is claimed, individualists such as Barth rarely deal with actual individuals and their decisions; rather, they create composite, ideal persons (Evens 1977). Individuals, they argue, also delude us into thinking that individuals have great independence of action and corresponding ability to manipulate situations, when in fact individuals make the choices they do primarily because of their locations in social structures--locations that predetermine the preferences that individuals have and establish the opportunities and limitations with which they must operate. Thus, in a reconsideration of Barth's (1959) analysis of Swat Pathan political economy, Talad Asad criticizes Barth's suggestion that Pathan political relationships are freely negotiated alliances between landowners and peasants. Asad (1972:90) concludes that, "In place of an organization which is dependent on the political choices of all persons (i.e., an organization created through voluntary individual transactions between those seeking political support and those able to provide such support), we find a structure in which political choices of the majority are largely illusory or irrelevant." Similarly, in a critique of my own claims for the advantages of actor-oriented strategic-choice models (Davis 1973), Scott Cook (1976) cites the following statement from Capital: ". . .individuals are dealt with only in so far as they are the personifications of economic categories, embodiments of particular class relations and class interests and which. . .can less than any other make the individual responsible for relations whose creature he socially remains, however much he may subjectively raise himself above them" (Marx 1967:10).

Marxist class analysis provides certain dimensions that commonly are overlooked, or given inadequate treatment, in actor-oriented models. In sum these call for greater attention to be paid to political, economic, and social structures that constrain individual action, and to the unintended consequences of aggregated behaviors. In effect, Asad's main criticisms of Barth's Swat Pathan study are that he paid insufficient attention to history, to the international forces impinging on Swat, and to the local system of distribution (resource allocation among social sectors). The conclusions about the character of Pathan political organization that may be drawn from Barth's analysis once those constraints are given more weight would be very different indeed.

On the other hand, there are some important analytical advantages that can be claimed for individualist, strategic-choice models, as well. First, such models provide for a refined analysis of social processes, since they do not automatically assume a high degree of internal integration among the members of societies or associations, such as social classes. Second, having an understanding of social situations in terms of the information, preferences, and alternatives that are acted upon consciously provides a substantive basis upon which the effects of policy changes may be assessed, and upon which policy changes may be made intelligible to actors. Third, choice models provide the basis for understanding the concrete processes by which structures themselves are altered--even if we choose to believe that decisions ultimately are produced by properties that are inherent at supra-individual societal levels. That, of course, was the feature of choice models that made them attractive to scholars such as Firth who sought ways of overcoming the limited capacity of functionalism for dealing with conflict and change. (See Greenfield and Strickon [1981] for a more elaborate defense of individualism).

These considerations of the differences between superorganic and individualist approaches are directly relevant to discussions of entrepreneurship, for although views differ in detail, anthropologists apparently agree that the essence of entrepreneurship is creative decision-making (e.g., Belshaw 1954-5; Barth 1963; Greenfield and Strickon 1979, 1981; Bennett 1982). That is, entrepreneurs are not viewed merely as persons who act as they do because of their relationship to structures; rather, they are seen as persons who perceive and take advantage of opportunities that are available to other person similarly located, but which are acted upon only by the creative few.[2] As Barth (1963:6) suggests, the modern view of the entrepreneur is not simply one of rights and duties, but one of choices and actions. Thus, the notion of the entrepreneur is more generally interesting theoretically because it has become a particularly acute instance of an individual choice model of action that is widely used to explain social

170

change. As such, it would seem especially important for those who employ the concept to take into account the criticisms of individualist approaches that have been offered by marxist scholarship. Unfortunately, none of the recent anthropological treatments of entrepreneurship have addressed the criticism raised, and Greenfield and Strickon (1981) even rebuke Barth for placing too much emphasis on the importance of structure in shaping transactions. Ironically, therefore, Barth's position has been assailed from both sides. Asad criticizes him for paying too little attention to the imposition of social structure, while Greenfield and Strickon argue the opposite.

These controversies should make us suspicious that just as superorganic analyses may profit from attention to individual choices, so should choice models gain by giving more weight to constraints. Furthermore, it is not satisfactory to allow the nature of constraints to remain unspecified as "selective factors" or the "influences on strategies and choices [that] come from the community" (cf. Bennett 1982:12). Rather, the nature of the selecting constraints, the patterns of interaction that exist between constraints and actors, and outcomes must be examined closely. Going further, marxist scholarship has suggested what the nature of some of the most important kinds of constraints may be: power differences that rise from the distribution of resource control. In short, environments are not entirely passive and one kind of constraint that decision-makers are likely to be obliged to evaluate in making choices is one or more sets of counterstrategies that are employed by other decision makers, some of whom may be superior in power. Unrelenting sensitivity to efforts by some social sectors to exploit others is one of the most important contributions of marxist theory.

III. Taking Barth Seriously: A Model of Constrained Choice

One obvious conceptual means of resolving the "levels of analysis" problem would be formulation of a model of social process that incorporates advantages associated with both structural and strategic-choice positions. There would be two immediate advantages to such a synthesis. First, it would be possible to overcome the neglect of history, social scale, and power relations that have diminished the usefulness of strategic choice models to this point. Second, it would be useful to provide a format that encourages systematic attention to the process of conflict within social classes and interest groups, as well as between them, thereby avoiding renditions of class relationships that overemphasize the functional unity of intraclass associations (Taylor 1979). Barth actually seems to hint at such a synthesis when he draws attention to the factors that "structure the activities" of entrepreneurs (1963:2) and the importance of the "context" and "restrictions" that limit the activities of enterprises (1963:6). In fact, he specifically advocated borrowing the concept of "constrained choice" from the theory of games (von Neumann and Morgenstern 1947:79-100) in order to formulate the nature of structure-decision relationships. However, nowhere did he develop that model, nor has he dealt specifically with the prior role of power and differential ownership of resources as factors that condition decision and negotiation (Paine 1974).

In the discussion to follow I attempt to develop the constrained choice model by refining the notion of "constraints" to include class relationships. A full explication of such a model, however, would oblige us to pay similar attention to such other elements as the biophysical environment, culture, and demography, along with the ways in which these elements feedback through the actors. Obviously, the complete development of the model is too ambitious to attempt here; thus, I limit consideration to constraints and opportunities derived from political relationships. The problem, then, is to describe and analyze the patterns of interaction that occur between political elites and petty market operators in Beguet City as the outcome of constrained choice. Before describing those patterns, I examine briefly the components of the model. More detailed description of the constraints also will follow in the discussion of the ethnographic situation.

The elements of the model are 1) two sets of actors who in several ways stand in opposition to each other, and who, in terms of the constraints of the system, find it mutually advantageous to exchange utilities in order to obtain what for each are distinct and highly desired end-states; 2) a set of high priority goals for each; 3) a set of constraints (here understood to include "opportunities") that condition decisions and interactions among actors; 4) strategies for each set of actors; and 5) outcomes, both intended and unintended. The actors are certain municipal political elites and small-scale merchants in the city marketplace. The high priority goals for the political elites are attaining public office (which in the Philippines means obtaining enough votes to be elected), or to build for future efforts at higher office. Marketplace sellers, on the other hand, seek to obtain operating capital and to increase their income by expanding the scale of their enterprises (which, for reasons that will become clear, translates to increasing the size of publicly-controlled selling sites). The major constraints include elements that are general for both sets of actors and specific for each. General constraints include cultural principles and values that define obligations and encumber participants in reciprocal exchanges in Philippine society (Hollnsteiner 1961, 1963; Lande 1964); and the fact that ownership of agricultural land in this region is concentrated in the hands of rural tribal minorities--a condition that inhibits entry of lowland Filipinos directly into production in the area concerned. Constraints specific to would-be holders of political power are: 1) a *de jure* political system that requires would-be holders of office to compete for and obtain votes; and 2) a large, ethnically and regionally diverse and dispersed electorate, members of which are difficult to contact for direct solicitation of votes. Constraints on the market operators are: 1) their limited capital and impeded access to public financial institutions, which are controlled by the political elites; 2) rules and ordinances--made by the holders of public office--that regulate the location and conditions of commerce; and 3) a tradition of highly personalized relations between suppliers, buyers, and sellers.

The constraints of each group, in turn, provide opportunities for members of the other that lead to a series of dyadic exchanges. Market sellers have direct access to large numbers of colleagues, suppliers and customers who are potential voters. The political elites, in turn, have control over public financial institutions and the rules governing trade. Individuals in each category make available to members of the other what they have in return for what they need. That is, the market sellers serve as middlemen-organizers of the votes of their colleagues, suppliers, and customers in return for access to financial institutions and preferential treatment by the political elites. The latter, to obtain the votes necessary for public office, grant preferential treatment to selected market sellers.

The case materials presented below are drawn from the activities of small-scale merchants in the city's public marketplace and the municipal officials with whom they interact. The events to be described occurred prior to the establishment of the Marcos dictatorship in 1972. To anticipate, economic entrepreneurship in this case does not involve direct control of production; rather, it consists of the creation of special relationships with landowning primary-producers that take advantage of an innovation in production that occurred some years prior, together with the creation of a new kind of enterprise and new political relationships and groups. The production innovation is the cultivation of mid-latitude vegetables expressly for the market, an economic activity that began about 1910 and expanded enormously during the 1960s. The commercial innovation is the creation, among the otherwise tiny firms of the public marketplace, of multi-stall wholesaling and retailing operations that approach in size and earnings some of the better elite-owned shops of the downtown business district of the city. The political innovations are the creation of interclass associations that are intended to further the interests of entrepreneurs of both kinds.

IV. City and Marketplace

Benguet City is an urban area of approximately 30,000 persons (the "city" boundaries actually include some countryside that adds to the population) that is located near the southern end of the Central Cordillera mountain ranges of Luzon. It is an administrative and marketing center that provides many services for the adjacent region, but very little manufacturing takes place within the city. There is, however, a thriving trade in native handicrafts, and tourism is an important aspect of the local economy.

The region within which the city is located is ethnically very diverse, as are most Philippine regions. Indigenous mountain peoples constitute the area's numerical majority. There include a number of different ethnolinguistic groups, especially Ibaloi and Kankanai, who usually reside well outside the city or in its "hutment" fringe. Historically the native peoples supported themselves by cultivating some combination of root crops and rice grown both in dry (swidden) and irrigated fields. After World War II market garden production expanded greatly and presently many rural households produce at least some vegetables for sale. Much of this market production moves through the public market in Benguet City, although a substantial proportion also is bulked by rural wholesalers who ship it directly to lowland markets, including Manila. The merchants most prominent in that long distance trade in the 1960s and early 1970s were ethnic Chinese. In the city itself, as in most other sizeable central places in the Luzon uplands, the majority of the population consists of Christian Filipinos of lowland origin. A number of lowland ethnic groups are present, but Ilocanos from the nearby provinces of Ilocos Norte, Ilocos Sur, and La Union are numerically dominant and tend to monopolize the town's political offices. However, diversity is so great that successful candidates for office cannot depend solely on support from members of their own ethnic/regional groups. Thus, conditions encourage the emergence of brokers who represent the interests of minority groups to candidates and officials. There exists in the city, therefore, a rough kind of ethnic division of labor. Both the town's major businesses and most of the petty enterprises of the public marketplace are owned by Filipinos of lowland extraction. The region's primary agricultural producers are indigenous mountain peoples, whose claim to land is long standing. Cultivators market produce partly by retailing it themselves on special market days when they are allowed into the public market; but more commonly, produce is sold to wholesalers, either at the farmstead or in the marketplace.

Until 1960 the city was part of a "special province," so designated because of the large proportion of indigenous minority peoples represented in the population who, presumably, could not comprehend the normal electoral process of Philippine government. During that period city officials were appointed by the national government in Manila; thus, if there was competition for offices it was conducted elsewhere and was relatively unaffected by deeply-felt local issues. From 1960 on, however, city officials have been elected. Top level city administration now consists of a mayor, vice-mayor, and six city councilmen, all of whom are elected for four-year terms. Councilmen are elected at large, rather than by district; the six leading candidates are elected regardless of party affiliation or regional representation. Political influence is as much a function of the number of votes the candidate receives as it is the office to which one is elected; e.g., a very popular councilman may be as influential as the mayor. Thus, each candidate is encouraged to try to win by as large a margin as possible.

In theory, any adult citizen who is a community resident may stand for office; but as is so often the case, in practice there is a wealth threshold involved--heavy election expenses--that prevents all but the wealthy from being serious contenders. In fact, councilors in the past have tended to be recruited again and again from a small number of families. Further, since leadership in formal political parties until recently has been the monopoly of local elites, it is unlikely that any non-elite could secure a party nomination. Election without the support of a political party has never been accomplished, although it has been attempted several times.

Political campaigns are conducted partly by general appeals made to the public at large (e.g., claims of honesty and efficiency made in public speeches). But more importantly, as is common in many social situations (Strickon and Greenfield 1972, Lande 1977, Scott 1977), campaigns also rely heavily on the formation of highly personalized patron-client relationships between power seekers and lower status persons in which very specific benefits are exchanged for votes. Ethnic and regional affiliations are important bases for the formation of these relationships, and both sides ideally are bound by norms that require meeting reciprocal obligations; but there is no doubt that the transactions involved are primarily instrumental.

As has been implied, the population of the city is stratified in complex ways that result from two key facts. First, the region being discussed is a frontier of capitalist market penetration in which local control of the primary means of production (agricultural land) remains mainly in the hands of rural small holders who are members of minority ethnic groups. Land has not become concentrated in the hands of the elite as is so commonly the case elsewhere in the Philippines; thus, this is not the simple class situation in which elites own local means of production. Second, the elites in Benguet City are "pioneers" who emigrated to Benguet to take advantage of local commercial opportunities. They are members of families that typically have extensive land holdings in adjacent lowland areas, and histories of political participation in those areas. Their source of power in Benguet historically is based on wealth, with an extra-regional source of origin, long-standing relationships with national political parties, and on their ability to use these advantages successfully in political and commercial ventures in Benguet. In brief, elite status and economic position in Benguet City is not so much based on the control of local production as it is on the monopoly of formal positions of authority, domination of public financial institutions, and the legal right to regulate the terms and conditions of trade that those extra-regional relationships help establish. In Benguet City elites use their wealth and influence economically virtually to monopolize the professions and ownership of the substantial businesses that comprise the city's "downtown" area--an economic sector that is emphatically distinguished from the public marketplace. Because elites share a market position, they have common economic interests that include limiting competition with their enterprises from marketplace firms. Furthermore, they are not merely a quasi-group; rather, they tend also to form a community by virtue of common membership in elite associations, the most significant of which for united political action is the Chamber of Commerce. The important point, however, is that members of elite families occupy all high public offices and have done so since the end of World War II.

The majority of the town's inhabitants are poor laborers, craftsmen, and petty merchants, and the public marketplace is the institution that organizes most of their sales and purchases. In the Philippines towns typically are arranged around a public marketplace, and marketplaces have come to have an important position in nationalistic ideologies regarding economic development. Public marketplaces were nationalized shortly after independence in order to provide a foothold for the development of Filipino-owned small businesses. Non-citizens legally are excluded from public marketplaces and public control of marketplaces is highly ranked ideologically as one important means of providing a competitive advantage to small-scale Philippine-owned commerce by setting aside for citizens locations from which commerce may be conducted at the cost of modest rents and fees. In Benguet City, however, that theoretical advantage has been counterbalanced by local officials who, despite stated nationalist ideals, have tended to regard the marketplace ambivalently as both competition for their own commercial interests and as an important source of city revenue. Until recently, officials had a history of insensitivity and opposition to the needs and interests of the citizens who depend upon the public market.

The public marketplace in Benguet City consists of approximately 1200 stalls (puestos) that are owned by the city and leased to individuals for weekly rents that range between $.75 and $6.00 U.S. Many different kinds of products and services are offered for sale, including imports that are manufactured in Japan, Germany, the United States, and other industrial metropoles. City ordinances have "zoned" the market by product so that it is partitioned into divisions in which the same products are sold in each section; sellers of the same products, therefore, are spatially adjacent. The rationale for this arrangement is that it is convenient for the public to know where specific products may be found; but it also facilitates the collection of market fees and rents since changes vary by product and location. Although very large quantities of goods move through the market daily, typical transactions are very small and most sellers' incomes are modest. Market vendors explain that they are content when, at the end of a day's trading, they have made a profit equal to the day's wage paid to ordinary labor (in particular, the market sweepers)--about one U.S. dollar.

The conduct of the market is supervised by a market superintendent and his staff of twelve employees who are appointed by the city council. The superintendent's office is responsible for allotting stalls, collecting rents and fees, maintaining zoning restrictions, and administering other regulations governing the market that are ordained by city government. Further, city administration has the right to establish commercial zones and has prohibited street vending; consequently, all poorly capitalized small traders have been forced to locate in the public marketplace where they fall under the superintendent's jurisdiction.

Space in the market is very scarce since demand far exceeds supply. Thus, once rights to operate a stall are acquired they are not relinquished easily. When a stall is vacated, the right to occupy it is reallocated, at least in theory, in accord with a procedure that is fixed by law. Each interested party files an application and pays an application fee. At the appropriate time, the names of all applicants are placed in a container and a winner is chosen by random draw. Any adult citizen and city resident may apply, with the limitation that no "family" may operate more than one stall simultaneously.

Of the many kinds of products offered for sale in the marketplace, the single commodity sold in the largest number of stalls is fresh produce, especially the vegetables and fruits that are grown locally. The market superintendent's zoning plan lists 300 stalls in that section of the market. In the discussion that follows I will, for the sake of simplicity, focus on the activities of the vegetable sellers, although many of my remarks also pertain to sellers of other products as well.

The usual way in which vegetable vendors conduct business is through retail sales, making every effort to develop a clientele of steady customers. Typically, this involves extending credit, granting small price concessions and guaranteeing top quality products to regular customers, and providing a range of additional small services. Regular trade relationships, regardless of whether they are with suppliers or consumers, are termed suki. The suki institution is very similar to pratik relationships described for Haitian marketplaces by Mintz (1961). I have described the practice at length elsewhere (Davis 1973), and Anderson (1969) has suggested that such relations are the very foundation of entrepreneurship in the Philippines.

Among the holders of the 300 vegetable stalls there are fifteen individuals who, in addition to the retail selling that is typical of all market vendors, for several years have used their marketplace stalls for wholesaling--selling both to other stallholders and to "agents" who bulk produce for resale in lowland markets. They are the marketplace vendors for whom I claim entrepreneurial status.

V. Entrepreneurship: A Market for Votes

Entrepreneurship, as Schumpeter (1973) has indicated, involves the formation of "new combinations." In the world of the vegetable merchants in the Beguet marketplace the new combination that have been created are simple in conception, but difficult to implement. Although all sellers might have selected this advantageous alternative, they did not, leading to the conclusion that entrepreneurship was not simply a matter of the sellers' common position in the local social system.

The key to the new strategy is a shift from traditional retail selling to a combination of retailing and wholesaling, with emphasis on the latter. This change in marketing behavior in turn requires changes in the way that produce is obtained by the seller, plus changes in the organization of the enterprise and its sales strategy. In some cases, it also involves increasing the variety of goods offered for sale--in spite of the constraints imposed by city zoning regulations.

To expand on these points, on the supply side the market vendor must acquire an assured source of produce from growers. That is necessary both to reduce the risks that accompany heavy investment in a single, specialized enterprise, and because the seller's regular customers expect him/her to be a certain source of supply. If the seller fails to provide produce for suki, he/she both loses the profit from that day's sales and jeopardizes future purchases by disappointed clients. Securing a source of supply may be accomplished either by providing cash advances ("crop loans") to producers in exchange for an agreement to deliver the harvest to the lender at a favorable price or, less frequently, by purchasing standing crops in the field before they are harvested.

Both modes of acquiring produce stand in sharp contrast to the common practice among vegetable sellers of purchasing vegetables daily from the many producers that bring small quantities to the market each morning.

The entrepreneurs that follow the new pattern must enlarge their firms in order to accommodate the increased volume. More specifically, they must to increase their respective share of the market (which means that they need more space in the marketplace), and to mobilize additional labor. Labor normally is the easiest factor to assemble. It is plentiful and usually recruited within the stall owner's own family. Few skills are required and a manager typically is close at hand to provide the necessary training and direction. Relatives generally are hired at low wages, on the grounds that they are partially compensated by being provided with an opportunity to learn about business. However, some of the larger-scale operations recently have hired non-relatives as clerks, thereby producing fully rationalized firm organizations.

The entrepreneurs attempt to expand their share of the market by increasing retail sales and/or wholesaling. On the retail side they try to increase the number of their regular customers by emphasizing how well prepared they are to be a good suki; but in practice they rely most heavily on the provision of credit. Credit is an important aspect of retailing and is most apt to be provided generously by sellers of perishable commodities such as vegetables. Selling on credit also is a technique for managing risks associated with heavy investment in a single enterprise, although it involves costs resulting from slowing the turnover velocity of capital. Successful innovators also offer a wider range of products, such as canned goods and/or handicrafts, to their regular customers. This, of course, is inconsistent with the market zoning regulations and brings the expanding firm into conflict with market authorities, a point to which I will return presently.

The wholesale strategy is conducted in several alternative ways. One method is to cultivate persons, referred to generally as "agents," who buy in large quantities for resale in other markets, or to sell to hotels, restaurants and other establishments.

However, one of the distinctive features of successful entrepreneurship is wholesaling to other marketplace retailers who have not had enough managerial creativity to obtain their own supply sources. Some of these "client" stall operators actually have become tenants of the major wholesalers, occupying stalls to which the wholesaler holds the use-rights, and selling stock owned by the wholesaler in exchange for a share of the profit. Through these relationships many of the smaller marketplace firms are deeply dependent on the few large-scale wholesaler-stallholders. Thus, the wholesalers themselves have become patrons in a patron-client network, and are in a position to exact concessions from client vendors.

Given the conditions that obtain, the entrepreneur's primary needs are to obtain working capital and more space in the marketplace. To return the discussion to the political constraints with which I began, the successful entrepreneurs have been those who have acquired capital and space by means of patronage from political elites.

Vendors in the marketplace typically are quite poor and the $2500 to $3000 necessary to implement the kind of program of expansive management described is usually beyond their means. To mobilize that much capital they must turn to external sources of funds. There are three alternatives that sellers have attempted to use. The first is borrowing from relatives, which is the capital source most frequently mentioned by all sellers queried. However, since relatives of vendors also are likely to be poor, that source has proved to be inadequate. Borrowing from moneylenders is another possibility. Money lenders are abundant in the marketplace, but the interest rates they charge are exorbitant and too high to make them a useful source of venture capital for the stall owners. A third alternative, which has proven most successful, has been the local branch of a certain national bank that offers loans to assist the development of Filipino-owned "small businesses." However, the category "small business" was never intended to include marketplace sellers, none of whom could meet the collateral requirements necessary to be eligible for such loans. The marketplace vendor, therefore, must overcome legal constraints in order to obtain a loan from the bank.

This is accomplished with the help of local political elites who have influence with bank officials. The politicians are able to persuade the bank officials not to enforce the legal requirements for collateral by personally assuring them that the market vendor is reliable and that the investment is sound. But why should a politician use his influence on behalf of a poor, although aspiring stall owner? To answer the question I must return to the structural constraints on political elites discussed above. As stated, elites need votes to remain in office and/or increase their influence, but the electorate is dispersed and difficult to reach. The stallowners, and especially those moving into wholesaling, come in personal contact with, and have considerable influence with, sizeable numbers of suppliers, customers, and other sellers (in addition to their friends and relatives), who also are potential voters. In exchange for their efforts as organizers or mobilizers of votes, certain political elites provide selected stall owners with access to the loan funds of the bank.

Ethnic and regional associations also constitute an "opportunity" for the marketplace participant, for when candidates have different ethnic affiliations than the voters to whom they wish to appeal, access to the latter is difficult, and often requires the services of an intermediary. Further, simple logistic problems render it difficult for the politician to maintain personal reciprocal relationships with the large number of voters that is required for successful candidacy. It is obviously much more practical for politicians to strike bargains with persons who are themselves the centers, on a more modest scale, of patron-client networks, and therefore capable of influencing the votes of a number of others. Thus, local political alliances have a "pyramidal" form (Scott 1977:125).

The motives underlying the willingness of marketplace operators to participate in patron-client organizations are quite apparent. Virtually all marketplace sellers understand that it is very useful for them to open avenues of personal access to officials by which the latter may be approached for favors. They also know that a broker who represents an aggregation of voters normally will be a more effective negotiator than the average individual stallholder. Therefore, operators tend to be quite susceptible to organization by political brokers. For the broker's part, once he has gained a reputation for being able to deliver votes, that reputation provides him with much greater chances of obtaining personal, as well as collective, benefits from officials. The main benefit acquired from these relationships by political figures is, of course, votes; but in some cases, elites also are tempted to negotiate with marketplace clients by the allure of direct financial incentives, as well. Some sellers with promising businesses reported that they were persuaded to accept a town official as a silent business partner as one of the costs of successful negotiation.

We have seen that small-scale commercial enterprises are confined to the public marketplace, and that each family of marketplace sellers is legally restricted to use-rights in a single stall. Since efforts to expand the size of the enterprise inevitably also require increasing marketplace space, the firm again encounters legal restrictions the avoidance of which creates still greater demand for the intercession of political patrons. That intervention takes two forms.

The simplest, though illegal, way of increasing the firm's space is to purchase de facto rights to occupy adjacent stalls from their legal holders. This is done with great delicacy so that the change in management does not embarrass the authorities. The new occupant appears more frequently in the "purchased" stall as the old occupant appears less frequently, until the latter disappears from the market. The new occupant also is careful to pay rents and other fees on time, and in general to avoid attracting any public attention to the substitution. In this particular strategy of expansion, the main role of the political patron is to prevent market authorities from enforcing the law. However, since the "sale" price of transferring use-rights is quite high (probably approaching the actual market value of the stall), acquiring very many stalls in this manner is prohibitively expensive. The more frequently used alternative, therefore, is to arrange for direct political interference in the selection process for vacant stalls. Stalls customarily are distributed to applicants by means of a random draw. Influential politicians, however, can direct the outcome of the draw in favor of a client. If a stall acquired in this way is not adjacent to the original, trades often can be arranged to make them so. By this means the fifteen stallholder-entrepreneurs being discussed have established operations combining from four to eight stalls. In fact, approximately one-third of the total number of vegetable stalls that appear in the official records as rental units have disappeared through this process of accumulation. Where there should be 300 independent stallholding firms, there actually are but 188.

Finally, increasing the size of the vendor's share of the market may involve other forms of political patronage. Logically, a seller may chose to expand by increasing the number of his customers, or by selling more, of perhaps diverse commodities, to a given set of buyers, or some mix of the two strategies. All sellers in the Benguet market attempt the first of those alternatives. The second, however, is in violation of the "zoning ordinance." It may be practiced only by those vendors who have the protection of an influential politician who can make the market officials look the other way. Marketplace entrepreneurship, therefore, necessarily involves the cooperation of political elites. The character of the cooperative process, however, allows considerable latitude for choice and negotiation.

V. Entrepreneurship and Social Change

As indicated earlier, one of the benefits claimed for adapting "individualist," actor-based analytical strategies, and especially the concept of the innovative entrepreneur, is an enhanced capacity for dealing with intra-societal variation and the process of social change. Thus, there remains the task of identifying some of the wider consequences of action, both intended and unintended, that have resulted from the patterns of political and economic entrepreneurship that I have described.

As I have argued, until 1960 an external elite from the lowlands controlled commerce in Benguet City, and formulated and enforced rules that maintained their favorable position. Successful access to public resources was available to non-elites only by means of exchanges made with elites. Sharp distinctions existed between the multitude of small-scale commercial operations in the marketplace and the shops of the town's main business district--the latter housing elite commercial interests. Though much smaller in number, the downtown businesses generally involved much larger investment, larger and better equipped establishments, and a much greater use of rational business and cost accounting procedures.

The principal alterations in the set of constraints on local behavior that occurred after 1960 were: 1) the imposition of an electoral political system from an external source, the national government; and 2) the penetration of a capitalist market in the form of the immigration of lowland traders and improved roads, transport, and marketing facilities that rendered feasible agricultural production for the market. Those changes encouraged varieties of entrepreneurial activities by individual elites and petty market operators that have, in turn, resulted in the formation of new relationships and organizations--in other words, changes in the structure of constraints.

First, marketplace sellers have provided the kind of articulation function that Barth (1963) speaks of as diagnostic feature of entrepreneurship. By gaining access to public sources of finance and using the funds obtained to provide operating capital for primary producers, venturesome marketplace sellers have integrated regional and local economic sectors. This connection has allowed ethnic minorities to take advantage of more productive methods of cultivation, but also has linked them intimately to cash crop production and the market. Furthermore, some of the risks associated with market-oriented production have been reduced for producers because the market operators limit uncertainties by contracting for specified products. In the long term that articulation may be disadvantageous to producers, especially if, as often occurs, it leads to the loss of lands by smallholders; but in the short run it has raised rural incomes.

Second, the efforts of entrepreneurs in both political and economic realms have increased intraclass conflict and generated interclass organizations. Petty merchants in the marketplace represent one of the few large categories of non-elites in the region with specific common interests, as the result of a common occupation and regulation by a common set of rules. Therefore, they represent a very large potential voting block for politicians who are clever enough to mobilize them by appealing to those interests. Knowledgeable local politicians estimated that there were approximately 3,000 eligible voters associated with the marketplace, in a situation in which 9,000 votes normally would assure the election of a city councilman and 12,000 votes would certainly elect a mayor.

Virtually from the introduction of electoral government a few enterprising elites adopted a strategy of appealing specifically to political activists in the marketplace as an aspect of campaigning. Initially that was effected through the kinds of dyadic relationships described; but they have also assisted marketplace sellers in the development of a market vendors' association (MVA). Their motivation in doing so was the hope that by consolidating marketplace organization they would render negotiations with marketplace personnel still more efficient. Simultaneously, on their side politically-astute marketplace sellers perceived that a formal organization which they led would, by unified action, have greater effect in adjusting public policy in ways that advanced their own interests. For that reason, economically aggressive marketers have been motivated to assume leadership roles in the MVA.

Electioneering by new politicians has badly divided the old class alignments. Among elites recent elections have been bitterly contested between old guard and new factions, and there are frequent reports of "dirty tricks" and even physical violence during campaigns. Among the marketplace vendors, the entrepreneurs have separated themselves from the majority of their less enterprising colleagues. They have accumulated retailing space and capital, thereby substantially reducing the number of sellers in competition with them. Furthermore, their functions as wholesalers and providers of credit have created for each a clientele of lesser traders who depend upon them for a major portion of their trading stock. As noted, some of their retailer-clients are, in effect, tenants--they occupy stalls to which the wholesalers possess use-rights and receive their trading stocks on credit terms from wholesalers. Indeed, such tenants are _de_ _facto_ employees of the wholesalers. But perversely, as one result of the process of accumulation, the political potential of the MVA has not been fully realized because smaller operators are aware that their interests are not necessarily those of the more successful entrepreneurs. Many small-scale vendors voice concern that the few successful entrepreneurs eventually will gain control of the public marketplace, thereby driving out the small operators.[3]

Nevertheless, the threat that marketplace sellers might ally as a voting block has not escaped those already elected to city administration. As one indication, a "Market Committee" that consists of representatives of the city administration and the MVA has been created to adjudicate vendor complaints and to provide a forum for discussion of city policy on marketplace regulation. As another, several councilmen publicly have advocated lower market rents and fees, and the use of rents and fees to refurbish the marketplace in ways that would render it more attractive and accessible to buyers. Finally, politicians have interfered so often in the legal proceedings being instituted by the market superintendent against the larger operators for non-payment of rent that the superintendent complains that the more influential marketplace merchants are preserving their selling sites virtually rent free. The city's income from rents and fees, therefore, is many thousands of dollars below what had been expected. One of the unanticipated outcomes of this situation is that by paying their taxes, the substantial merchants of the town's main business district are subsidizing their marketplace competitors. These kinds of intraclass conflicts are, of course, not news to modern marxist analysis (e.g., Singelman 1981); but by incorporating a rational choice dimension in the model, our understanding of the process by which such conflict appears--and even by which new classes perhaps emerge--is considerably sharpened.

In summary, it seems evident that to grasp the processes that underlie patron-client relationships in this case it is necessary first to have an understanding of the local system of resource distribution and the social means by which that pattern is maintained--in short, the system of class relations. A rational actor model alone appears to be of limited value in understanding why elites exist in the first instance, and therefore why clients require patrons, or why patrons and clients have different kinds of utilities to transact. On the other hand, it seems equally clear that individual members of social classes have by no means acted consistently to preserve collective class interests. For instance, the very political institutions that should, in theory, advance elite shared interests, in practice frequently are rendered ineffective by the behavior of entrepreneurial elites who in their actions give greater priority to their individual interests. In a similar manner, the strategies of entrepreneurial marketplace sellers express more concern for the welfare of their enterprises than for the prosperity of other members of their class--although their actions often are clothed in claims to the contrary. In that context, the Market Vendor's Association is particularly significant because it has become an interclass association that challenges the interests of both elite and non-elite classes. It is an example of the process by means of which the actions of individuals, taken collectively, have altered the external constraints that affect their individual choices and behaviors. The value of the concept of the entrepreneur in the model of constrained choice, therefore, is that it requires consideration of the interplay between creative individuals that carry the process and the constraints that both affect their choices and in turn are affected by them.

Finally, an additional benefit of such a model is that it can be manipulated to produce hypotheses that may clarify the conditions under which alternatives to the patron-client relations observed may emerge. For example, it may be proposed that if constraints were altered in a manner that made bank credits easily available to marketplace entrepreneurs, clients would lose their major incentive to seek political patrons--thereby weakening or eliminating clientelist politics. Alternatively, it might be hypothesized that if local elections were suspended in favor of centrally appointed authority, officials would have no need of personal clienteles drawn from non-elites. Therefore, uses of the model might be extended to include an examination of the conditions under which patronage politics emerge, flourish, and disappear.

NOTES

(1) Paul DiSenso, Tom Love, James Peoples, Benjamin Orlove, and Susan Russell all discussed with me some of the issues addressed in this paper, and I gratefully acknowledge their contributions. Sidney Greenfield, Gary Hamilton, Suad Joseph, Bonnie McCay, Peter Richarson, Henry Rutz, and Miriam Wells all generously offered detailed comments on an early draft, for which I am particularly appreciative. I alone am responsible for any errors in interpretation.

(2) Hagen (1962) and McClelland (1963) both have attempted to determine the personal qualities that entrepreneurs have that allow them to make creative perceptions.

(3) More recent field work in this area by Susan D. Russell (personal communication) suggests that the process of accumulation described has been amplified considerably, as increasing numbers of ethnic minority sellers have entered the market as tenants of major marketplace entrepreneurs.

REFERENCES

ANDERSON, James N. 1969. Buy and sell and economic personalism: foundations for Philippine entrepreneurship. Asian Survey 9:641-668.

ASAD, Talal. 1972. Market model, class structure and consent: a reconsideration of Swat political organization. Man 7:74-94.

BARTH, Fredrik. 1959. Political Leadership Among Swat Pathans. London: Athlone Press.

_____. 1963. "Introduction." In Fredrik Barth, Ed., The Role of the Entrepreneur in Social Change in Northern Norway. Oslo: Norwegian University Press.

_____. 1966. Models of Social Organization. Royal Anthropological Institute Occasional Papers, No. 24. London: Royal Anthropological Institute.

BELSHAW, Cyril S. 1954-5. "The cultural milieu of the entrepreneur: a critical essay." Explorations in Entrepreneurial History. 7:146-163.

BENNETT, John W. 1982. Of Time and the Enterprise. Minneapolis: University of Minnesota Press.

BLAU, Peter M. 1964. Exchange and Power in Social Life. New York: Wiley.

COOK, Scott. 1976. Review article: "Social Relations in a Philippine market." Journal of Development Studies. 12:442-445.

DALTON, George. 1969. "Theoretical issues in economic anthropology." Current Anthropology. 10:63-102.

DAVIS, William G. 1973. Social Relations in a Philippine Market: Self-interest and Subjectivity. Berkeley: University of California Press.

DUPRE, G. and P. P. Rey. 1973. "Reflections on the pertinence of a theory of the history of exchange." Economy and Society. 2:131-163.

EVENS, Terrence M.S. 1977. "Prediction of the individual in anthropological interactionism." American Anthropologist. 79:579-597.

FIRTH, Raymond. 1954. "Social organization and social change." Journal of the Royal Anthropological Institute. 84:1-20.

FRASER, L. M. 1937. Economic Thought and Language. London: Black.

GREENFIELD, Sidney M. and Arnold Strickon. 1979. "Entrepreneurship and social change: toward a populational, decision-making approach." In Greenfield, Sidney M., Arnold Strickon, and Robert Aubey, Eds., Entrepreneurs in Cultural Context. Albuquerque: University of New Mexico Press.

_____. 1981. "A new paradigm for the study of entrepreneurship and social change." Economic Development and Cultural Change. 29:467-499.

HAGEN, Everett E. 1962. On the Theory of Social Change. Homewood, Illinois: Dorsey Press.

HALPERIN, Rhoda. 1977. "The substantive economy in peasant societies." In Halperin, Rhoda and James Dow, Eds., Peasant Livelihood. New York: St. Martin's Press.

HOLLNSTEINER, Mary R. 1961. "Reciprocity in the lowland Philippines.: Quezon City: Ateneo de Manila, Institute of Philippine Culture Papers, No. 1.

_____. 1963. "The Dynamics of Power in a Philippine Municipality." Quezon City: Community Development Research Council, University of the Philippines.

HOMANS, George C. 1958. "Social behavior as exchange." American Journal of Sociology. 63:597-606.

_____. 1961. Social Behavior: Its Elementary Forms. New York: Harcourt, Brace and World.

LANDE, Carl H. 1964. *Leaders, Factions, and Parties: the Structure of Philippine Politics.* Yale University Southeast Asia Studies Monograph Series, No. 6. New Haven: Yale University Press.

_____. 1977. "Networks and groups in Southeast Asia. some observations on the group theory of politics." In S. W. Schmidt, Laura Guasti, C. H. Lande, and J. C. Scott, Eds., *Friends, Followers, and Factions.* Berkeley: University of California Press.

LONG, Norman. 1977. *An Introduction to the Sociology of Rural Development.* London: Tavistock Publications, Ltd.

MARX, Karl. 1967. *Capital, Volume I.* New York: International Publishers.

MC CLELLAND, David C. 1963. "The achievement motive in economic growth." In Bert Hoselitz and W. E. Moore, Eds., *Industrialization and Society.* Paris: Mouton.

MINTZ, Sidney M. 1961. "Pratik: Haitian personal economic relationships." *Proceedings of the American Ethnological Society.* Seattle: University of Washington Press.

NEUMANN, J. von and O. Morgenstern. 1947. *The Theory of Games and Economic Behavior.* Princeton: Princeton University Press.

ORTIZ, Sutti. 1967. "The structure of decision making among the Indians of Columbia." In Raymond Firth, Ed., *Themes in Economic Anthropology.* Association of Social Anthropology Monograph No. 6. London: Tavistock Publications, Ltd.

_____. 1976. "Uncertainties in peasant farming: a Columbian case." In R. Apthorpe, Ed., *People, Planning and Development Studies.* London: Frank Cass.

PAINE, Robert. 1974. "Second Thoughts About Barth's Models." Royal Anthropological Institute Occasional Paper, No. 32. London: Royal Anthropological Institute.

POLYANI, Karl. 1957. "The economy as instituted process." In Karl Polanyi, Conrad Arensberg, and Harry Pearson, Eds., Trade and Market in the Early Empires. New York: Free Press.

RAPPAPORT, Roy. 1968. Pigs for the Ancestors. New Haven: Yale University Press.

RUSSELL, Susan D. 1982. Personal Communication.

SAHLINS, Marshall. 1977. Culture and Practical Reason. Chicago: University of Chicago Press.

SALISBURY, Richard F. 1962. From Stone to Steel. Melbourne: University of Melbourne Press.

_____. 1970. "Vunamami: Economic Transformation in a Traditional Society." Berkeley: University of California Press.

SCHNEIDER, Harold K. 1964. "Economic in East African aboriginal societies." In Melville Herskovits and Mitchell Horwitz, Eds., Economic Transition in Africa. Evanston: Northwestern University Press.

1973 Economic Man. New York: Free Press.

SCHUMPETER, Joseph A. 1936. The Theory of Economic Development. Cambridge: Harvard University Press.

SCOTT, James C. 1977. "Patron-client politics and political change in Southeast Asia." In S. W. Schmidt, Laura Guasti, C. H. Lande, and J. C. Scott, Eds., Friends, Followers, and Factions. Berkeley: University of California Press.

STRICKON, Arnold and Sidney M. Greenfield. 1972. "The analysis of patron-client relationships: an introduction." In Strickon, Arnold and Sidney M. Greenfield, Eds., Structure and Process in Latin America. Albuquerque: University of New Mexico Press.

SINGELMAN, Peter. 1981. Structures of Domination and Peasant Movements in Latin America. Columbia: University of Missouri Press.

TAYLOR, John G. 1979. From Modernization to Modes of Production. Atlantic Highlands, New Jersey: Humanities Press.

IX. CHILDREN AS ENTREPRENEURS: CASE STUDIES FROM KANO, NIGERIA[1]

Enid Schildkrout

Entrepreneurs are usually assumed to be adults. Those social scientists who study economic activities rarely look at the behavior of children, except in terms of their patterns of consumption or, more frequently, their labor contribution (Rodgers and Standing 1981:bibliography; Ward, Wackman and Wartella 1977). While these aspects of children's behavior are indeed important, it is also possible to look at children as economic decision makers. Of course, the extent to which children make decisions about the expenditure and investment of resources and about the allocation of labor and other factors of production varies from one society to another. In those societies in which children are significant economic actors, as among the Hausa of northern Nigeria, it is impossible to fully understand the economic system without taking into account the behavior of children. Not only do they facilitate adult entrepreneurial activity, they are often entrepreneurs in their own right. Moreover, much can be learned about the Hausa economy in general by studying the way in which children learn the alternatives available to them and how to manipulate them.

From a behavioral point of view, the Hausa economic system can be conceptualized as a series of interdependent sexually segregated domains. The division of labor as well as certain aspects of production and consumption can best to understood in these terms. Although I have discussed this at greater length elsewhere, I will summarize the argument here and elaborate on the ways in which the stratification of economic behavior by age fits into this system (Schildkrout 1983). Differentation of economic behavior by sex and age is crucial to Hausa domestic economy and an understanding of this is requisite to understanding the economic system as a whole. In this paper, I will review this argument and describe the economic roles of children in some detail. I will do this by presenting and analyzing a series of case studies which demonstrate the roles of children in the economic system, the interdependence between children and adults, and the ways in which children learn accepted forms of economic behavior.[2] These case histories also demonstrate some of the possibilities for innovation which children are able to seize and manipulate. In these examples we are looking at children in two ways: as participants in adult economic (including entrepreneurial) activity and as entrepreneurs in their own right. The latter is perhaps the most surprising and interesting aspect of Hausa children's economic activity; and it is also the one which has been most ignored.[3]

This paper is based on research focusing on the interdependence of the economic roles of women and children conducted in Kano, a city in nothern Nigeria between 1976 and 1981. Before turning to the entrepreneurial activities of the children in the community, however, I shall present a summary of that research which will serve as a context within which to examine childhood entrepreneurship.

A Brief Sketch of Hausa Domestic Economy

The Hausa of northern Nigeria have for centuries been involved in a complex economy based on rural and urban trade. Although the majority of Hausa can be described as peasants, long distance and local trade, wage labor, and complex mercantile relationships have characterized Hausaland for several centuries (Hill 1969,1971,1972; Paden 1973; Smith 1952). Their assiduity as traders has made the Hausa language the lingua franca of much of West Africa and has given Hausa traders control of a significant portion of the indigenous West African economy (Adamu 1978; Cohen 1969; Hopkins 1973; Works 1972).

The research on which this paper is based was done in urban Kano. However, writings on rural Hausaland suggest that urban/rural differences are not significant with respect to the operation of the domestic economy and the involvement of most Hausa people in the cash economy (Hill 1969, 1971, 1972; Raynaut 1977). The two neighborhoods in which this study was conducted are long settled communities with stable populations. Most of the children in the study were born in Kano, as were many of their parents; indeed, many of the adults were born in the same neighborhoods where they later lived as adults. Perhaps the major difference between the Kano urban population and the population of rural Hausaland is in the occupations of the men. While most Hausa men, including farmers, are involved with the cash economy in one way or another, the men living in Kano are all wage workers or merchants -- either self-employed or clients of more prosperous merchants. The populations in the two neighborhoods we studied differed in just this respect: in one neighborhood most of the men were wage workers, in state government offices, in the Emir's administration (the traditional administration which now has taken over many local government functions), or in small private businesses;[4] in the other neighborhood most of the men were involved in local or long-distance trade and marketing, a few were building contractors, and a few owned transport vehicles. In either case, they worked away from their homes, for the most part, without the assistance of members of their households. In relation to their families, the obligations of the men were similar: they were expected to provide housing, food and clothing for their wives and children, and to offer support for their parents in old age. While Kano children generally do not participate in their fathers' occupational activities, boys often grow closer to their fathers in adolescence and in some cases they become apprentices to them. This is obviously more common in families where the men are self-employed merchants. Western education, on the other hand, is increasing the occupational options for young Hausa men and may mean that in the future fewer Hausa men pursue the same occupations as their fathers.

I have argued elsewhere that it is the particular cultural definition given to Hausa married women's roles which shapes the lives of Hausa children (Schildkrout 1978, 1979, 1981). Hausa girls marry at or before puberty, traditionally by twelve years of age. Although the increase in western education is delaying marriage for many, most girls are still married around puberty.[5]

As soon as they are married, all Hausa girls - considered adults once married regardless of their age - enter purdah, or seclusion (see Smith 1954). Seclusion is interpreted by the Hausa much more literally and strictly than in many other parts of the Islamic world, where women can often move about outside their own homes as long as they are veiled.

The veil is less important in northern Nigeria then in North Africa; instead the walls of the compound or homestead are used as a barrier between the domestic world of women and the public world of men. Prepubescent children, however, are not restricted by gender, and they are able to move freely between these two domains. Because they can act as intermediaries between the domestic domain, controlled by women, and the public "outside" world dominated by men, children have a crucial place as intermediaries in Hausa society. As we will see below, children physically carry out most of the transactions which link the marketplace and the home.

The interpretation of the Koran ascribed to in Kano stipulates that Hausa married women only leave their homes to attend ceremonies, such as marriages and naming ceremonies, to visit relatives, and to obtain medical care. They sometimes go to market at night, but only with their husbands' permission and always accompanied by an escort, who more often than not is a child. The degree to which seclusion is enforced varies somewhat from one household to another, but in the great majority of cases, married Hausa women do not go out of their homes during the day to attend to their domestic chores. They rely on children, their husbands, and sometimes on clients or hired help, for all communication with the world outside their homes including shopping, selling (see below) and exchanging information.

While women are responsible for preparing food for their familes to eat, their husbands are responsible for providing the raw materials for its preparation. A few husbands bring home all of the family's food supplies: thirty or fifty pound sacs of guinea corn and rice - which last from two to six weeks depending on the size of the family, and daily rations of meat and vegetables. Most men, however, buy staples such as rice and guinea corn by the sac and provide daily cash allowances for the purchase of meat, condiments, and other perishables. Although most men expect their wives to cook the evening meal themselves, virtually no men stipulate how women should provide the afternoon meal for themselves and their children. The money men provide can therefore to used either to purchase cooking ingredients or to purchase cooked food. Regardless of how she does it, a woman's obligation is to turn raw materials or cash, usually provided by her husband, into daily meals for the family.

The above description of the division of labor is obviously a somewhat "idealized" version of the Hausa domestic economy which describes sex and marital roles very much from the male point of view.[6] In reality, the domestic economy is much more complicated. For one thing, in very poor families women generally contribute directly to subsistence. For another thing, Hausa women can and do have income-producing occupations from within the confines of purdah. It is through their control of domestic labor - their own and that of children - that women are able to transform their unpaid domestic labor into entrepreneurial activity. They also control the relationship between the household fund, which comes from their husbands, and their own earnings. These funds are very distinct, and their distinctness generates a dichotomy between what I have referred to as male and female spheres of exchange. In managing the complex relationship between the two funds, women are able to control debt and credit relationships between them. Women occasionally borrow from household money or their own investments, or lend the household money or food from their businesses. Thus while men provide the means of subsistence in most families, women control the economic activity that takes place within the household. This gives them a great deal of leverage, for it enables them to utilize the resources provided by men as a source of capital for further investment.

The notion of male and female economic domains only makes sense when one appreciates the way in which women actually control production at the domestic level, and the way in which they transform the cash earnings of men into savings and investments for themselves. Rather than simply cooking food for consumption, women - except in the poorest families where they are providing bare subsistence - are in fact inflating the price of food by charging for their labor in cooking it. The income thus generated is then invested in goods, in the form of dowries, that circulate almost exclusively among women.

Women are able to transfer wealth from a male to a female domain by taking their daily obligatory activity - providing cooked food for their families -

and seeing that this is not simply the product of their unpaid labor. In both rural and urban Hausaland (Raynaut 1977), very few women, including married women with children, actually cook three meals a day, although the dietary pattern requires this. Most women take the money their husbands give them for food and buy cooked food from other women, and most women also cook food for sale to other women. Some women buy food from themselves (a practice also noted by Hill 1972:25).

When women sell cooked food - as opposed to simply consuming the food that they cook - the income generated is their own to keep. Cooking food for sale is, not surprisingly, the most common occupation among Hausa women. The food is either sold to children who are sent with bowls and money to the producer's house, or it is sold for women by children who set up stalls outside their houses or move about in the street with bowls of food on trays on their heads. While cooked food is purchased with the money men provide for household consumption, the seller places the income in her personal account[7] rather than in the household fund. Since the majority of Hausa women do this at one time or another, this is the means by which funds which men allocate for consumption are transferred to what I have called a female sphere of exchange. Many women who start their businesses in this way go on to trade in other commodities besides cooked food; cloth, or raw food stuffs, for example, are profitable when a woman has built up some working capital and when labor is in short supply, as for example, when an older or childless[8] woman has no available assistance from children.

While women spend some of their income for supplementary support - on food and clothing - for themselves and their children, most of it is invested in gifts for other women and in their daughters' dowries. These dowries traditionally consist of large numbers of enamel bowls and pots, only a few of which are ever used. Nowadays glassware has become a significant part of the dowry, and electrical appliances are found in the more westernized households. These dowries represent a form of economic security for women since they remain their personal property even in the event of marital dissolution; and at any time they can be sold for cash. They are very important status symbols for women; when a marriage takes place friends and neighbors visit and admire the new bride's kayan daki. So important are these items that women will borrow them in order to impress their peers (Bashir 1972). There is, however, very little evidence to suggest that the amount spent on dowry has any effect on a girl's ability to contract a more advantageous marriage. Men profess to be uninterested in the subject, and they get no direct benefit from it. In the context of our analysis of the sexual dichotomy of economic domains, this is not very surprising: a woman's kayan daki is an indication to other women of her wealth, her industriousness, and her ability to raise capital at any time through the sale of these goods. It is a measure of a woman's potential independence since she maintains control over these assets throughout her lifetime.

The Role of Children

Women are able to have income-producing occupations and meet their domestic marital obligations because, within the limits of purdah, they can control their own labor and, at least in part, that of their children. All over West Africa, as in many other parts of the world, women rely on children in carrying out their economic activities. In Hausaland, however, because of the strict practice of purdah, the dependence of women on children is particularly acute. From about the age of four, and sometimes even earlier, children are expected to particpate in many adult activities. They are sent on errands as soon as they can understand the tasks assigned.[9] Children help their mothers and other women who live in their houses with domestic tasks such as cooking, minding babies, taking out trash, cleaning the open drains which wind their way in and out of old Kano houses, and washing clothes and dishes. They also escort women on the occasions when they do go outside to visit friends or go for medical treatment. They take messages from one house to the next; they go to market and to neighboring houses to make purchases for their mothers, their caretakers, or for other adults or older children. Children also sell the items - food, raw ingredients, or handiwork (mats, embroidery, knitting, machine sewn cloths, for example) which women produce.

Children have the obligation to perform these services for their mothers, caretakers, or other adults to whom they are related, through kinship or even just through family friendship or neighborhood ties. There is a clear hierarchy of command in which an older person can order a younger person to do something. Children almost never refuse to obey an order given by an older person, although there are ways in which they can avoid compliance. For example, they sometimes will claim that they have been sent on another errand by someone else; occasionally they will simply absent themselves and accept a reprimand or punishment; often they will delegate the job to a younger child.

Children are involved in the cash economy from a very early age since women depend upon them for carrying out most of their cash transactions. Money is also used as a reward for children's services, and children have considerable discretion in spending their own money. They also are highly motivated to obtain and save money since, unless their families are wealthy, much of the burden of saving for their marriage expenses falls on the children themselves.

Children receive several different kinds of gifts for performing the tasks adults assign to them. The more distinct the relationship between the person who sends a child on an errand and the child, the more likely is the child to receive some form of remuneration. Mothers, fathers or other primary caretakers do not usually pay a child for services, but others are expected to offer some form of reward. When a child completes an errand, the person who requested it usually gives the child a <u>lada</u>, a gift of cash or food.[10]

In addition to these forms of income, children also earn income through entrepreneurial activities of their own. They trade, cook food for sale, work for a specified sum (piece work) or commission, and even rent their own property - e.g., their bicycles or toys. Because children have discretionary spending money, some children, as well as some adults, orient their economic activities towards this market. In the samples below, we have included several instances of children cooking food for sale to other children. Since the units of money children spend are often very small,[11] they can only buy food from those people who sell in very tiny quantities. One of the most common activities of nine and ten year old girls, for

202

example, is cooking pancakes for sale to children. In their fantasy play still younger girls experiment with this form of enterprise by making mud pies to "sell" to other children (see case 1 below).

Hausa children often become involved in credit and debt relationships with other children as well as with adults. The younger the child, the more he or she is likely to spend money on immediate satisfactions: small children buy candy, small quantities of food, chewing gum, small toys such as balloons (even damaged balloons, for a reduced price) or playing cards; older children, particularly girls who are attempting to assemble their dowries, often give their earnings to an older woman to save for the purchase of kayan daki, the collection of enamel bowls Hausa girls traditionally amass for their marriages.

The most obvious form of children's economic activity performed outside the house is street trading, or talla. Girls are more likely than boys to be found doing talla, and children from some neighborhoods do it more frequently than those from others. In our study, we noted considerable differences between the two neighborhoods in this respect: in one most of the girls were engaged in street trading, while in the other, they were attending primary school. A growing antithesis exists in the minds of many Kano people between hawking and school, and many parents have strong preferential views about their childrens' activities one way or the other.

Most of the children's trading is done for a parent or caretaker. The child turns over the profit to the parent or caretaker who then uses it for immediate household expenses, if the family is very poor, or saves it for the child's marriage expenses. Whether the income from talla is for subsistence or for savings depends to a large extent on the wealth of the husband. Nevertheless, in general women whose children engage in hawking are found to have higher incomes than the women whose children do not trade (Schildkrout 1979, 1981). Street hawking is not, among the Hausa, necessarily associated with poverty. If one were to envisage a hierarchy of children's careers, based upon the economic status of their parents, begging would be at the bottom and street hawking would be found to occur primarily in "middle income" families, although exceptions to such a schema would no doubt abound.

Both boys and girls engage in street trading, although boys do it less frequently than girls. There are a number of reasons for this. First, more boys are enrolled in primary school and therefore have less time. Second, by the onset of puberty, the age at which talla is most often done, boys are beginning to break away from their mothers. Unlike girls who marry immediately after the onset of puberty, boys have a long period in their teens and twenties in which they are moving out of the domestic domain, out of their mothers' control, and into the working world of men. They spend this time either in apprenticeships or in school. Since most street trading is organized by women, boys are less likely to do it than are girls.

Some boys, however, do engage in talla. Many of these are living away from their own families and are trading on a commission basis in order to earn their own subsistence. Some of these boys are almajirai, students sent by their parents who live elsewhere to study the Koran in Kano with a particular teacher. Few boys who live with their own families hawk on a regular basis; those who do so do not usually attend western schools; in our study there was only one such family. The father was a driver, vehemently opposed to western education, who had three wives who were all in the business of selling cooked food. All of the boys looked forward to other types of apprenticeships.

Even if they trade less frequently than do girls, young boys are still economically active. They shop and do errands for their secluded female caretakers. They mind younger children, and they escort women when they go out. Boys' and girls' activities are not sexually differentiated until about the age of five or six, although sex differences become apparent in imitative play even earlier. Women feel free to call on both boys and girls to do household errands but the allocation of tasks to children gradually becomes sexually differentiated. Just when this occurs depends upon a number of factors including the number, sexes and ages of the children resident in a particular compound or household. For example, boys will not be expected to help in food preparation if girls are present, but if there are no girls in a household, a young boy will be given tasks related to food preparation.

There are four categories of boys who are economically active throughout childhood, beyond the routine household tasks mentioned above. None of these attend western schools and none live with their own families. There are the Koranic students, or *almajirai*, who are expected to support themselves by begging, doing odd jobs, or regularly working for their teacher or for a woman in his house. Many people give these boys leftover food, which constitutes a gift of alms (*sadaka*), and hire them to do odd chores. Similar to the *almajirai* are those boys who support themselves by joining a particular household and exchanging services for room and board. These boys also come from rural areas to study the Koran. Third, there are those boys who apprentice themselves to their fathers or to other men often learning a particular trade. Lastly, there are the professional beggars. These are the most deprived children; quite a few of them are physically handicapped and many are orphans. They generally live with or work for men who are professional organizers of beggars. The government occasionally attempts to end this type of activity and in 1981 many of the Kano child beggars had been placed in government camps where they were supposedly being given vocational training.

All of these forms of behavior can be seen in case studies of Kano children, examples of which have been selected from interviews conducted with a sample of one hundred and ten children between the ages of five and fourteen. Each child was interviewed once or twice a day for a week. The children were asked to recount all of their activities; when they described economic transactions they were asked more detailed questions: who had sent them on the errand?; what was the amount of the transaction?; what was done with the money?; how much was the profit?; and so on. These interviews are supplemented by biographical data on the children, census data on their households, biographical and occupational data on their caretakers, and observations of the children's behavior.

The Case Studies

1: Jummai

Jummai is a seven year old girl whose parents live in Jos, over two hundred miles from Kano. At the time of the study she had been living for several years with her widowed grandmother. The family is one of butchers, or <u>mahauta</u>, an endogamous occupational group in Hausa society. Jummai's grandmother sells cooked meat, is not in <u>purdah</u>, and has a relatively high income compared to other women in her neighborhood; she has paid for her own pilgrimage to Mecca. Jummai attends Koranic school, but does not go to primary school. In this respect she is similar to all but one of the girls studied in her neighborhood. She related the following account of a day's activities:

"I went to buy chewing gum with the money, but there wasn't any in the first shop so I went to another place and bought "bazooka" for 2 k. (kobo). Then I did <u>talla</u> of <u>sire</u> (skewered meat). I went with a friend of mine. The <u>tsire</u> owner gave me meat to sell for two Niara [N.]. He also gave me one skewer of meat to eat. First I went to Hajia Kalwa's house and people there bought some; Hajia bought some for her guests. She needed change for 10k., but we couldn't find it so I went on my way and sold more and later went back with her change. When I finished I took the <u>tsire</u> money and gave it to the meat seller and he gave me my <u>lada</u> of 20 k. I bought chewing gum again and then I sat down and drank porridge. Then I asked my grandmother for money to buy rice. She gave me 5 k. I came here and bought the rice from Hassana. I was also given a piece of chicken so I added it to my rice and ate them all. Then I taped this interview."

She later continued her account of the same day:

"While I was at Hassana's house for the interview, Hassana called her daughter, Hajia, but she refused to come because she was playing. Her sister, Shamau, was making <u>kosai</u>, bean cakes, with sand. She was just playing. I said I would buy two n. of <u>kosai</u> from her and I gave her two pieces of white paper pretending to give her two n. I was then given a very little <u>kosai</u> so I said that I would not buy it at that price; I said it was too expensive. So she took it back and I asked for my money back. When she finished she put it down and went to get some water. I took her <u>kosai</u> away and when she came back I told her that we also had sand and would make our own <u>kosai</u>. She sat down and asked where hers was. She was about to cry so I gave her back her property.

"When I want home my grandmother was about to go out to do _talla_. I asked her to give me one piece of liver, but she said she would not because one piece cost 20 k. But she said there was another piece in the meat she was going to sell and she said I could have that piece. I asked her to give me some _gurasa_ (fried wheat cakes) and I ate the two together..."

2: A'i

A'i's mother is a divorced woman with two daughters. She and A'i live with a family to whom she is distantly related through one of the wives. The other daughter lives with another relative. A'i's mother is not in seclusion and she usually goes to the market and buys various food items to sell. A'i does not go to school, and her mother attempts to engage her in hawking. A'i's account nicely illustrates how children learn entrepreneurial skills; it therefore is excerpted here for a period of one week.

January 25:

"Late in the morning I got 50 k. from my mother and went to the market to buy garden eggs (small aubergines which people eat raw as snacks). I got many but I did not count them. When I came home I went to Mamudu's house where I sold them for 1 k. each. From there I went to other houses and I did not come back until they were all sold, for 70 k. I made 20 k. profit, but I was tired. I do not like doing _talla_."

January 27:

"I went to the market and came back with 28 garden eggs for 50 k. I sold each of them for 2 k. I went to do _talla_ at 11:15; at 12:45 I had sold only 30 k. worth. After I ate lunch I went back. This time I did 22k. and had two garden eggs left so I ate them and came home. The total I made was 52 k. - a profit of 2 k."

January 28:

"When I went to the market there were no garden eggs so I bought lemons, fifty-two for 60 k. The lemons were all green so when I went to sell them people refused to buy. Out of 60 k. I only sold 11 k.

worth. In the evening I was tired and hungry from going from one place to another. I had been in four neighborhoods. So when I returned I took the lemons to Hansetu's room (an elderly woman in whose household she and her mother live) and left them there. I saw Yawa (another resident) sweeping her room and so I helped her. While sweeping, the 11 k. fell down and I began to search for them but I couldn't find them. I told Yawa that it was all her bad luck that caused this, and people began to laugh at me. At night my mother came back and asked me for the money I had made. I told her that I had already put it in the tin where we keep our money."

January 29:

"Early in the morning I went to get money for garden eggs. My mother asked me to bring 60 k. and she said she would give me a 50 k. note rather than coins. There was nothing I could say because I knew I didn't have a single kobo. I began to look around and I said I couldn't find the money. Then I told my mother that the money was with her. My mother could not remember if this was true or not so she gave me 60 k. and I then went to the market.

"From the market I went to do talla. After I sold all of it for 61 k. the profit was only 1 k. When I returned I saw my mother and when she asked for the money I had made I said I had sold 61 k. worth. My mother said that she had given me 60 k. which meant that the profit was only 1 k. I said no, that in fact when she had given me 60 k. I had given Hansetu 10 k. to keep for me and I had bought garden eggs for only 50 k. which meant I made 11 k. profit. My mother believed me so she agreed and took the money (61 k.)."

February 1:

"My mother and I went to market and my mother bought the usual things: lamsir (a kind of leaf eaten raw with spices), kuli-kuli (a sweet made of gound nuts, sugar and pepper), and garden eggs. My mother decided to sell the garden eggs herself since I was not making any profit. The only thing I bought was cabbage for 5 k. and tomatoes for 5 k.

"At noon I went outside our house and sold the cabbage and the tomatoes. Children came to buy it.

By the time I came home and washed the bowls I had made 15 k. profit.

"In the evening I asked my mother for 5 k. because I wanted to make wainar kwai (fried flour and eggs). I went to the store and bought flour for 2 k.; I bought palm oil for 3 k. from Dodo's house. I then mixed the flour with water and salt and collected all the things I needed and went outside to sell it. I stayed out until around 6:30 pm and when I had sold all of it I went home. This time I sold 16 k. worth - 11 k. profit."

February 2:

"Late in the morning I went to the market with my mother and bought two eggs for 15 k., 7 k of cabbage, 5 k. of tomatoes, and 2 k. of onions. When we came home I washed and cut up these ingredients. Then I went out to sell the salad and I made 25 k. - 11 k. profit. When I came home I ate lunch and then I sent Atiku (a seven year old boy who lived in the same compound) to buy flour for me for 3 k. while I washed the bowls and then went out again to sell the fried eggs. When Atiku returned, I mixed the flour and eggs and began to fry it in groundnut oil. I stayed up late at night to sell all of it, and made 26 1/2 k. profit."

Case 3: Lami

Another example of children's involvement in trade comes from the diary of Lami, a fourteen year old girl who both attended primary school and actively helped her mother shop, cook, and sell food. Unlike Jummai and A'i, Lami's mother is a married woman in seclusion. On the morning of June 14 Lami related the following:

"When I woke up, I performed ablution and prayed. After bathing I went and helped my mother with work, that is, with cooking food for sale. I bought the ingredients in Sabon Gari market. My mother gave me the money to buy peppers, 20 k., ataruga (a leaf vegetable), 20 k., onions, 20 k., tomatoes, 20 k., and n5.80 of yams and n5.00 of rice. When I came back home I washed the rice. After it was cooked the students came to buy it and I helped my mother serve it. When we finished I washed the bowls and did my homework. I finished it in time for school."

June 22:

"When the bell rang at school I left for home. I found that my mother was asleep although she had put the meat on the fire, but the fire had gone out. I fixed the fire and put oil and salt on the meat. Later I cleaned the pot and when Maiwada (her eight year old brother) came back from school I gave him raw vegetables to take to the grinder.

"When he was gone my younger sister, Sabuwa, came back from market. I took the beans and washed them and sat down. I told Sabuwa to put the beans on the fire while I rested. She refused but she didn't tell me. At night, when I asked her if she had put in salt and onions she said no. I was very worried and I slapped her. I got up and put in on the fire and performed my prayers.

"Then a woman who sells rice to my mother came. She sold us a sack of rice for n32, whereas the price had been decreased to n28. That's why my mother sent for her. The woman said that she could not sell it for n28; we would have to add something. I said we could only add 50 k. Sabuwa then told me shut up since the matter did not concern me, but I said that since it concerned money it did concern me. Since the woman refused to accept 50 k., my mother raised the offer to n1.00. Then the woman went to inform the actual owner of the rice and later she came back and told us that he had agreed. So my mother gave her part of the money and told her to come back to collect the rest in two days."

4: Sabo

Sabo is a nine year old boy whose parents live in a village outside Kano. He has been sent to Kano to study the Koran with a Mallam, and he has attached himself to one of the most affluent houses in the neighborhood of this teacher. Sabo sleeps in an annex to the house with Idi, the washman. This is Sabo's account for March 14, 1977.

"When I woke up I prayed and Idi came and told me that the wives of Alhaji (the houseowner and household head) were looking for me. When I went to the house I was sent to take food to Hajia Yarinya's (one of the wives) parents in another neighborhood. When I returned I took my own share of food and ate it. When I finished eating I gave the remaining food to the almajirai and told one of them to return the bowl to the house when he finished.

"When I went back inside I was sent by Hajia Yarinya to buy pepper for 40 k., attaruga for 5 k., onions for 3 k., and okra for 40 k. When I went to buy the okra the seller said she only had dried ones. I said I would buy it and the woman said that if she sold it to me for 40 k. the women in the house shouldn't complain because it is very expensive now. When I bought it to Hajia Yarinya she said she would not buy it for 40 k. and she sent me back to the woman. The okra seller was angry but she gave me the money and I returned it to Hajia Yarinya. She sent me to another place where they sell it but I couldn't find any there. Then she sent me to the market to buy karkashi (a plant whose leaves are used in soup) for 50 k. When I brought it back she began to complain again because there were too many seeds inside; she sent me to another place to buy it and I had to return the first bunch.

"When I returned she told me to go and do the washing. After the first interview (to narrate this account) Hajia Rukaya (another wife in the house) sent me to buy karkashi for 10 k. from Nayawale's shop. When I brought it to her she complained that it wasn't good so I had to return it and get the money back. When I returned it, the shopkeeper said that the reason he did not like to sell things to the wives of Alhaji was that they always complained.

"Then Hajia Yarinya called me and sent me to buy 5 k. of kunu (a sweet drink made from grain); the others also asked for some - 4 k. for Hajia Rukaya, 3 k. for Hajia Nasara. On my way back from buying kunu a man sent me to call an almajiri for him and he gave me 3 k. for this and I thanked him. Then I carried the kunu home and Hajia Yarinya sent me to look for Jumma (her younger sister).

"In the evening I carried food to Hajia Yarinya's parents in Madatai ward and also to Isuhu's house and to Alhaji Basiru's house (the father and son of the household head). When I took the food to Hajia Yarinya's parents I told them that Hajia greeted them.

"When I returned I ate and took the food to the watchman. Then the watchman sent me to buy bean cakes for 3 k.

"Then I went and watched TV. Later I went out to Idi and I met Hadi, Alhaji's son, who was teaching Idi how to read. Idi said I should go home because a policeman had been killed in a nearby ward and they were catching anyone they saw on the street. But then one of the children said this was not true. Then I went to Alhaji's house and said goodnight to the wives and went home to sleep."

5: Saraki

Nine year old Saraki lives with his grandparents. His grandmother is in <u>purdah</u>. His parents live in a nearby ward. He attends both primary school and Islamic school.

"When I woke up (March 7, 1977) I performed ablution, prayed, put on my uniform and went to school. We worked on English, math, Hausa and Arabic. During break I came home and got 10 k. from my grandmother and bought food with it. Back at school we did some work and came out for short break. I gave my friend Isuhu one k. to go and ride a bicycle, and I bought 1 k. of groundnuts with my other kobo.

"At 1:00 p.m. when school was over I came home, changed my clothes and ate lunch.

"At 2:30 I came for an interview with you and when I left here I bought ingredients for my grandmother from Dan Sarki's house: 10 k. green leaves, 5 k. tomatoes, and 3 k. onions. When I returned I went to Garba's house, my grandfather's son, and took bowls there. I was sent by Yelwa, my grandmother's co-wife. At night when I went home I bought bean cakes from a woman outside for 5 k. Then a relative of a woman in my house gave me 10 k. so I bought a wheat cake with 5 k. and saved 5 k. Later I played with the boys in the next house; we played hide and seek, and then we watched T.V. in my uncle's house. Then I went home to sleep."

<u>Analysis</u>

In analyzing the five case studies presented, there are three issues which bear comment: the variables which affect all children's lives and which account for the differences in the expectations placed upon particular children; the nature of the symbiosis between women's and children's economic roles; and the degree to which children have autonomy in implementing their assigned tasks. The first of these questions will be discussed in this section, and the others will be addressed in the concluding section of this paper.

The general expectation that chldren assist in household chores and facilitate secluded women's economic activities has been discussed above. However, as these five examples illustrate, there is considerable variation in the daily routines of different children. Some children do a great deal of housework; others spend most of their time street trading; still others have considerable time for school and play. There is no doubt a relationship between the extent of variability in children's roles in any society and the complexity of social structure. Parental occupations, education, as well as the wealth, sex, age, residence, education and birth order of the child all enter into defining the status of the child. This may seem obvious, but much of the ethnographic and economic literaure on children has greatly oversimplified the depiction of children's lives. It is frequently assumed that children's roles are solely determined by age and sex and are otherwise homogeneous within the same society.[12] The variables which these five examples illustrate are sex, age, parental marital status, family economic status, fostered versus non-fostered children, birth order, mother's occupation, number of children in the household and school attendance. In addition, there are other underlying variables which are less easily documented than the above: parental "lineage" status in terms of traditional categories of social ranking, paternal education, and occupation, and others.

The cases above include three girls and two boys. The most obvious difference between them is the girls' involvement with cooking. Neither Sabo nor Saraki, the two boys, do any cooking. They are quite typical in this respect, although as Jummai's account showed, the seller of barbecued meat was a man. As in other parts of the world, this is the main exception to the general rule that men do not cook. Boys are only asked to help in food preparation if there are no girls available. Among the Hausa, roles first become differentiated on the basis of sex with reference to cooking. In Jummai's account we can see how, in play, very young girls imitate adult female roles, when five year old Shamau is busy making and selling mud pies and Jummai haggles with her over the price. Both boys and girls are involved in shopping for cooking ingredients and cooked food; through this activity they acquire knowledge of the cash value of various commodities, as well as the skills necessary to carry out market transactions. These skills include evaluating the quality and quantity of merchandise, bargaining, making change, and giving and receiving credit. Children also establish relationships with particular merchants and customers and learn how to build up a clientele.

In these examples only the girls did any street and trading, as explained earlier, girls trade more frequently than boys. This is partly related to the higher frequency of school attendance among boys. While boys sometimes sell cooked food, when they do the food is already divided into individual portions; a boy which he is to sell for a pre-established price, will be given a headtray full of bowls of food whereas a girl will be given a large pot of food which she will divide as she sells it in variable quantities. In other words, except for barbecued meat, boys are not expected to handle food except to eat it. They also are given less responsibility in handling economic transactions.

In these particular examples the only child involved in the care of a younger child was Sabo, a boy, who was required to care for a ten month old baby. In general, however, both boys and girls care for younger children, although girls do so with more frequency. They spend a lot of time learning how to carry babies on their backs, both through imitative play and real practice. Sabo had somewhat less discretion in the roles he performed than other boys because he was in the position of a "houseboy."

Children are given as much responsibility as they can handle from a very young age within the sexually defined paramters mentioned above. Well before they understand the notion of making change, they may be given a coin, a bowl, and a shopping order in the vicinity of their own house. Cooking and child care also are delegated to young children, with their responsibilities increasing as soon as their mothers or caretakers see that they can handle it. Since girls get married as early as eleven years of age (and this is later than it used to be in some areas of rural Hausaland), by that time they are expected to be able to assume virtually all adult responsibilities. Boys are given more time to grow up, but they too are given household responsibilities before puberty. Fourteen year old Lami, the oldest child in these examples, takes as much responsibility for the purchase, preparation and sale of food as does her mother.

In Lami's case we can also see the significance of a child's relative age and birth order. Lami assumed authority over her younger brothers and sisters and acted towards them in much the same way as adult Hausa women act towards children, even threatening them with physical punishment. Lami was the oldest child in her family and was old enough for marriage at the time of the study (and in fact was married the next year). Her account shows how she has learned how to control the labor of those younger than herself, and how she takes a direct role in calculating the investments and profits of her mother's business. A'i also delegated a task to Atiku, a younger boy in her compound. Whereas Hausa men generally have formal authority over women, among children age rather than sex determines dominance.

In the examples above the only child whose parents were divorced was A'i, who lived with her mother. The general rule in Hausa society is that children stay with the father when the parents are divorced, but men sometimes allow their wives to keep one daughter with them as was the case here. Divorced women who do not remarry must become self-supporting or must depend upon other relatives. Their daughters, like A'i, are relied upon for assistance even though the mothers, being unmarried, are not in seclusion. In A'i's case, although her mother needed her help, A'i was so bad at trading that the mother finally had to acknowledge that the attempts to involve her in trade were only an educational experience. A'i was adamantly unsuccesful and freely admitted that she hated doing <u>talla</u>. However, A'i's story is interesting because it shows how a child who was unsuccessful at one task began to learn the skills that enabled her to setup her own tiny profitable business. In the week in late January described here, A'i's fortunes changed significantly. In March, she was still cooking food for sale to children. Because she was willing to sell in very tiny quantities and because children frequently have small sums of money, her business contined to thrive. She began to save her profit in an empty milk tin and finally, by the end of March, had made enough to buy herself a new pair of shoes. This account shows the detail in which children learn to calculate expenditures and income. It also shows how A'i manipulated her mother, but eventually got her mother's assistance.

Whereas A'i was living with her mother, most children of divorce remain in their father's house but live as foster children under the care of another of their father's wives. They are frequently given more than an equal share of the housework. Hausa folktales abound with such stories and women frequently mention this as one of the reasons they hesitate to get divorced.

Divorce of parents is not the only reason children are fostered. As in many other parts of West Africa (see Goody 1978; Schildkrout 1973), Hausa children are frequently sent to live with relatives even when the parents' marriage is intact. Jummai, Saraki, and Sabo all were foster children whose parents were still married. The first two were living with grandparents and the last with an unrelated family. Children are often sent to live with their grandmothers when the parents agree that the grandmother needs help in her economic activity. Saraki's grandmother was an active koko (porridge) maker, while Jummai's grandmother sold meat. Parents and siblings have an acknowledged right to request to foster children of their offspring and siblings, and the request is rarely refused.

Whether or not foster children do more work than non-fostered children is an important question which cannot be answered from the case studies presented above. Some have argued that fostering is a major factor in defining the roles of West African children; the Hausa deny this but the evidence has not yet been adequately considered.[13] Sabo, who had no kinship connection to the people in those house he lived, was clearly regarded as a servant. Were we to present accounts of the activities of other children in that same house, it would be evident that they did very little work. But this house is one of the wealthiest in the sample; children in less affluent households, where there are no houseboys or servants, clearly do more work than children in wealthy households. In the case of Jummai, her position was effected by the fact that her caretaker had no other children on whom to rely; but since this is frequently a reason that children are fostered, these variables are not independent.

Only two of the children in these examples attended western school: Lami and Saraki. The effects of school attendance on children's roles may not be as evident from these accounts as it is in reality. Street trading definitely diminishes with school attendance for girls; in fact many people see these as alternative careers for children. While school children still help with housework and shop for ingredients, on the whole they seem to be less active economically than children who do not attend school. The change in children's roles consequent to school enrollment definitely does affect women, however.

In comparing the occupations and incomes of women whose children were in and out of school, it became very apparent that these women who were able to "exploit" the services of children had more labor intensive businesses. Their incomes were significantly higher than those of women whose children were in school (Schildkrout 1979, 1981) and who generally did not trade. While these women also had income producing occupations, such as sewing, embroidering, or hair plaiting, their earnings were much less than those of women who, relying on the assistance of children, cooked food for sale or utilized children to trade other commodities. Given the low level of capitalization and the paucity of investment options open to women, labor intensive businesses were the most profitable ones.

Conclusion

Children gain great understanding of the operation of the Hausa domestic economy through their interaction with women. At a very early age they learn the principles of investment and profit making; they learn about credit and debt, about savings and investments. However, they learn all of this in the context of women's activity. They learn very little about the Hausa economy from the male point of view, about the world of formal sector employment, for example. Most women know very little about their husbands' business lives, and almost none know their husbands' incomes. In contrast, boys have a long transition period before marriage in which they have to leave their mothers and learn many other skills. Although the skills they learn as children help them, they must acquire others; which skills they learn depends upon their occupational choices, but there are many more options for boys than for girls.

In childhood, many Hausa girls learn as much about the economic opportunities open to them, as females, as they will learn the rest of their lives. The skills they learn as children are immediately useful to them as adults, but when they enter purdah their opportunities almost always diminish. From that point on they become dependent upon their children and their husbands; they have to seek out opportunities for money-making activity from within the confines of purdah. Their capital is usually meager and many husbands are only tolerant, not supportive, of their wives' economic activities. In fact, it is often the case that the weathier the husband, the less supportive he is of his wives' independent economic activities.

Much of the work that children do under women's supervision is, in fact, for themselves. This is often true when the children seem to be working for the women. Since most of the money girls make from street trading is saved for their marriage expenses, they regard this work as an investment in their own futures, capitalized by their mothers. Immediately after marriage most women engage in very little economic activity for a number of years, while they are raising young children. When they are older they begin to work again, this time to save for the marriage expenses of their children.

Since both men and women are restricted by the institution of purdah, Hausa children have more freedom than both. Just as women cannot physically move about outside of their own houses, men cannot freely enter any houses but their own. Children, however, are able to move between the "private" world of women and the "public" world of men. They carry out the transactions that link these two domains. In doing this, Hausa children can and do become entrepreneurs in their own right. Their clients are men, women and children, and they can deal directly with all of them.

At this point one must ask the inevitable question about what this all adds up to. Obviously, Hausa children learn a lot about economic transactions very early; they learn many skills that will be useful to them as adults. By western standards they are indeed precocious. However, through their activity they also support the rigid division between male and female economic sectors; without children women could not remain in purdah. They could not carry out their expected roles as wives and housekeepers, not to speak of their income earning activities. There is a kind of paradox in this, because it is this very system, which children's economic activity perpetuates, which limits the application that female children, at least, can make of their skills once they grow up.

While there are indeed opportunities for both men and women in Hausa society - and the fame of Hausa men as traders throughout West Africa is well known (Adamu 1978; Cohen 1969; Hopkins 1973) - the system of purdah confines women to exercising their business skills in a very limited number of ways. It is not surprising, then, that the only Hausa women who are able to become "wealthy" relative to their peers are those who are not in purdah, because they are divorced or widowed, or those married women who have been very significantly helped by their husbands, fathers or brothers (see Schildkrout 1985). Children's economic activities enable the majority of women to earn money to help pay for their children's marriage expenses or to help make ends meet. The industrious child is also able to amass a sizable dowry which can be used as an investment in further income-earning activities, or as a kind of insurance in the event that his or her marriage is dissolved. Aside from the money invested in dowries, however, children earn only enough money to buy such things as a new pair of shoes or an item of clothing. After all, when most of a child's clients are other children, the amounts of capital and profit are indeed miniscule. When we are dealing with money, it is still more than the principle than counts.

NOTES

(1) This paper is based on research conducted in Kano between 1976 and 1978, and a revisit in 1981. The project has been supported by the American Museum of Natural History, The National Science Foundation (grant no. BNS 76-11174 AND BNS 8014089), the Wenner-Gren Foundation, the Ford Foundation and the Social Science Research Council. I am grateful to Carol Gelber for assisting in the final phase of the fieldwork and for continuing help with the analysis.

(2) Children are excellent informants; through their accounts of their activities and through daily observations of their behavior, social patterns become very obvious. In their play children clearly express the "rules" - that is, the social expectations - by which they and others are expected to operate; they are very conscious of mastering rules and learning the sanctions which enforce them.

(3) This is due primarily to the tendency to view childhood as a rehearsal for adult life, and to view children as passive actors in a social system defined by adults. Recent anthropological and developmental studies of children are beginning to alter this view; to my knowledge there are no published studies of children as entrepreneurs; although there are many of children as workers.

(4) None of them, however, worked in factories or large expatriate-owned firms.

(5) In studying a group of children over a five year period, we found that while girls who attended school were still in school and not married by age fourteen or fifteen, those who never attended school (other than Koranic school) were married by age twelve.

(6) Divorce is quite common and quite a number of women, those who do not remarry as well as elderly widows, are in fact often self-supporting.

(7) Few women have bank accounts but many invest their money in rotating credit clubs run by women. Other women simply keep cash, but keep their own money physically separate from the money given by the husband for household expenses.

(8) Women often exchange children in fostering relationships in Hausal society and elsewhere in West Africa. The need for child labor is one of the major motivations for these relationships. See Schildkrout 1973, Goody 1978.

(9) I have seen a two year old, for example, enter a neighbor's house with a coin and bowl and ask for rice, which the child then carried back to his mother.

(10) <u>Lada</u> differs from <u>kyauta</u>, a present, or <u>sadaka</u>, a gift of alms, both of which are also given to children, often in the form of cash. Another form of cash gift which children frequently receive is <u>tukwici</u>, a gratuity given to the bearer of a present or message by the recipient.

(11) A kobo or a half kabo (100 kobo = 1 Niara; 1 Niara = $1.50 in 1977).

(12) It is interesting to speculate on why it is that children's roles have become much more homogeneous in some societies than in others, particularly in those that have had formal education for a long time and have abolished child labor. This also has to do with a certain conception of the nature of childhood, as Aries (1962) and others have pointed out.

(13) Caroline Bledsoe is engaged in research in Sierra Leone on the relationship between child fosterage, child mortality, and fertility. Her project should provide some interesting data about a range of variables considered in relation to child fosterage. When my own data is fully analyzed it should also contribute to this discussion.

REFERENCES

ADAMU, M. 1978. *The Hausa Factor in West African History*. Ibadan: Oxford University Press.

BASHIR, M. K. 1972. *The Economic Activities of Secluded Married Women in Kurawa and Lallokin Lemu, Kano City*. B.Sc. Thesis, Ahmadu Bello University, Zaria.

COHEN, A. 1969. *Custom and Politics in Urban Africa*. London: Routledge and Kegan Paul.

GOODY, E. 1978. "Some Theoretical and Empirical Aspects of Parenthood in West Africa." In *Marriage, Fertility and Parenthood in West Africa*. C. Oppong, G. Adaba, M. Bekombo-Priso, J. Mogey, Eds. pp. 227-273. Canberra: The Australian National University.

HILL, P. 1969. *Hidden Trade in Hausaland*. Man 4(3): 392-409.

_____. 1971. "Two Types of West African House Trade." In *The Development of African Trade and Markets in West Africa*. C. Meillassoux, Ed. London: Oxford University Press.

_____. 1972. *Rural Hausa: A Village and a Setting*. Cambridge: Cambridge University Press.

HOPKINS, A. G. 1973. *An Economic History of West Africa*. London: Longman.

PADEN, J. 1973. *Religion and Political Culture in Kano*. Berkeley: University of California Press.

RAYNAUT, C. 1977. "Aspects socio-economiques de la preparation et de la circulation do la nourriture dans un village hausa (Niger)." *Cahiers d'Etudes Africaines*. 68 (XVII-4): 569-597.

RODGERS, G. and C. Standing. 1981. *Child Work, Poverty and Underdevelopment*. Geneva: International Labor Office.

SCHILDKROUT, E. 1973. "The Fostering of Children in Urban Ghana: Problems of Ethnographic Analysis is a Multi-Cultural Context." *Urban Anthropology*. 2(1): 48-73.

_____. 1978. "Age and Gender in Hausa Society: Socio-Economic Roles of Children in Urban Kano." In Sex and Age as Principles of Social Differentiation. J. S. LaFontaine, Ed. pp. 109-137. New York: Academic Press.

_____. 1979. "Women's Work and Children's Work: Variations among Moslems in Kano." In Social Anthropology of Work. S. Wallman, Ed. A.S.A. Monograph 19. pp. 69-85. London: Academic Press.

_____. 1981. "The Employment of Children in Kano." In Child Work, Poverty and Underdevelopment. G. Rodgers and G. Standing, Ed. pp. 81-112. Geneva: International Labour Office.

_____. 1983. "Dependence and Autonomy: The Economic Activities of Secluded Hausa Women in Kano, Nigeria." In Female and Male in West Africa. C. Oppong, Ed. pp. 107-127. London: George Allen and Unwin Ltd.

SMITH, M. 1954. Baba of Karo: A Woman of the Muslim Hausa. London: Faber and Faber.

SMITH, M. G. 1952. A Study of Hausa Domestic Economy in Northern Zaria. Africa 22: 333-347.

WARD, S., D. Wackman and E. Wartella. 1977. How Children Learn to Buy. Beverly Hills: Sage Publications.

WORKS, J. A. Jr. 1976. Pilgrims in a Strange Land: Hausa Communities in Chad. New York: Columbia University Press.

POLITICAL ENTREPRENEURS IN A WEST AFRICAN CITY[1]

Sandra T. Barnes

It is well known that in many new nations a relatively small, highly educated elite class controls national political institutions and, by virtue of that control, major economic resources.[2] Access to the state's political and economic institutions for the general public is, accordingly, relatively restricted.[3] This essay describes one of the few ways in which members of the general public have found access to the dominant institutions of the state. The places where they are particularly successful are large cities where major bureaucratic, industrial, and commercial establishments are located and where, as a result, elites and masses come together.

The movement of people to urban places in the new nations is one of this century's most profound, to say nothing of problematic, demographic shifts. In Africa, the least urbanized continent, only one percent of the people lived in cities at the turn of the century, whereas today the number has jumped to more than twenty-eight percent. Much of this growth has focused on primate cities where populations explode in just a few years time. The most dramatic examples are Kinshasa, capital of Zaire, which grew tenfold--from 208,000 to 2,049,000--in the 25-year period between 1950 and 1975, and metropolitan Lagos, where this study was conducted, which nearly trebled between 1963, when it was estimated to have 1.2 million, and 1977, when it reached 3.5 million, people (Abate 1978:27 and *Business Times* 11 Jan. 1977:1). Both places, it should be noted, are expected to exceed 9 million by the year 2000.

The problems that growth rates of this magnitude present are themselves monumental. Here I am particularly concerned with two of them. The first is that urban governments and other official institutions are gravely restricted in funds, personnel, and organizational elasticity to the extent that they are neither able to meet the needs of their mushrooming constituencies nor are they able to communicate effectively with them. The second is that urban resources, mainly government controlled, are in exceedingly short supply. These include education (or in the Nigerian case, quality education), training, and jobs; housing, social services, and physical amenities such as water and electricity; and even information and expertise concerning public processes. These problems indicate that there are significant structural gaps in urban social systems. Certainly this is confirmed by the feelings of estrangement which are felt by many city dwellers with respect to their local bureaucracies (Peil 1976:144-7).

In response to these problems a body of people, whom I call political entrepreneurs, informally bridge the structural gaps which exist between the public and the governing elite and in the process fill some of the vacuum which formal institutions of the state are unable to fill. They do so by cultivating the role of patron and middleman to fellow urbanites who then become their clients.

In the following pages I describe the services for clients which are performed by political entrepreneurs and then I analyze the skills they develop in performing them. The point I wish to stress in this essay is that successful political entrepreneurs are able to transform social relationships of patronage and dependency into political power and, in some cases, relative economic wealth. As Schumpeter suggests (1949:74), their entrepreneurship is demonstrated in their ability to make new combinations. In the process two sets of needs are satisfied: the survival needs of the new urban dwellers and the political goals of established urbanites who aspire to positions of influence in their society's dominant institutions. Before turning to the actual examination of political entrepreneurship, it is necessary to summarize briefly the setting in which it occurs and the circumstances out of which it arises.

Background

The urban area where this study is situated is metropolitan Lagos. Lagos is both a federal and a state capital, and thus it houses a large bureaucratic establishment. It enjoys the heaviest concentrations of industrial and manufacturing establishments, and it also serves as the commercial nexus of the nation, with headquarters of banks and most foreign and indigenous business establishments, and the only stock exchange. Except for oil, the bulk of Nigeria's import and export trade passes through Lagos' ports. Consequently the metropolis is the gathering point for the country's most talented people--indeed it has the most highly educated population of any Nigerian city-- and for its largest assemblage of wage-earning, working-class people.

At the time of this study, metropolitan Lagos was divided into four administrative districts: the city proper and three suburbs. Research was concentrated in suburban Mushin, the largest of these four districts.[4] Mushin was officially created in 1955 when its population was roughly 32,000; by 1977 it had grown to 1.5 million people (compared to the city's 1.2 million and the .8 million divided betweeen the other two suburbs). Mushin's incoming population represents a broad spectrum of Nigeria's peoples, but at least 60 percent are Yoruba-speaking. Although the Yoruba peoples are divided into more than 10 sub-groups which are politically competitive and structurally diverse, cultural similarities, together with a long Yoruba tradition of urbanism, have facilitated their coming together to form a dominant supra-ethnic stratum which does not block the assimilation of non-Yoruba into it, but which does monopolize urban politics.

Mushin houses one of the largest concentrations of low-income residents in the metropolis. It has neither a shanty-town nor a spontaneous squatter settlement, both of which are limited in Lagos; much of its housing, however, is the least desirable and room rents the least costly in the city. Wage workers, most of whom are men, had an average annual income of $900 in the mid-1970s. Self-employed workers--about 50 percent of all working-age men and women, both of whom engage in trade, crafts, and other "informal" occupations--had annual incomes that, on the average, fell below those of wage-employed workers (Fapohunda 1978:51-8).

Unlike the rest of the metropolitan area, very few industrial or large-scale governmental and commercial establishments actually are located in Mushin. It is, rather, a residential community whose major resource is housing, as indicated by the Mushin Town Council's emblem of crossed door keys. Mushin's large houses are built primarily by private owners on houseplots purchased from indigenous descent groups. Real estate is, therefore, one of the few resources which is not government controlled, and which is available on the open market for any member of the public who is able to pay for it. Houses are almost always designed to accommodate both owners and their tenants, and therefore they are rent-producing, a form of savings, and an investment from which all or part of an income can be derived. In point of fact, houseowning often serves as an occupation in and of itself. In the mid-1970s there were nearly 35,000 privately-owned houses in Mushin, each with an average of 40 to 45 inhabitants living in some 13 rooms, 11 of which, roughly speaking, were let to tenants.

Real estate is the material base from which residents of Mushin can derive power. First, housing is a resource which is vitally important in the urban economy; in the mid-1960s revenue derived from taxes on privately owned houses accounted for 43 percent of the annual Mushin Town Council budget--the largest single source of revenue outside state grants and subsidies (Nigeria 1975a:1). Second, housing is scarce; although it is almost all privately built,[5] the construction industry is unable to keep pace with the public's demand for it.[6]

Mushin's houses, and the residential neighborhoods they form, represent far more than mere shelter to city dwellers. Neighborhoods draw people together in many ways to the extent that residence is a significant component in the urban social organization. Outside of the work place and a few voluntary organizations, the large houses and their immediate neighborhoods are, for example, among the only places outside of work and some voluntary associations where people of different ethnic backgrounds and socio-economic statuses are brought together in intense, long-term relationships. There is a high density of house and neighborhood interaction necessitated by close living--tenant families rarely rent more than one room, and cooking, washing, and sanitary facilities are shared. More than four-fifths of the women in a survey I conducted of 360 adults spend most of their time in their residential neighborhoods, trading at street-side stalls. Neighbors are, in fact, one another's prime customers. About one-fifth of the working men stay in their residential neighborhoods, and nearly the same number work within one to two miles of them. The religious activity, moreover, of two-thirds of the residents is neighborhood-centered. Finally, much leisure time activity--gaming, drinking, socializing--centers on neighborhood friends and acquaintances (Barnes 1978:76-9).

In this relatively closely integrated neighborhood environment, owners occupy the topmost position. They are permanent; tenants are transient. Owners have high status; tenants have low status. As one resident put it, "Where a man rents he considers himself small." Owners dominate a resource which tenants need and which owners can use as a mechanism of control. Tenants are forced into a position of dependence since the demand for housing far exceeds the supply and, therefore, undesirable tenants easily can be evicted and replaced. More important is the fact that owners are seen *ipso facto* as authority figures. According to long-standing custom among Yoruba and many neighboring peoples, the senior person in a residential group is empowered with rights to settle disputes, take decisions concerning household responsibilities, and keep order. Transposed onto the contemporary urban setting, the landlord or landlady is by virtue of that status the senior person of the residence and hence an authority figure inside the house.

An important point about owners in Mushin is that in the residential setting they constitute the stratum out of which political entrepreneurship often arises.[8] An equally important point is that most of the owners, hence most of the political entrepreneurs, begin their careers as fairly typical representatives of Mushin's low socioeconomic-status population and not as members of the highly-educated elite.

Two Neighborhood Political Entrepreneurs

The following profiles examine the ways in which two Mushin landlords perform the roles of patron, middleman, and dispute settler for tenants and other owners. In so doing they acquired a client-following, acquired local prestige, and became known as authority figures and leaders.

Profile 1

I. A. Adeyemi[9] began his entrepreneurial career in Mushin in 1950. His first step was to purchase a houseplot near the railroad tracks on which he built a small mud-block, pan-roofed structure. His family occupied part of the building while the rest was rented to four or five families. At the time, the site was distant from the town and therefore inexpensive; it cost approximately fourteen dollars, well above a month's wages. Adeyemi borrowed half of this amount from an in-law; the other half he saved from his earnings.[10] He paid for the house construction step-by-step as he was able to accumulate the necessary amounts for building a foundation, erecting walls, and so on. As he recounted it a quarter of a century later, a bundle of corrugated metal sheets for the roof cost $2.52; a bag of cement for flooring was eighteen cents, and a laborer could be hired at seven cents a day if a relative were not available or suitable to the task. A more accurate estimate made in the early 1960s indicated rooms such as those in Adeyemi's house could be built for about $25.50 each (Koenigsberger et al. 1964:134). It took several years, however, to build a house in this way.

As a second step, Adeyemi familiarized himself with the area and with other opportunities for purchasing houseplots. Thus, he was able to assist others with information concerning available houseplots or potential purchase risks in case they should have problems. In a few cases, two being distant relatives, Adeyemi provided the buyers with small loans ($2.80 to $5.60) like the one he had received. The monetary assistance, however, was insignificant compared to the information he provided. I cannot emphasize sufficiently the lack of information that was available to people interested in the purchase of a houseplot. Knowledge pertaining to real estate was, therefore, an extremely valuable commodity. Adeyemi consequently was as likely to receive a small monetary gift for the information he gave, as he was to provide a loan to the party he advised.

As a third step, Adeyemi attached himself as a client to his neighborhood headman, performing a number of services for him.

Finally, he joined others in the neighborhood landlords' association. There are many such groups in Mushin. Roughly 10 to 15 percent of the resident owners are active in them at various times. For the most part they draw owners who have political aspirations and who use the neighborhood arena either as an end in itself or as a first step in establishing political careers. The functions of such groups include settling disputes between tenants, between tenants and owners, and between other owners. In the absence of governmental services, especially police protection, they hire night guards to prevent theft; they try to keep neighborhood order by seeing to it that troublesome tenants are evicted; and they sometimes lobby as groups for administrative attentions. Indeed, landlords such as Adeyemi and his landlords' association are largely responsible for securing a customary court, a town planning authority, and finally the Mushin Town Council itself (see Barnes 1977 and forthcoming). I mention these things because it was partly through membership in such an association that Adeyemi established himself as an authority figure in his neighborhood. More importantly, it was through contacts made in the association that he was able to expand his network of relationships outside his own neighborhood to important members of the larger community.

When I met Adeyemi in 1972, he was at the peak of his political career. I was taken to him at the direction of the head of the Mushin Town Council, who recommended him as a leader who could assist me in one neighborhood I had chosen for research purposes. Certainly he had the kind of take-charge personality that inspired confidence, but his economic circumstances were not what one would expect of a successful leader. He was reluctant to discuss his income as much from embarrassment over its smallness as from cultural proscriptions against revealing this kind of information. From various pieces of evidence it appeared his income hardly reached $700 per annum. He received a monthly income from a few shabby rooms let to tenants (probably no more than $30 per month), from contributions made by his adult sons who lived with him, and from occasional cash gratuities from clients. Given the strong correlation between relative wealth and political power, I was curious to see how a person whose income was below the average for skilled, and even unskilled, wage-earners became a well-known community authority figure.

Adeyemi's network of clients, and the connections he had made in his own and in adjacent neighborhoods, were remarkable. Aside from the usual participant-type research, my own project required a large number of interviews. In a city the size of Lagos, where strangers are suspect, and relationships of trust take time and effort to develop, finding the diverse categories of people I wished to interview would have been impossible alone. Adeyemi, however, introduced me to 123 people he knew personally and who readily agreed to submit to my questions.[11]

The relationships between Adeyemi and the people in his network were developed primarily on the basis of residential familiarity. The residences of these people with respect to Adeyemi's house are shown in Figure 1. The actors represent a fair cross-section of the population with the exception of the national elite. They do not represent the full range of Adeyemi's primary network; rather, they happen to be some of the people in his network who fit certain criteria I had pre-established. Most of the 123 people--55 men and 26 women for a total of 81--were simply clients. The others were colleagues from his own or nearby landlords associations, his former political party, or his local market. These colleagues were in some cases Adeyemi's clients, in others his patrons, and in still others simply acquantances with whom there had been no previous transactions but merely co-participation in the same groups or events. For the most part, however, this network represented former transactions which had created varying levels of indebtedness between Adeyemi and his neighborhood clients and on which he was subsequently able to draw in order to further his own ends.

The exact nature of Adeyemi's transactions with people who had become his clients was not entirely clear. What kinds of requests were actually made of this neighborhood leader? Who made the requests? How did a patron handle the transactions he engaged in with his clients? To answer these questions, I kept a record of Adeyemi's activities for ten weeks. During this time he was involved in 68 separate transactions with, or on behalf of, his clients. They are listed in Table 1. The integrative role of residence, it should be pointed out, was attested to by the fact that the majority of the requests (74 percent) came from people who belonged to Yoruba sub-groups or ethnic groups different from Adeyemi's own. These neighbors, then, asked Adeyemi most frequently to settle their disputes: domestic, neighborhood, and community-wide. Next in frequency were requests for bureaucratic interventions, followed by requests for therapeutic services, and then assistance with land and housing problems (many of which took the form of disputes). On a few occasions, Adeyemi was asked to assist clients by "managing" their neighborhood reputations, and, most rarely, they asked him for direct patronage.

The following narrative account examines these requests in greater detail. Taken from field notes, this sequence of events concentrates on Adeyemi's activities, and is an expansion of Cases 24 to 32 in Table 1.

>Years ago, one of Adeyemi's loyal clients was Alhaji Adebola. When the authenticity of Adebola's houseplot purchase was questioned by Yinka, the daughter of the seller, Adeyemi helped Alhaji Adebola successfully defend the legality of his purchase. He did so by arranging for Adebola to make a second payment to the daughter in return for which she gave Adebola a court-validated conveyance.

>Later, after Adebola's death, his son, Mustapha, perpetuated the tie with his father's patron. Mustapha was educated by his father and became a clerk in the treasury of the Mushin Town Council, where he loyally responded to Adeyemi's requests on behalf of other clients. At one point, Adeyemi was asked to intervene with the Town Council to lower the property taxes of Yinka, the daughter who earlier challenged the authenticity of Mustapha's father's land title, and which Mustapha and his siblings had inherited. Adeyemi did not intervene since his Council contact in this request would have been Mustapha.

>Mustapha Adebola felt that the treasury clerkship at the Mushin Town Council was a stressful job. There were constant

pressures to "fix" things like property tax assessments, and as a consequence, there was a high rate of dismissals from his office. Therefore, Mustapha wanted to transfer to another post. Yet requests such as this were difficult to process internally without assistance from a superior which, because of his youth, Mustapha had not yet developed. Instead Mustapha turned to Adeyemi, who contacted a landlords' association colleague who was serving as head of the Town Council Committee of Management, and whose suggestions to the personnel manager did not go unheeded. Within a few weeks time, Mustapha was transferred to another office.

Meantime, Adeyemi's interaction with Mustapha was noticed by the Council's sanitary inspector, who was in charge of Adeyemi's neighborhood. Building code violations were monitored by the sanitary inspector. He wished to enlist the help of Adeyemi in order to increase his effectiveness in dealing with violators and levying fines in his (Adeyemi's) neighborhood. In return for assistance in finding and citing violators who were not Adeyemi's clients, the inspector was prepared to be lenient with those who were his clients. In this way, the sanitary inspector became another link in Adeyemi's chain between neighborhood residents and the bureaucracy.

Mrs. Cole was one of the sanitary inspector's problems. She had become Adeyemi's client a few years earlier when her mother--also Adeyemi's client--died. Mrs. Cole wanted to bury her mother in the compound of the house her mother built, and which Mrs. Cole and her brother jointly inherited. For health reasons, home burial was reserved as the privilege of notables; only a chief could authorize it. Adeyemi successfully petitioned the chief of his division to allow Mrs. Cole's mother to be buried in her house compound, and then he supervised the digging of the grave himself. In return, Adeyemi asked Mrs. Cole to join the neighborhood landlords' association to become its secretary.

Mrs. Cole was more interested in business than in being a clerk. After inheriting her mother's house she and her brother built a row of stalls at the edge of their property and rented them to traders and artisans. The stalls, however, violated planning ordinances. The violations fell within the jurisdiction of the sanitary inspector. Adeyemi arranged for Mrs. Cole and her brother to pay the sanitary inspector an annual gratuity in exchange for which he did not report the violations. One year, because of the distractions growing out of a dispute with her brother's wife--which Adeyemi later settled--neither Mrs. Cole nor her brother offered the prearranged gratuity to the sanitary inspector. They were summoned to appear in court. If convicted, the fine would exceed their ability to pay. Adeyemi responded to Mrs. Cole's plea for help by agreeing to ask the presiding judge of the customary court--whom he met through partisan activities and who subsequently became an in-law--to adjourn the case.

Before Adeyemi reached the customary court judge, he learned that Mrs. Cole had also asked his neighborhood rival to intervene in the case. Angered by what he saw as a threat to his dominance in patronage matters, Adeyemi confronted Mrs. Cole with her "duplicity" and announced he had "washed his hands" of her; if she desired help from him in the future, she must deal with him exclusively. Adeyemi then suggested to the sanitary inspector that he allow any other interventions on Mrs. Cole's behalf to go unnoticed, and to let her case run its full course in the court.

The transactions in this brief series of cases vividly illustrate the way in which each is a link in a chain of many, one inevitably leading to another. Through Adeyemi these clients were brought under the influence of some of the important, official connections Adeyemi had been able to make over the years: Mushin's only Native Court judge, the chairman of its Town Council, and one of its paramount chiefs. Thanks to his visibility in the community, and his visibility in official circles, this same series of transactions provided Adeyemi with a way to expand his own contracts, specifically to include the sanitary inspector. This contact, in turn, gave him an ability to exercise additional power among his neighbors, i.e. to influence the sanitary inspector's decisions as to whether or not residents could build (illegal) stalls for trading or other business purposes.

Client relationships are not institutionalized in Mushin as they are in many other places, such as northern Nigeria or Ruanda. In Mushin they are highly self-interested, instrumental, and often ephemeral. Indeed, clients are always looking for many sources of support, and therefore it is incumbent upon the political entrepreneurs to sell themselves or to make themselves invaluable in their client's lives. They use several tactics in order to intensify their relationships with clients whom they value. One way is through frequent exchanges which create strong bonds and potentially instill a sense of solidarity between the parties involved. An advantage for the middleman is that, by giving much in many ways, he can increase the sense of indebtedness on the part of clients and their obligation to repay. The more beholden a client is, the greater the use he is to an aspiring leader.

Another aspect of these relationships which increases their intensity is that there is frequent contact among the parties. Clients are expected to, and do, visit their benefactors frequently, even when they have no problems to be solved. Adeyemi, for example, was visited by Mrs. Cole, Yinka, and the sanitary inspector at least once a week and sometimes more often. The nature of the visiting relationship, it should be noted, is a prime indicator of the status of the parties to a relationship for it is the subordinate party who inevitably visits the superordinate party.

Client ties also increase in intensity if they extend over long periods of time. Adeyemi's relationship with the late Alhaji Adebola and his son,

Mustapha, spanned two generations and had begun at least 15 years before the above incidents. The same was true of the two-generation relationship with Mrs. Cole and her deceased mother, which had begun about 10 years earlier. Both relationships had developed in such a way that they later included several other members of each family, not just single members. Related to this, and another factor which increased the intensity of relationships, was that each client lived with family members who consequently became known to Adeyemi and *vice versa* and thus involved with him.

The relationships, furthermore, include many transactions of quite different content. This, of course, is another of the ways of increasing the intensity of the patron-client ties. Adeyemi assisted Mrs. Cole with three quite unrelated problems: a ritual matter, a bureaucratic intervention, and a domestic quarrel. The same was true in the Adebola family, where he addressed both land and employment problems. Finally, he assisted Yinka and her siblings in many different types of land disputes; in fact Cases 52 and 57 involved Yinka.

Adeyemi, therefore, was known for his ability to deal with the whole individual. He had a strong sense of human nature and of human response to stress. Consequently he devoted all or part of 20 days to healing and therapeutic services. Problems of this sort ranged from a simple headache to severe mental illness. Adeyemi's ability to blend his social and psychological approaches in meeting client needs was epitomized in his treatment of a client who believed that her physical illness (diabetes) was associated with ill feeling directed to her by a co-tenant (see Cases 41, 44, 45, and 47). Adeyemi administered several medicines to his diabetic client--prepared by another healer 50 miles away--and he climaxed her treatment with the sacrifice of a goat. Throughout the process, Adeyemi spread information about his client's problems and his ministrations to her throughout the neighborhood. His goal was to create pressure on the co-tenant so that she would restore harmony in her house and indirectly help to restore her co-tenant's feelings of well-being. Using a combination of approaches, Adeyemi thus saw to the psychic and physical well being of his client as conscientiously as he saw, on other occasions, to her material and social needs. Indeed, he consciously cultivated a reputation for dealing with a broad range of problems.

Adeyemi was additionally known for his ability to secure medicines which protected clients when they were involved in property disputes, as in Case 42. Anyone who had a land case, Adeyemi explained, could be helped by one of at least ten different preparations, depending on the particulars of the dispute.

It is necessary at this point to describe, as briefly as possible, the problems involved in securing a houseplot for migrant settlers. This process was highly competitive and risky (Barnes 1979:61-2). The greatest problem, as attested to by thousands of court cases, was to secure a clear title to the land on which a house was built. The primary reason for this was that the burden of proof for establishing ownership was, largely, on the purchaser. The range of problems is too complex to be dealt with here. Suffice it to say that some houseplots, owned by large lineages, were sold, often unwittingly, either by more than one member or one segment, or to more than one buyer. Furthermore there were false estate agents, imposters, or squatters with forged receipts. According to Nigerian law, any structure erected on a piece of land had to be forfeited if the title was later found to be invalid. Protection of a land purchase often entailed "repurchasing" the property one or more times (as shown below) in order to satisfy the various people or groups claiming to be the rightful owner-sellers. Protection also rested in great measure on a buyer's ability to gain support as a legitimate owner in his or her neighborhood. This was often done with the help of an older owner acting as patron to the newcomer. Each time Adeyemi helped an owner protect his property purchase he was assisting a new and permanent member of the neighborhood to establish a legitimate presence. Needless to say these were intense ties.

All in all, each of the aspects of the patron-client relationships pointed to here accounts for the relative ease with which client networks in neighborhoods can be mobilized by political entrepreneurs when they, in turn, have needs which they wish to fulfill.

Profile 2

Unlike Adeyemi whose strength in politically entrepreneurial activities rested on his breadth, other patrons and middlemen are known for their expertise, connections, or information in very specific domains. One of the most successful neighborhood leaders I knew, S. A. Ojo, used his knowledge of property problems to achieve upward political mobility.

Ojo bought land in another Mushin neighborhood in 1944. As a railway worker, Ojo had a steady wage income. The $49 he paid for his 50' x 100' houseplot in a kolanut grove came solely from savings derived over many years from his job. Construction for Ojo also was a slow, room-by-room process. As soon as he completed the first room, he rented it for between 70 and 41.40 per month, saved the rent, and eventually built a second room, and so on until six rooms were finished.[12] Ojo's father gave him a hunting gun, and thus protected, he moved to the remote house with his wife and child. He was quickly followed by a number of new settlers who heard that the area was now being populated.

From the beginning, Ojo attracted a high-status owner clientele by concentrating on the things which had the greatest value to them: their property investments. Ojo, like Adeyemi, familiarized himself with his locale, and with other opportunities for purchasing houseplots in it. He recalled assisting more than 20 people to purchase plots near his own. Ojo became a hero to his owner-neighbors when he defended their and his property rights in a series of litigations which repeatedly threatened them with the loss of their houseplots and the houses they had built on them. In Ojo's words, this is what happened:

> We bought our houseplots from a member of the original Awori landowning family. Later, a man called Olesanya claimed that the same Awori family sold this area to him. Court action came, and due to a legal technicality Olesanya was declared the owner of the land. We were compelled to pay his younger sister (his heir) because Olesanya died before the final court decision was made. By that time the worth of the plots

had increased in value and we each were asked to pay 100 ($280). I begged the sister's lawyer on our behalf, and the cost was finally reduced to 40 each ($112).

The sister was made guardian of Olesanya's minor children. But she spent the money we paid to her on her own children and did not use the money to care for the rightful heirs. When Olesanya's children were older, they filed a motion in court saying that they had realized no benefits from the land. They wanted the property returned to them. This time the court referred the case to the Administrator General. He ruled that the children must benefit from the sale. If we each paid the children 100 immediately, the Administrator General would sign legal conveyances. Thereafter no court action would be taken against any of us. Because I was the leader of the group, the Administrator General said I must set an example and pay my own 100 at once, or he would confiscate the land and sell it to someone else. I did, and we have been left alone since that time.

The repeated demands of sellers on Ojo and his neighbors led him to master the complex land tenure system of the then Colony--a system which had come to combine customary and introduced English law. He learned how to deal with lawyers and court judges, so as to work effectively and knowledgeably with them. He also found sources from which his neighbors could borrow money in order to pay the extra sums that were levied against them. The loans were made by other neighbors, friends, Ojo himself, and a moneylender.[13] In order to get the loans, especially from the moneylender,[14] it was necessary for an intermediary who was known personally to the lender to vouch for the borrower and to apply sanctions against him if he defaulted on the payments. Ojo played this intermediary role. The reward to him, as might be expected, was a loyal following of neighbors.

Ojo's celebrity, however, reached greater proportions following a neighborhood drama which occurred a few years later. He described the incident as follows:

Mr. Coker bought two plots of land side-by-side. He developed one and left the other vacant. Mr. Coker was a quiet man who kept to himself, but he came to me as a neighbor and we were friends. When he died a few years ago his only child inherited both plots, but he was too poor to develop the empty land that stood alongside his house. Another neighbor we knew to be unscrupulous decided to do his own friend a favor and "sell" him the empty plot. I awoke one night to hear workers behind my house on Coker's land and realized it was a case of land stealing. Coker's son ran to me in great fear. Construction proceeded and intermediaries offered Coker's son money for the land. I told him to take nothing and led him to court where my testimony resulted in an injunction to cease all construction.

Ojo benefited from this incident primarily because his testimony was accepted by the court as the "correct" version of the dispute. He would not have received as much acclaim if his testimony had been interpreted as just one version among several. There had been no written land conveyances in the original transaction. Yet Ojo's recollections that Mr. Coker had been the "rightful" purchaser, was recognized as the valid version of what had transpired. This recognition contributed to establishing Ojo as a local authority on land matters and it significantly enhanced his reputation as a person who had credit in official circles.

The Skills of the Political Entrepreneur

It takes many skills, developed through experience, to move from a political aspirant to a successful leader. Three roles around which skills are developed are those of dispute settler, middleman, and patron. Political entrepreneurs such as Adeyemi welcome the opportunity to settle disputes. In cultural terms, elders are expected to take on this role, particularly within the kinship domain. But it is important to be able to go beyond this relatively circumscribed domain and to be able to attract unrelated clients for two reasons: an individual's reputation is enhanced when outsiders come to him, and an individual's legitimacy as an authority figure is attested to when disputing parties signal their willingness--mainly by seeking his services--to comply with his judgments. The dispute settler role also broadens the political entrepreneur's following, since, in key respects, acting as a dispute settler and intervening with the bureaucracy are similar. The dispute settler-client relationship, like that between the patron or middleman and his client,[15] is maintained between people of unequal status, and it is based on the fact that the exchanges of goods and services are personal, contractual, and informal (not legal). Furthermore, the relationship creates an indebtedness and this, of course, is the desired goal since this indebtedness can constitute the basis for a future political exchange. Inasmuch as the end product of the three kinds of relationships--dispute settler, middleman, or patron-client--are similar, I do not wish to elaborate further on the dispute settler role, but turn instead to the middleman and patron roles and the skills associated with them.

Both the patron and the middleman allocate resources or direct people to the places where resources can be obtained. The difference between them is that patrons allocate resources directly and middlemen indirectly. In Mushin, middlemanship and patronage are combined to greater degrees as one moves up in the political system. Therefore direct patronage became quite important to Ojo when he was more and more obliged to use economic power in order to expand his political base. Middlemanship, on the other hand, is more often found at lower levels of the political system where economic incentives are no less desirable but where they are less critical to the exercise and expansion of power. The middleman role in Mushin fills an important niche, providing access to resources for the less privileged members of the society while at the same time serving as a political outlet for political entrepreneurs who are not relatively affluent. Hence a person such as Adeyemi was far more involved in acting as a middleman or dispute settler than as a patron.

Whichever role is being played, however, one of the skills which Mushin's political entrepreneurs develop is the ability to balance the conflicting demands which clients make on the patron's own goals, or on the goals of their other clients, without alienating them. When Adeyemi was asked to fix the property tax of his client, Yinka, there was a conflict of interest. Clearly, he was unable to ask a favor of a man (Mustapha) whose father was once cheated by the very person (Yinka) who was now asking for a tax reduction. At the same time he did not wish to turn his client away. Yinka was a wealthy woman who brought many members of her family and of her Islamic prayer group to him for assistance. Adeyemi therefore quickly paid his own property tax. He then informed Yinka that it was impossible for him to petition the tax assessor's office on her behalf, inasmuch as he had himself already paid that same amount.

The ability to understand and to use communications channels to their own advantage is another skill which is related to the success of neighborhood patrons and middlemen. Both Ojo and Adeyemi consciously molded public opinion by spreading information about their cases through their neighborhoods. Adeyemi's treatment of the diabetic woman was one example. Following his usual routine, Adeyemi visited friends, shopkeepers, and prayer groups during the late afternoon and early evening hours and casually discussed the case. Later he reported to them that his treatment had been successful: the co-tenant had made amends.

Clearly it is important for a patron or middleman to maintain the upper hand in his dealings with clients. His reputation rests in large measure on his ability to control them. When Mrs. Cole asked his rival to solve the same problem she had asked Adeyemi to solve, Adeyemi countered by publicly complaining that she had violated an agreement between the two of them. He immediately withdrew from the case so that an evaluation could neither be made of him nor could he be measured against his rival. The loss of a client lowers a patron's reputation, particularly if that loss is laid to the patron's lack of effectiveness. However, the patron who drops a client first has then controlled the situation. Adeyemi felt secure in taking action against Mrs. Cole. There had been a long, involved series of transactions between them, and he felt from experience that she would return to his fold. Meantime, the knowledge of his action against her warned other clients of the consequences of disloyalty.

As can be seen, part of the skill of a patron or a middleman is to disseminate information that is beneficial to clients. Much of the capital with which a political entrepreneur trades in a rapidly expanding city where there is a relatively new, transient, and little-educated public, is knowledge--knowledge of how to deal with a host of institutions, systems, and situations and of who can be tapped for favors within or about them. The one constant is that in order to maintain credibility and one's clientele, information must be reliable. One of the side benefits of this type of service, it should be pointed out, is that the political entrepreneur, by virtue of his mastery of urban information, is one of the key figures responsible for socializing newcomers to the new environment.

The political entrepreneur also manages reputations of clients. In the process, there is an accompanying need to protect and manage one's own reputation. When the manager of a pools and lottery establishment (Case 65) asked Adeyemi to inform people of the neighborhood that he was a fair businessman and not, as his competitors would have it, an "unscrupulous scoundrel", Adeyemi did not take the request lightly. He explained:

> You cannot lead your friends astray. When you act, you take responsibility on your shoulders, and you must be accountable for your recommendations. I do not take this responsibility lightly; I consider requests carefully.

In this case Adeyemi's investigations revealed that the pools' manager had once been jailed for fraud. Consequently he did not attempt to clear the man's reputation through his neighborhood gossip channels. Adeyemi was reluctant to risk his own reputation, and in this instance, unlike others he described, he let pass an opportunity to secure a new client.

It should be clear by this point that the reputation of political entrepreneurs is, additionally, linked to the status of the people with whom they deal. This is true both of their contacts and their clients. Adeyemi gained prestige by making it known that he had connections to the Town Council, a court judge, practicing lawyers, the police, and other useful people. Ojo did the same. Connections of this nature assisted patrons in attracting clients who themselves had high standing in the community. Both Ojo and Adeyemi gained prestige from the fact that many of their clients were owners like themselves.

Skillful political entrepreneurs make public display of their connections whenever possible. The usual strategy is to invite important people to one's private ceremonies. One of Mushin's most successful political entrepreneurs staged a lavish reception, following his daughter's marriage, in an open courtyard next to a hotel. The person who agreed to act as master of ceremonies was the Commissioner (head) of a Lagos State Ministry. Other honored guests and speakers came from among the community's most distinguished notables and officials. They were seated behind a long table on a raised platform at the center of the courtyard, and introduced with abundant praise. Their names also were printed on a program which was distributed to every guest present and to every visitor to the host's home for the next few weeks.

Political entrepreneurs also are assessed on the effectiveness of their services and ministrations. This places pressure on them to perform, but the pressure is ameliorated by one feature. A leader who can in some way indicate that he has at least "tried" to help his client is given credit for his efforts. It is, therefore, important to be visible in one's actions and, unless privacy is demanded by the circumstances of a particular case, to bring public witness to bear on one's attempts to act on behalf of others. Needless to say this need again draws on patrons' abilities to manage effectively the neighborhood communications and gossip channels.

Converting Non-Political Resources into Political Capital

One of the greatest skills of the neighborhood patron or middleman is the ability to convert non-political resources into political gains. Adeyemi's successes as a political entrepreneur brought him a neighborhood chieftaincy title. His reputation, moreover, was such that he eventually was called to the Mushin Town Council for periodic consultations. Here he was able to influence in small ways the decisions and policies which guided the affairs of a large urban population. As for Ojo, he was elected to serve a three-year term as a Town Councillor. He was elected by his fellow ward residents who were, in fact, the neighborhood owners whose land rights he had defended over the years. Ojo's election illustrates in a pointed way how a political entrepreneur can mobilize his clientele for support. The owners he had defended earlier constituted a neighborhood clique--brought together through adversity and the need to work as a group to defend their land rights--which acted as the nominating board of his ward's political party committee and which nominated Ojo as the candidated for the post. After this, they campaigned among other neighbors and their tenants to vote for him.

Political successes such as the ones described here are possible for people of widely varying economic circumstances. But upward mobility in the political system is usually--not inevitably--restricted by factors of wealth. In this respect, the careers of Adeyemi and Ojo took sharply different turns. Political entrepreneurs who wish to move up in the system are expected to exhibit the qualities of a high public figure and to meet the responsibilities of such a figure, both of which can require large amounts of cash. People who wish to move ahead, therefore, find it necessary to display their entrepreneurial talents in other directions--by amassing economic resources. In some instances, like that of Ojo, it is possible to convert political gain into economic assets.

Ojo capitalized on his expertise in land matters and his reputation as a trusted defender of property rights to expand his personal economic base. He left his job with the railway and opened a private business as a caretaker and rent collector for other, sometimes absent, owners. His reputation in property matters brought many owners to contract his services. At the height of his business career, Ojo managed more than 50 properties, and his income placed him at the lower end of the income scale of the nation's governmental elite.[16]

Ojo reinvested his wealth in other political ventures. Like high public figures, he spent lavishly

245

on gifts and hospitality, and he supported a large number of dependents. He also constructed a house in his hometown as a sign of his interest in that place. When the highest title in his hometown chieftaincy system fell vacant he used his wealth and the status gained from serving on the Mushin Town Council to secure the title. He valued his new chiefly role more than that of local councillor, and eventually he withdrew from the Mushin political scene.

Finally, another of the most significant skills of political entrepreneurs is their ability to convert their entrepreneurial activities into legitimate political activities. If information and connections are the resources which attract people to political aspirants, people are the resources which aspirants need in order to attract legitimacy to their actions. At the beginning of their political careers Mushin's neighborhood patrons and middlemen are not legitimated by formal institutions; neither do most of them hold offices or titles. The free-floating quality of authority in Mushin's neighborhoods is different from authority in formal institutions: there are no statutory sanctions at their command that there are no official resources for them to distribute. Their main source of strength in carrying out their entrepreneurial roles, therefore, comes from being accepted by the people. Given the uncertainties and struggles they face in a new place, and buttressed by the belief that nothing is accomplished without the intervention of authority figures,[17] ordinary residents are only too willing to exchange support and compliance for the help they need in establishing and keeping a secure place in the urban milieu.

Conclusion

Gellner points out (1977:4) that clientelism of the kind described here stands out as a prominent way of conducting political and economic transactions under certain conditions, particularly when the power of the state is incompletely centralized. The inability of a government to provide its administrative services and duties to all sectors of the population is one form of incomplete centralization, and the inability to provide official information to the full population is another. As in other parts of the world,[17] clientelism in metropolitan Lagos is a prominent solution to the needs created by both forms of incomplete centralization.

Clientelism, however, has profound political ramifications which exceed its prominence as a style of conducting political and economic transactions in incompletely centralized politics. Clientelism, and the political entrepreneurship associated with it, is a way of securing and wielding political power. In the case presented here, political entrepreneurship serves as a vehicle with which ordinary people who are not members of the privileged elite class of their society are able, nevertheless, to move into positions which influence the official institutions that are governing the lives of an ever-increasing number of people who are moving into the cities of the new nations of the world.

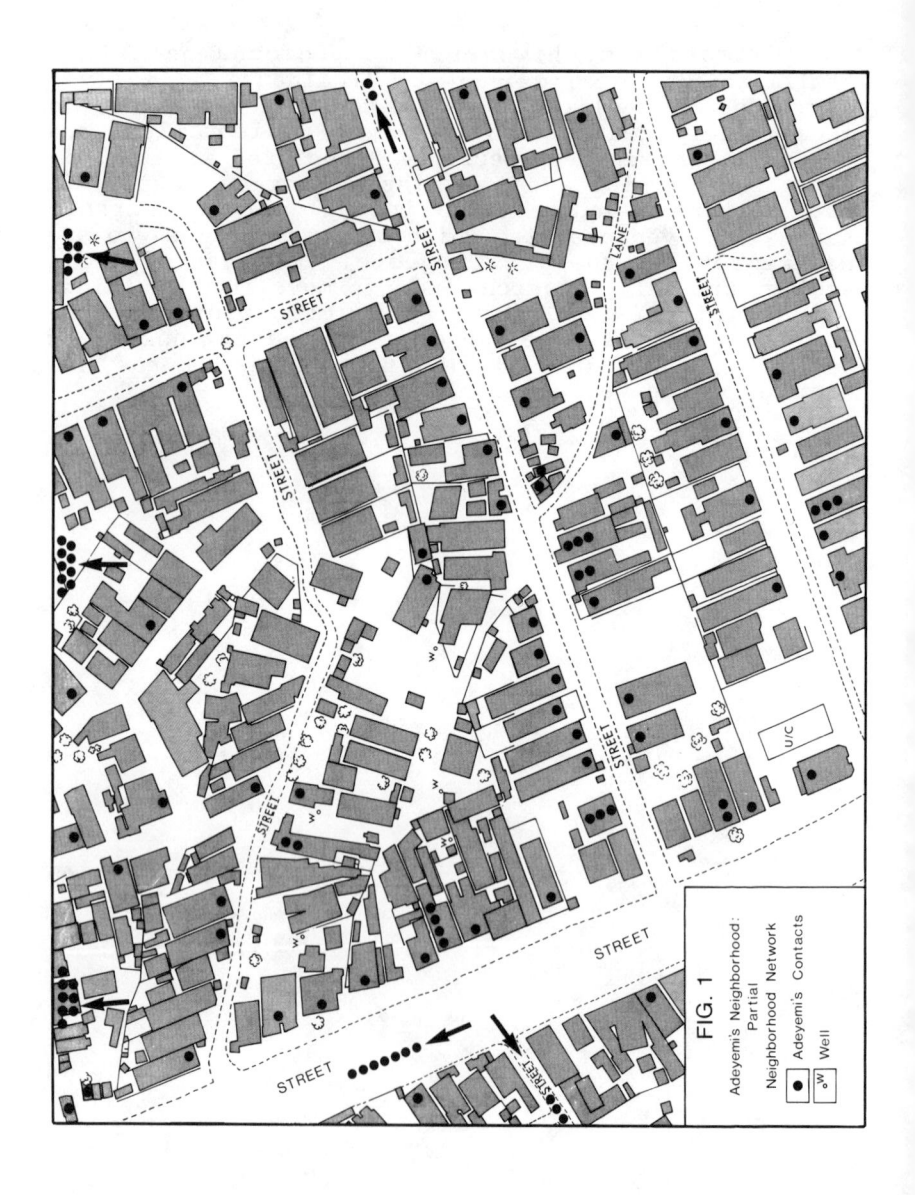

FIG. 1
Adeyemi's Neighborhood: Partial Neighborhood Network

● Adeyemi's Contacts
ₒW Well

TABLE 1

Cases Handled by I. A. Adeyemi

July 5 - September 22, 1972

DISPUTES
Domestic
1. July 5 -- Neighbor called Adeyemi to settle a marital dispute.

2. 9 -- Adeyemi was called to Ijebu Ode (another city) to settle a father-son dispute.

3. 21 -- Adeyemi returned to Ijebu Ode to continue hearing the father-son dispute.

4. ? -- Adeyemi was called to admonish four disobedient children of a deceased neighbor whose sister was left as guardian of the children, but of whose estate Adeyemi was made executor.

5. 26 -- Adeyemi was called to settle a neighbor's marital dispute (see nararative).

6. Aug. 18 -- Adeyemi was called by Mrs. Cole to settle a household dispute (see narrative).

7. 23 -- Adeyemi was called to reassure the new wife of a neighbor's son that her mother-in-law would not harm her. He advised the new wife to put her faith in the neighborhood elders who would protect her and support her marriage.

8. Sept. 11 -- Adeyemi was called to Ijebu Ode to settle a domestic dispute.

Neighborhood
9. July ? -- A neighboring landlord called Adeyemi to deal with his tenant

			who owed back rent. Adeyemi asked the tenant's father to remove his son from the premises.
10.	?	--	Adeyemi returned to his landlord-neighbor to deal with the tenant who refused to leave with his father.
11.	?	--	Adeyemi consulted the customary court judge regarding the above problem. The judge advised the landlord to sue the father.
12.	Aug. 4	--	A neighboring landlord, above, informed Adeyemi his rent case had been taken to a lawyer whom Adeyemi had recommended, and Adeyemi then withdrew from the case.
13.	5	--	Adeyemi was called to hear the grievance of a landlord who was not appointed to a neighborhood landlords' association committee on which he wanted to serve.
14.	8	--	Adeyemi made two visits to landlords' association officials to solve the above grievance.
15.	Sept. 20	--	Adeyemi was called to Shomolu (part of Mushin) to help a tenant with an eviction dispute. Adeyemi suggested the tenant go to customary court where he would support her (and where the judge was Adeyemi's in-law).

Wider
Community
16. Aug. 8 -- Adeyemi was summoned to a chieftaincy meeting to help settle a market dispute. The problem involved a factional struggle over control of the market. The matter was not resolved.

17.		16	--	Adeyemi was again summoned to a chieftaincy meeting to continue settling the market dispute.
18.	Sept.	8	--	Adeyemi was summoned to the Mushin Town Council to give expert testimony and advice on chieftaincy succession rules.
19.		11	--	Adeyemi was summoned to a chieftaincy meeting to hear again the market dispute.
20.		15	--	Adeyemi was summoned again to a chieftaincy meeting to hear a dispute over succession rules of Mushin chiefs.
21.		20	--	Adeyemi was called to the market to hear another dispute.
22.		22	--	Adeyemi was called back to the market to continue hearing the dispute.

BUREAUCRATIC INTERVENTIONS

23.	July	?	--	Adeyemi was asked to help a man secure a taxi license from the Mushin Town Council.
24.		?	--	Mustapha Adebola asked Adeyemi to help him get a transfer in the Muschin Town Council (see narrative).
25.		24	--	The sanitary inspector met with Adeyemi. The latter used the occasion to speak on behalf of a neighbor who needed a building permit for a shed (see narrative).
26.		26	--	The sanitary inspector asked Adeyemi to help him investigate a violation.
27.	Aug.	4	--	The sanitary inspector asked Adeyemi to investigate the illegal construction of a shop.

28.   5 -- A neighbor asked Adeyemi to help her secure a lower property tax rating. He declined. (See narrative.)

29.   16 -- Adeyemi saw the Mushin Town Council head, and Mustapha Adebola was subsequently transferred.

30.   18 -- Mrs. Cole called Adeyemi to secure help with the sanitary inspector over her illegal trading stalls (see narrative).

31.   23 -- Adeyemi visited the customary court judge to secure advice regarding Mrs. Cole's problem with the sanitary inspector.

32.   28 -- Adeyemi confronted Mrs. Cole with her attempt to get help from two sources at once. He then told the sanitary inspector to pursue her case in court.

33. Sept. 21 -- The chief of a neighboring ward sought out Adeyemi to get help from the Mushin Town Council to solve a flooding problem.

34.   21 -- Adeyemi was asked by a neighbor to help obtain a license from the Mushin Town Council to sacrifice a cow for a funeral ceremony.

THERAPEUTIC SERVICES
35. July 6 -- Adeyemi was asked to pray for two women with personal problems.

36.   27 -- Adeyemi went to Ijebu Ode for two days to secure medicine for a mentally ill client.

37.   30 -- Adeyemi was called to a nearby neighborhood to administer medicines to the family of a mentally ill client.

38.	Aug. 2	-- Adeyemi was called to the above family to check on the client.
39.	6	-- Adeyemi went to Ijebu Ode to secure more help for the above family.
40.	10	-- Adeyemi went to Ijebu Ode for more medicine for two other clients.
41.	11	-- Adeyemi was summoned by a neighbor who suffered from diabetes and co-tenant problems. She sought curative medicines (see text).
42.	12	-- Adeyemi was summoned by a policeman to secure medicine to protect him in a land problem (i.e. the threat of the loss of his title).
43.	15	-- Adeyemi was asked by a tailor how to cure his headache.
44.	17	-- Adeyemi went to Ijebu Ode for curative soap for the diabetic client.
45.	19	-- Adeyemi held a ceremony for the diabetic client. The cotenant made amends.
46.	20	-- Adeyemi went to the family of the mentally ill client to check on its progress.
47.	21	-- Adeyemi went to Ijebu Ode for more medicine for the diabetic neighbor.
48.	25	-- Adeyemi was asked to pray for an Islamic group which was concerned over its members' problems.
49.	Sept. 5	-- Adeyemi went to Ijebu Ode for more medicine for the family of the mentally ill client.

50.   12   -- Adeyemi returned to Ijebu Ode for a different medicine for the first mentally ill man.

51.   17   -- Adeyemi went to the latter person to check his progress.

LAND AND HOUSING PROBLEMS/DISPUTES
52. July 6   -- Adeyemi was called to settle a boundary dispute between two neighbors.

53.   7   -- Adeyemi accompanied a friend to court (in Ijebu Ode) for a land case.

54.   17   -- Adeyemi was called to a nearby neighborhood to settle a dispute between brothers over the management of a house they inherited from their father.

55.   24   -- Adeyemi was called to the house of an Alhaji on a land matter.

56. Aug. 4   -- Adeyemi was called again to the Alhaji who wanted a small plot of land to lease or buy. Adeyemi searched for a plot.

57.   8   -- Adeyemi was called to help a neighbor who complained that a hotel owner illegally erected a fence on her property.

58.   16   -- Adeyemi was again called to hear the dispute between brothers.

59.   29   -- Adeyemi was called to get one brother out of jail, after the dispute became violent.

60. Sept. 2   -- Adeyemi called on a lawyer friend to seek help for the jailed brother.

61.   11   -- Adeyemi went to a neighboring chief to intervene in the case of the brothers.

62. 18 -- Adeyemi returned to Ijebu Ode to attend the court case of his friend involved in the land dispute.

PUBLIC OPINION MANAGEMENT
63. Aug. 2 -- Adeyemi was asked to speak to landlords in a neighboring ward to clear up a misunderstanding which was impeding the research of the author. He did, and the matter was resolved.

64. 4 -- Adeyemi was asked to speak to the landlords regarding a rumor which interfered with research. He did, and the second problem was resolved.

65. 15 -- Adeyemi was asked by a pools and lottery manager to tell neighbors the manager was an honest businessman. He refused (see text).

PATRONAGE
66. July 27 -- Adeyemi was asked to arrange an apprenticeship (paid) for a client, and he did.

67. 29 -- Adeyemi was asked to house and feed an unemployed man, and did for many months.

68. Sept. 10 -- Adeyemi gave money to a poor neighbor.

FOOTNOTES

(1) Thanks are due to Sidney Greenfield, Josef Gugler, and Arnold Strickon who offered valuable suggestions for improving an earlier draft of this essay.

(2) This is, of course, a reversal of the Marxist proposition that control of the political institutions of the state derives from control of major economic resources.

(3) For a discussion of elite dominance in West Africa see Gugler and Flanagan (1978:173-5).

(4) Research was carried out in 1971-2 and 1975 and, therefore, the study refers to a period when Mushin was a single governmental unit. In 1976 Mushin was subdivided into several administrative units.

(5) The ratio of private to public housing in metropolitan Lagos is estimated to be 100:1 (Okpala 1979:26).

(6) Houses are usually built at the behest of owners who either supervise the work themselves or hire contractors to supervise it. The construction industry, also part of the private sector, makes a significant contribution to the metropolitan economy. At least 24,000 workers are directly involved in it (Nigeria 1975b:2), and a host of others are employed in construction-related capacities such as sub-contracting, supplying building materials, and collecting rents.

(7) In cases of absentee ownership--when owners live in other towns or when they own several properties--a relative, senior tenant, or caretaker performs the landlord's duties.

(8) My emphasis on real estate is not intended to negate the fact that sheer wealth and success in business--transporting, contracting, or large-scale merchandising--are significant resources in the political arena for the non-elite. Rather, it reflects the fact that the basic common denominator among political activists in Mushin is property ownership (Barnes, forthcoming).

This is the case whether or not the owners are relatively affluent.

A random survey that I conducted among 360 adult men and women in Mushin in 1972 revealed that most of the owners of the 150 houses in which these people lived were self-employed artisans, traders, or merchants. About 26 percent attended at least a few years of secondary school, but most had only a few years of primary education (47 percent) or no education at all (25 percent). (The educational attainments of 2 percent were unknown.) By contrast the national elite was at least secondary school-educated. Income figures are instructive. Interviews with 126 urban house owners in 8 West African cities in the 1970s, taken from a random sample, showed only 35 percent had incomes over $1400 per annum; 40 percent earned between $280 and $1400; 15 percent earned less that $280; and 10 percent were unknown. In an area of Lagos where housing standards are similar to those of Mushin, incomes of owners rarely exceeded $1400 (Peil 1981:134). By contrast, a Nigerian manager in a Lagos industrial firm, no doubt a secondary school graduate, earned on the average $3365 per annum. An unskilled worker in Lagos earned an annual wage the averaged $540 (Fapohunda et al 1978:53, 55).

(9) Pseudonyms are used.

(10) Residents of Mushin like Adeyemi earned very small salaries at the time. However, the income of the family came from several sources. Women, for example, often engaged in petty trade, contributing some of their earnings to the family enterprise; adult children were obliged to make regular contributions to their parents; also, employed men could earn additional income from subsidiary occupations, such as shoe repairing, barbering, or trading, which they undertook in the evening or on weekends; in addition, friends, relatives, and neighbors commonly contributed to "special projects"; furthermore, rotating credit associations provided opportunities for relatively systematic savings.

(11) In the interviews I wished to elicit information about kinship, occupation, and the migration histories of the interviewees.

(12) Ojo then saved enough money for a second, nearby houseplot on which he constructed a 16-room rental property. In time, he built nine plank rooms behind the first house for rental purposes, and he built a second-story addition on the original structure for his own use. Each addition came from savings acquired through rental income.

(13) It is possible to get bank loans or mortgages for real estate or other business activities. Neither Ojo nor Adeyemi did this, but a third entrepreneur whose career is not described here, but who was a client to Ojo, did mortgage his first and subsequent properties with a bank. (It is almost impossible to acquire a loan or mortgage without real estate as collateral; hence a first purchase almost always is owner-financed.) A study of house-funding in Nigeria shows that low-income groups, at least the bottom 75 percent of the population, have only limited sources of financing available to them, and these sources rarely are institutional (Okpala 1979:33).

(14) Two landlords stated that the moneylender in Ojo's neighborhood charged as much as 6 shilling interest on each pound (84¢ on $2.80) per month. On a large loan, the borrower usually puts up a house or houseplot as security. This is forfeited if (s)he defaults on payments. The moneylender in question acquired several properties in this manner.

(15) Discussions of these political roles which have guided my thinking are found in Bailey (1969:167) and Boissevain (1975:147-8).

(16) A conservative estimate of Ojo's income was $7,300 per annum. The salary range for high civil servants, business executives, and professional people in Lagos, c. 1970, was between $5,600 and $11,200 (Baker 1974:40-1).

(17) Several useful collections document this worldwide phenomenon: Clapham (1982), Gellner and Waterbury (1977), Schmidt et al. (1977), and Strickon and Greenfield (1972). Additional Mboya (1969:91), and Sandbrook (1972 and 1982:195-8).

258

REFERENCES

ABATE, Yohannis. 1978. "Urbanism and Urbanization." Issue VIII (4):23-29.

BAILEY, F. O. 1969. Stratagems and Spoils. New York: Schocken Books.

BAKER, Pauline. 1974. Urbanization and Political Change: The Politics of Lagos, 1917-1697. Berkeley and Los Angeles: University of California Press.

BARNES, Sandra T. 1977. "Political Transition in Urban Affair." Annals of the AAPSS. 432:26-41.

_____. 1978. "Social and Economic Ties Among Neighbors in Mushin, Lagos." J. Gugler and W. G. Flanagan, eds. Urbanization and Social Change in West Africa. Cambridge: Cambridge University Press, pp. 76-9.

_____. 1979. "Migration and Land Acquisition: The New Landowners of Lagos." American Urban Studies. 4(Spring): 59-70.

_____. Forthcoming. Urban Chiefs: The Politics of Clientelism in West Africa.

BOISSEVAIN, Jeremy. 1975. Friends of Friends. Oxford: Blackwell.

BUSINESS Times. 1977. January.

CLAPHAM, Christopher, ed. 1982. Private Patronage and Public Power: Political Clientelism in the Modern State. New York: St. Martin's.

FAPOHUNDA, O. J. et al. 1978. Lagos: Urban Development and Employment. Geneva: International Labour Office.

GELLNER, Ernest. 1977. "Patrons and Clients." E. Gellner and J. Waterbury, eds. Patrons and Clients in Mediterranean Societies. London: Duckworth, pp. 1-6.

_____ and John Waterbury, eds. 1977. Patrons and Clients in Mediterranean Societies. London: Duckworth.

GUGLER, Josef and William G. Flanagan. 1978. *Urbanization and Social Change in West Africa.* Cambridge: Cambridge University Press.

KASFIR, Nelson. 1976. *The Shrinking Political Arena.* Berkeley and Los Angeles: University of California Press.

KOENIGSBERGER, Otto et al. 1964. *Metropolitan Lagos.* New York: UN Programme of Technical Assistance.

MBOYA, Tom. 1969. "The Impact of Modern Institutions on the East African." P. H. Gulliver, ed., *Tradition and Transition in East Africa.* Berkeley and Los Angeles: University of California Press, pp. 89-103.

NIGERIA. 1975a. Draft Estimates, 1975-76. Mushin: Mushin Town Council (mimeo).

_____. 1975b. *Third National Development Plan 1975-80: Lagos State Programme.* Lagos: Lagos State Government (mimeo).

OKPALA, D. C. I. 1979. "Accessibility Distribution Aspects of Public Urban Land Management: A Nigerian Case." *African Urban Studies.* N.S. 5:25-44.

PEIL, Margaret. 1976. *Nigerian Politics: The People's View.* London: Cassell.

_____. 1981. *Cities and Suburbs: Urban Life in West Africa.* London: Holmes & Meier.

SANDBROOK, Richard. 1972. "Patrons, Clients and Factions: New Dimensions of Conflict Analysis in Africa." *Canadian Journal of Political Science.* 5(1):104-119.

SANDBROOK, Richard. 1982. *The Politics of Basic Needs: Urban Aspects of Assaulting Poverty in Africa.* Toronto: University of Toronto Press.

SCHMIDT, S. W. et al. 1977. *Friends, Followers, and Factions: A Reader in Political Clientelism.* Berkeley and Los Angeles: University of California Press.

SCHUMPETER, Joseph A. 1961. The Theory of Economic Development. Cambridge, Mass: Harvard University Press.

STRICKON, Arnold and Sidney M. Greenfield, eds. 1972. Structure and Process in Latin American Patronage, Clientage, and Power Systems. Albuquerque: University of New Mexico Press.

KEY WORDS

accumulation, 1, 19, 20, 21, 37, 54, 60, 61, 65, 66, 67, 78, 79, 80, 81, 83, 90, 185, 188, 190

action groups, 130, 131

agriculture,(-al), 1, 63, 64, 71, 72, 78, 80, 81, 83, 84, 91, 96, 97, 99, 102, 103, 105, 106, 109, 110, 111, 115, 116, 117, 118, 121, 173, 175, 177

apprentice(ship), 89, 90, 197, 204, 255

Argentina, 137, 159, 165

Aston group, 41

beggars, 205

bourgeois(ie), 65, 67, 79, 126, 131

Brazil, 99, 159, 163, 165

brick production, 67

broker(s), 15, 151, 152, 183, 184

bureaucracy, (-ies), 23, 49, 130, 163, 225, 232, 241

bureaucrat(ic), 21, 68, 101, 107, 152, 224, 225, 232, 236, 251

business cycles, 21, 44

business success, 20

butchers, 206

capital accumulation, 19, 20, 54, 60, 78, 80, 81, 83, 85, 90

capital intensive, 67, 86

capitalist, 20, 37, 39, 54, 56, 63, 64, 79, 81, 83, 84, 85, 86, 88, 89, 96, 177, 186

causal effects, 29

causal lags, 38

causal models, 28, 38, 40

causal processes, 38

central satellite plantation system, 109, 110, 111, 118, 123

centrales, 109

chieftaincy, 244, 246, 250, 251

children, 1, 15, 126, 195, 196, 197, 198, 200, 201, 202, 203, 204, 207, 208, 209, 213, 214, 215, 216, 217, 218, 219, 220, 222, 223, 239, 257

Chile, 159

city (-ies), 1, 138, 149, 175, 176, 178, 179, 180, 188, 224, 225, 226, 231, 247, 249, 260

class analysis, 166

class relations, 169, 188, 189

class structure, 168, 191

commodity production 1, 54, 81

connections, 246

control, 16, 27, 30, 31, 33, 36, 38, 39, 119

corporations, 12, 37, 134

Cosmopolite, 102, 106, 107, 110, 112, 113, 114, 115

credit, 7, 21, 41, 179, 181, 187, 199, 203, 214, 221, 244, 257

decisions, 5, 8, 11, 12, 13, 14, 15, 21

dependency theory, 97, 98, 99, 100

dependistas, 100, 117

depeasantization, 69

development, 5, 6, 7, 8, 9, 10, 12, 17, 18, 19, 20, 36, 37, 40, 41, 97 developmentalism, (-t), 10, 82

diffusion theory, 97, 98, 99

division of labor, 63

divorce, 207, 215, 216, 219, 220

domestic economy, 195, 196, 199, 223

dowries, 199, 200, 201, 203, 219

Economic Commission on Latin America, 98

economic historians, 13, 83, 98

ejido, 56, 103

elites, 1, 12, 15, 16, 17, 99, 102, 103, 106, 107, 111, 112, 114, 115, 128, 129, 133, 136, 137, 149, 151, 166, 73, 174, 177, 182, 184, 185, 186, 187, 189, 224, 225, 228, 231, 245, 247, 256

enterprise, 7, 12, 20, 40, 45, 47, 54, 55, 60, 61, 63, 66, 71, 80, 86, 87, 89, 109, 124, 125, 126, 129, 130, 131, 133, 134, 137, 138, 149, 158, 159, 160, 161, 162, 163, 164, 165, 174, 175, 180, 181, 182, 184, 185, 191, 203

entrepreneur (-ship), 1, 2, 5, 6, 7, 8, 9, 10, 11, 12, 13, 14, 15, 16, 17, 19, 20, 21, 22, 23, 24, 25, 28, 29, 30, 32, 33, 34, 35, 36, 37, 40, 41, 43, 44, 45, 46, 47, 48, 49, 50, 52, 54, 60, 68, 77, 82, 87, 88, 89, 90, 96, 97, 98, 100, 101, 102, 105, 106, 109, 110, 113, 114, 115, 116, 119, 121, 124, 125, 126, 127, 128, 129, 130, 131, 132, 133, 134, 136, 137, 149, 152, 153, 158, 159, 160, 161, 162, 163, 166, 167, 170, 172, 174, 180, 181, 182, 185, 186, 188, 189, 190, 191, 192, 195, 196, 199, 224, 225, 228, 229, 237, 238, 240, 241, 243, 244, 245, 246, 247

equilibrium, 5, 6, 8, 11, 20, 21

evolution, 8, 11, 18

factors of production, 19, 28, 30, 33, 34, 38

family, (ies), 1, 11, 12, 17, 57, 64, 65, 66, 76, 77, 78, 90, 103, 107, 114, 1225, 126, 127, 128, 132, 133, 134, 137, 158, 176, 177, 179, 181, 197, 198, 199, 202, 203, 204, 205, 229, 236, 242, 253

firm, 1, 5, 7, 8, 9, 11, 17, 19, 21, 23, 24, 26, 27, 28, 29, 30, 37, 40, 41, 45, 46, 47, 48, 51, 159, 160, 161, 162, 163, 181, 185, 220

fixed assets, 31, 32, 33, 35, 36, 37, 38, 39, 41, 42

flat yarn, 26

food, 24, 48

functional specialization, 38

goals, 14, 54, 241

government, 10, 23, 26, 34, 67, 133, 158, 161, 163, 165, 175, 179, 185, 197, 205, 224, 226, 227, 230, 245, 246, 256, 260

guano industry, 99

Guatemala, 8, 96, 97, 101, 102, 105, 106, 107, 109, 110, 111, 112, 115, 116, 117, 118, 119, 120, 122, 123

Hausa, 1, 1967, 197, 199, 200, 203, 206, 213, 215, 216, 217, 218, 219, 221, 222, 223

houses, 246, 256, 258

housing, 254, 257

ideology, 63, 65, 67, 72, 119, 130, 131

image, 36, 161, 178

indigo, 103

industry, 22, 24, 25, 27, 41, 59, 64, 67, 68, 69, 78, 79, 81, 83, 85, 86, 89, 90, 93, 124, 130

information, 13, 24, 41, 132

ingenios, 110

innovation, 7, 8, 14, 15, 16, 19, 20, 21, 22, 23, 25, 26, 32, 33, 34, 35, 36, 37, 38, 39, 40, 132, 133, 166, 174, 196

inputs, 28, 33, 35

international debt, 115

investment, 12, 17, 19, 21, 23, 35, 59, 63, 65, 81, 83, 99, 117, 180, 181, 195, 199, 215, 217, 218, 219

involution, 1, 117, 118

Islam, 253

Japanese factories, 24, 26, 29, 34, 35, 37, 39, 40

Juglar cycles, 21

jute, 25, 26

kinship network, 128, 131, 132, 134

kitchin cycle, 21

Kondratieff cycle, 21

labor, 1, 8, 12, 19, 28, 29, 30, 31, 32, 33, 34, 35, 36, 38, 54, 57, 60, 61, 63, 64, 65, 67, 71, 72, 76, 77, 78, 79, 80, 81, 83, 84, 85, 86, 87, 90, 91, 103, 115, 116, 118, 119, 121, 127, 152, 175, 178, 181, 196, 199, 200, 215, 217, 222

Lagos, 15, 224, 225, 226, 231, 244, 247, 256, 257, 258, 259

lifestyle, 132

management, 5, 8, 9, 20, 22

managerial function 54, 55, 77, 82, 86

market efficiency, 1, 45, 48, 49, 52

marriage, (-ied), 60, 107, 127, 197, 201, 202, 203, 215, 216, 218, 219, 220, 244

Marx (-ist, -ism), 8, 20, 82, 83, 84, 92, 96, 168, 169, 171, 188, 256

metaphors, 13, 14, 16, 18

methods, 23, 40

Mexican revolution, 137

middlemen, 174, 225, 235, 238, 241, 242, 243, 244, 246

minifundios, 97, 106, 114

minority, (-ies), 10, 11, 175, 186

motivation, 10

multinationals, 124, 130, 133, 134

multiple regression analysis, 29, 33

neighborhood, 16, 227, 228, 229, 230, 231, 232, 233, 234, 237, 242, 243, 244, 245, 248, 249, 252, 258

Nigeria, 1, 15, 43, 195, 196, 198, 223, 225, 226, 227, 235, 237, 256, 258, 260

objectives, 22, 24

opportunity structure, 12

ordinary least squares analysis, 29

organization, 7, 12, 14, 17, 22, 23, 24, 28, 29, 30, 32, 35, 36, 39, 41, 42, 43

output, 19, 27, 28, 29, 30, 31, 32, 33, 34, 36, 37, 38, 43

owners, 21, 27, 29, 39, 40

patent applications, 25, 26, 27, 28, 33, 40, 41

paradigm, 13, 14, 15, 17

patron-client networks, (relationships), 131, 182, 183, 188, 189, 194 patrones, 79

peasant, 45, 59, 60, 63, 64, 80, 81, 82, 83, 84, 92, 93, 94, 95, 116, 119, 123, 169, 193, 196

performance, 24

personnel, 33, 35, 39, 41, 140, 144, 146, 152, 160, 187, 224

personnel turnover, 33, 35, 41

Peru, 121, 137, 160, 161

petroleum, 24

piece rate, 56, 59, 69, 76, 77, 78

piece work, (-er), 64, 90

plantation agriculture, 102, 103 109, 110, 111, 113, 117, 118

political entrepreneurs, 1, 224, 225, 228, 235, 237, 241, 243, 244, 245, 246, 247

power, 6, 15

prestige, 74, 141, 142, 243, 244

productivity, 27

profit, 5, 12, 21, 44, 66, 106, 162, 180, 182, 203, 208, 209, 215, 217

proletarian(t), 69, 78, 80

public enterprise, 1, 158, 159, 161, 162, 163, 165

purdah, 15, 197, 199, 201, 206, 218, 219

ratchet effect, 39

raw materials, 22, 28, 54

real estate, 227, 258

religion, 4, 13

rent, (-al), (-er), 178, 179, 188, 226, 228, 245, 250, 256, 258

research and development, 8, 40

resources, 10, 11, 13, 16, 22, 40, 54, 69, 124, 130, 132, 134, 135, 152, 158, 163, 166, 167, 169, 171, 172, 185, 188, 195, 199, 224, 226, 227, 241, 245, 246, 256

risk, 12, 19, 20, 21, 22, 63, 158, 159, 163, 164, 180, 181, 229

rituals, 134

Schumpeter, 5, 6, 7, 9, 18, 20, 21, 22, 28, 29, 38, 39, 40, 41, 44, 54, 83, 84, 85, 88, 94, 96, 109, 123, 132, 137, 180, 194, 225, 260

Siquinala, 102, 106, 107, 109, 110, 112, 115, 116, 117, 118, 119

social networks, 130, 133

solidarity, 134

span of control, 31, 32, 34, 35, 36, 41, 42

technocrats, 130, 163

technology, 7, 14, 23, 24, 28, 29, 30, 32, 33, 35, 43, 53, 89, 112, 129, 132, 133, 134,

technicos, 163, 164

trade, 64, 65, 66, 142, 174, 179, 196, 197, 202, 226

transactions, 16, 45, 48, 125, 176, 178, 198, 202, 205, 214, 219, 231, 234, 235, 236, 240, 246, 247

transactions costs, 45, 48, 50

uncertainty, 21

underdevelopment, 93, 94, 97, 117, 223

United Fruit, 102, 105, 114

urban, 55, 67, 68, 72, 80, 124, 137, 138, 174, 196, 200, 222, 223, 224, 225, 226, 227, 243, 245, 246, 259

value added, 28, 30, 33, 34, 35, 37, 38, 39, 42

variation, 15, 16

wage(s), 56, 57, 60, 76, 77, 78, 90, 113, 115, 160, 178, 181, 196, 197, 226, 229, 230, 257

wage-price spiral, 77

weaving, 26, 27, 54, 55, 56, 57, 59, 60, 61, 63, 64, 65, 68, 72, 79, 80, 85, 86, 88, 89, 90, 91

widow(s), 219, 220

Oliver Williamson, 48, 53

women, 1, 15, 65, 107, 128, 196, 197, 198, 199, 200, 201, 202, 203, 204, 213, 215, 216, 217, 218, 219, 220, 221, 242, 257

Yoruba, 226, 228, 232

Zaibatsu, 23

AUTHOR INDEX

ABATE, Yohannis, 259, 224, 259,
ACHESON, James M., 1, 7, 8, 12, 45, 50, 53,
ADAMS, Richard N., 118, 120,
ADAMU, M., 196, 219, 222,
ADAR, Z., 163, 164,
AHARONI, Y., 162, 163, 164,
ANDERSON, Charles W., 127, 136,
ANDERSON, James N., 179, 191,
ASAD, Talal, 169, 191,
AUBEY, R., 3, 12, 13, 17, 124, 132, 133, 136, 164, 192
BAILEY, David, 126, 136
BAILEY, F. O., 258, 259
BAKER, Pauline, 258, 259
BANTON, M., 157
BARAN, P., 87, 02
BARLETTI, B., 163, 164
BARNES, Sandra T., 1, 15, 16, 47, 224, 228, 230, 237, 256, 259
BARTA, R., 84, 92
BARTH, Frederik, 12, 13, 14, 17, 101, 120, 133, 136, 138, 157, 168, 169, 170, 171, 172, 186, 191
BASHIR, M. K., 201, 222
BEALS, Ralph L., 90, 92
BECKER, Gary, 52, 53
BELASCO, Bernard I., 20, 43
BELSHAW, Cyril S., 170, 191
BENEDICT, Burton, 12, 133
BENNETT, John W. 2, 17, 101, 102, 120, 170, 171, 191
BERGER, Peter, 99, 100, 101, 120
BEVERIDGE, Andrew A., 22, 23, 43
BIANCHI, A., 164
BING, Sir Rudolph, 155, 157
BLAU, Peter M., 43, 191
BODENHEIMER, Suzanne, 98, 120
BOISSEVAIN, Jeremy, 258, 259
BUSINESS TIMES, 224
CHANCE, J., 86, 92
CHANDLER, Alfred D., 49, 53
CHAPIN, Schuyler, 155, 157
CHAYANOV, A. V., 90, 92, 93
CHILCOTE, Ronald, 97, 118
CHIROT, Daniel, 96, 118
CLAPHAM, Christopher, 258, 259
COASE, R. H., 48, 53
COATSWORTH, John, 97, 98, 99, 118
COCHRAN, Thomas C., 20, 41, 43

COHEN, A., 219, 222
COLLINS, J., 98, 109, 115, 122
COMMONS, John R., 20
COOK, Scott, 1, 7, 8, 47, 54, 55, 65, 78, 80, 81, 83, 84, 88, 91, 92, 169, 191
DALTON, George, 168, 191
DAVIS, William G., 1, 15, 166, 168, 169, 179, 191
DE MARQUEZ, Viviane B. 127, 136
DEAN, Warren, 99, 118
DIENER, Paul, 111, 118
DOBB, M., 79, 83, 84, 92
DOS SANTOS, Teodosius, 98, 121
DUNCAN, Kenneth, 99, 121
DUPRE, G., 168, 191
EDELSTEIN, J. C., 97, 118
EVENS, Terrence M.S., 192
FAPOHUNDA, O. J., 226, 257, 259
FERNANDEZ, L., 163, 164
FIRTH, Raymond, 12, 13, 17, 168, 192
FISHLOW, Albert, 99, 121
FLANAGAN, William G., 256
FLETCHER, L., 97, 121
FORTES, Meyer, 60, 92
FOSTER, George, 82, 84, 92
FRANK, Andre G., 98, 99, 121
FRASER, L. M, 192
FREEMAN, John, 39, 43
FURTADO, Celso, 98, 121
GARCIA de Enterria, E., 163, 164
GEERTZ, Clifford, 47, 53, 82, 83, 93, 96, 118, 121
GELLNER, Ernest, 246, 258, 259
GLADE, W. P. Jr., 11, 13, 14, 17, 127, 133, 136, 163, 164
GODAU, Rainer, 127, 136
GOODY, E., 79, 93, 222
GRABER, W. C., 97, 121
GREENFIELD, Sidney M., 4, 5, 6, 10, 13, 17, 100, 101, 121, 124, 132, 136, 164, 170, 171, 176, 192, 194, 256, 258, 260
GUGLER, Josef, 256, 260
HAGEN, Everett E., 10, 17, 82, 93, 190, 192
HALPERIN, Rhoda, 168, 192
HALTRECHT, Montague, 155, 157
HANNAN, Michael T., 39, 43
HANSEN, Roger D., 127, 136
HARRISON, M., 84, 93
HICKSON, D. J., 41, 43, 44
HILL, P., 196, 200, 222

HIRSCHMEIER, Johannes, 23, 43
HOBSHAWN, E. J., 93
HOLLNSTEINER, Mary R., 173, 192
HOLLOWAY, Thomas, 99, 121
HOMANS, George C., 169, 192
HOPKINS, A. G., 196, 217, 222
HOSELITZ, Bert F., 19, 41, 43, 44, 97, 121, 193
HUNT, Shane, 99, 121
INKSON, J. H., 39, 43
JOHNSON, Edwin H., 1, 138
KASFIR, Nelson, 260
KAUTSKY, Karl, 83, 87, 93
KELLEY, G., 163, 164
KHANDAWALLA Pradip N., 32, 43
KILBY, P., 44, 160, 164
KITCHING, G., 87, 93
KNIGHT, Rolf, 109, 111, 122
KNOWLTON, Robert J., 126, 136
KOENIGSBERGER, Otto, 229, 260
KUHN, Thomas S., 13, 17
KYLE, John, 12, 17, 132, 133, 136
LA BEAU, Francis, 102, 122
LANDE, Carl H., 173, 176, 193
LAPPE, Thomas, 98, 109, 115, 122
LARSON, Henrietta, 18
LAYTON, Aviva, 155, 157
LEFF, Nathaniel, 99, 122
LENIN, V. I., 83, 93
LEVY, Marion, 96, 122
LEWIS, W. A., 83, 93, 97, 117, 122
LIPSET, Seymour, 124, 137
LOMNITZ, Larissa, 1, 11, 47, 124, 128, 132, 134, 137
LONG, Norman, 124, 133, 137, 166, 193
MANARI, Hiroshi, 1, 7, 19, 47
MANSOURI, Lotfi, 155, 157
MARSH, Robert, 1, 7, 19, 47, 89
MARX, Karl, 6, 20, 84, 85, 93, 168, 169, 193
MAYR, Ernst, 13, 14, 18
MBOYA, Tom, 258, 260
MC CLELLAND, David C., 10, 18, 82, 94, 190, 193
MC FALBE, Cecilia, 43
MC GREEVY, William, 99, 122
MC GUIGAN, James R., 28, 43
MC KINLEY, William, 43
MEDICK, Hans, 60, 93
MERRILL, E., 97, 121
MORSE, R., 83, 94
MOYER, Charles R., 28, 43

MORGENSTERN, O., 172, 193
MERCER, Ruby, 155, 157
MINTZ, Sidney M., 179, 193
MURPHY, Arthur, 2
MURTHY, K., 162, 164
NAFINSA, 127, 137
NAIRN, Allan, 116, 122
NEAL, Walter, 2
NIETO, A., 163
NIGERIA, 227, 256
NISBET, Robert A., 13, 18
NODA, Kazuo, 23, 44
OBERSCHALL, Anthony R., 22, 23, 43
OKPALA, D. C. I., 256, 258, 260
ORTIZ, Sutti, 168, 193
PADEN, J., 196, 222
PAINE, Robert, 172, 193
PARSONS, James, 99, 122
PEIL, Margaret, 225, 257, 260
PEREZ-LIZAUR, Marisol, 1, 11, 124, 128, 132, 137
PETRAS, James, 98, 122
POLYANI, Karl, 101, 122, 168, 194
POPPER, Karl, 13, 18
PREBISCH, Raul, 117, 123
PUGH, D. S., 41, 43, 44
PURCELL, J. F. H., 127, 137
PURCELL, S. K., 127, 137
QUIRK, Robert E., 126, 137
RAPPAPORT, Roy, 168, 194
RAYNAUT, C., 196, 200, 222
REDFIELD, R., 84, 94
REY, P. P., 168, 191
RICH, Maria F., 139, 149, 157
RODGERS, G., 195, 222
ROSTOW, W. W., 82, 94, 97, 117, 118, 123
ROTHSTEIN, Morton, 17
ROXBOROUGH, I., 82, 94
RUSSELL, Susan D., 190, 194
RUTLEDGE, I., 99, 121
SAHLENS, Marshall D., 138, 155, 157, 168, 194
SALISBURY, Richard F., 168, 194
SANDBROOK, Richard, 258, 260
SAULNIERS, A., 1, 12, 158, 160, 161, 165
SCHILDKROUT, E., 1, 15, 47, 195, 197, 203, 217, 219, 221, 222
SCHMIDT, S. W., 258, 260
SCHNEIDER, Harold K., 168, 194
SCHULTZ, Theodore, 52, 53

SCHUMPETER, Joseph A., 5, 6, 7, 9, 18, 20, 21, 22, 29, 38, 39, 40, 41, 44, 54, 83, 84, 85, 88, 94, 96, 109, 123, 132, 137, 180, 194, 225, 260
SCOTT, James C., 176, 183, 194
SHINOHARA, Miyohei, 23, 44
SILLS, Beverly, 155, 157
SINGELMAN, Peter, 188, 194
SINGER, M., 83, 94
SMITH, Carol, 111, 123
SMITH, M. G., 196, 197, 223
SMITH, Sheldon, 1, 7, 8, 96, 102, 109, 110, 123
SOLBERG, C., 163, 165
SPAULDING, Karen, 99, 123
STALEY, E., 83, 94
STANDING, C., 195, 222
STAVENHAGEN, R., 84, 94
STOLPER, Wolfgang F., 22, 44
STONE, Irving, 99, 123
STRICKON, Arnold, 4, 6, 12, 13, 17, 100, 101, 121, 124, 132, 133, 136, 164, 170, 171, 176, 192, 194, 256, 258, 260
TANDON, P., 163, 165
TAYLOR, John G., 82, 94, 168, 172, 194
THOMPSON, E. P., 83, 94
THORBECKE, E., 97, 121
TRACEY, Phelps K., 43
TURBAYNE, Colin M., 13, 16, 18
VERSIANA, Flavio Rabelo, 99, 123
VILLANVEVA, M., 86, 94
VON NEUMANN, J., 172, 193
WACKMAN, D., 195, 223
WALLERSTEIN, Immanual, 96, 123
WALSH, A. H., 158, 165
WARD, S., 195, 223
WARMAN, A., 84, 94
WARTELLA, E., 195, 223
WARWICK, D., 161, 163, 165
WATERBURY, J., 258, 259
WEBER, Max, 10, 18, 20
WHITE, Leslie, 118, 123
WILLIAMSON, Oliver, 48, 53
WIRTH, J., 163, 165
WOLF, Eric, 82, 83, 84, 85, 94, 96, 97, 116, 123
WORKS, J. A. Jr., 196, 223
YUI, Tsunehiko, 23, 43